BAD DATA

BAD
DATA

Why We Measure the Wrong Things and Often Miss the Metrics That Matter

PETER SCHRYVERS

Prometheus Books
Guilford, Connecticut

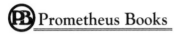

Prometheus Books

Prometheus Books
An imprint of The Rowman & Littlefield Publishing Group, Inc.
4501 Forbes Blvd., Ste. 200
Lanham, MD 20706
www.rowman.com

Distributed by NATIONAL BOOK NETWORK

Cover design by Liz Mills | Cover design Copyright © 2020 Prometheus Books

British Library Cataloguing in Publication Information available

Library of Congress Cataloging-in-Publication Data

Names: Schryvers, Peter, 1983– author.
Title: Bad data : why we measure the wrong things and often miss the metrics that matter / by Peter Schryvers.
Description: Lanham : Rowman & Littlefield International, 2019. | Includes index.
Identifiers: LCCN 2019012234 (print) | LCCN 2019980461 (ebook) | ISBN 9781633885905 (cloth) | ISBN 9781633885912 (epub)
Subjects: Quantitative research--Evaluation. | Performance—Measurement.
Classification: LCC QA76.9.Q36 S37 2019 (print) | LCC QA76.9.Q36 (ebook)
LC record available at https://lccn.loc.gov/2019012234
LC ebook record available at https://lccn.loc.gov/2019980461

CONTENTS

CONTENTS

Not everything that counts can be counted, and not every-thing that can be counted counts.

—William Bruce Cameron

INTRODUCTION

Man is a measurer of all things.
                                        —Herbert Arthur Klein

There is a species on this planet that has dominated nearly every ecosystem it has come into contact with. From arid deserts to lush rain forests, from high mountains to low valleys, and everything in between, it has spread and conquered. There is almost nowhere you cannot find it. It has learned to grow and harvest plants, to domesticate other animals to serve its needs, to create intricate and purposeful structures and habitats, to build complex societies with a division of labor and separate classes, and even has gone to war and enslaved members of its own species.

I am, of course, talking about ants.

To say that ants are merely a successful species would be an understatement. Not only have they colonized nearly every ecosystem and climate on our planet, they have done so in large numbers. In almost any ecosystem, if you were to count up all the animals present, ants would most likely be the most numerous. In some habitats ants make up not only the largest number of animals, but outweigh the others in total body mass.

The success of ants can be attributed to something that sets them apart from most other insects: They are social. They work together. Through elaborate divisions of labor and complex methods of communication and adaptations, ants have found a way to cooperate like few other species, humans being one of a few exceptions.

Ants work together so well because they communicate. Ants use an intricate web of signals to identify food sources and potential enemies, provide day-to-day maintenance and care for the colony, and accomplish a host of other tasks. These signals are then used to allocate resources to those tasks accordingly, which ensures the continual survival of the colony. No individual ant (not even the queen) understands the system they are part of; they just blindly follow the signals provided to them. Yet there is a purpose and strategy to this interaction. This creates an unusual paradox: While individual ants are dumb, the colony is smart. We can get a glimpse of this system from how ants handle a simple task: finding food.

In Australia there is an ant, *Onychomyrmex*, that specializes in hunting centipedes and other large arthropods in the rain forests of the northeast. When *Onychomyrmex* ants search for food, they excrete a pheromone every few feet by extending their hind legs backward and lowering their abdomen to the ground.[1] These pheromones signal other ants to follow.

The excretion by the *Onychomyrmex*, in the language of myrmecologists (the scientists who study ants), is called a recruitment pheromone. Recruitment pheromones signal to other ants to follow—to a food source, a new nest location, or a potential threat that needs to be attacked.

When this system plays out on the scale of a colony, the result is remarkable. Numerous scouts leave each morning in search of food. Once they find food, they return to the nest, excreting a recruitment trail as they return. Back at the nest they "recruit" other ants to follow them to the food source: a piece of fallen fruit, a particularly leafy branch of a tree, or perhaps a centipede if they are army ants, which specialize in hunting en masse. This simple system of chemical detection has allowed ants to achieve a staggering level of efficiency, albeit unthinking efficiency. This unthinking efficiency works often enough that ant colonies thrive all over the world. When it fails, however, it does so catastrophically.

When army ants leave the colony to exploit a food source that has been located, they do so in a large group, following behind each other closely. It is imperative that the group sticks together. Sometimes they are following a recruitment trail left by the ants in front of them, other times they are using their antennae to physically locate and follow the ant before them. In these cases, the recruitment trails are not laid down as a path to food, but simply as an instruction: "Hey, follow me."

Rarely a situation develops where the ants unintentionally double back on their trail. The lead ants begin to follow the ants at the rear. The trail is continuously reinforced, as each ant lays down a recruitment path, growing stronger and stronger each minute. The ants follow the trail in a giant loop, marching for hours and hours. But this journey will not end at a centipede to be attacked or a piece of decomposing fruit to be harvested. It will simply continue in a loop until it reaches its ultimate and devastating conclusion: the death of every single ant by exhaustion. The phenomenon has been observed numerous times in nature and has been reproduced in the laboratory. Myrmecologists call it an "ant mill." I prefer to call it the "ant death spiral."

Some myrmecologists have stumbled upon circles of deceased ants in the wild, grisly monuments to the catastrophe of their blind adherence to a signal. It is a tragic consequence of the very adaptation that allows ant colonies to be so successful. For ants, the death spiral is an unfortunate, but unavoidable, cost of being the most successful insect species on our planet.

Like ants, we understand our world through signals, through observation then action. We measure nearly everything we do. Performance at work. Quality of healthcare. Competitiveness in sports. Advantage in the market. Effectiveness of a product. Strength of the economy. Quality of education. Congestion of roads. Profits, revenue, and growth of a business.

Are our children learning in school? Test them. Are we productive at work? Tally our hours. Are professional athletes worth the money they are paid? Track every action they take and convert it into a stat. Is a business successful? Slice and dice its profits, revenue, growth, and other numbers until you're certain.

These measures, evaluations, and performance indicators are our metrics. They are the tools we use to quantitatively understand not only our own lives, but the rest of our world. We use metrics in our schools, our workplaces, our houses of government, and our homes. We use metrics to measure our productivity at work and measure how well our children are learning in school. Metrics help us gauge the size of our economy, the effectiveness of our healthcare, and the impact of congestion in our cities.

Metrics aid in our decisions about what things we value and prioritize over others. Metrics shape our understanding of the world: We spend tremendous amounts of time and resources choosing, collecting, and analyzing the data that make up these metrics. There is almost nothing that we do not measure.

There is an important distinction to be made here. In this book we will talk a lot about metrics. We will also mention measurement. How are the two different? Measurements are simply anything you can quantify. The speed of a cheetah is a measurement. The height of the Empire State Building is a measurement. The number of cheese pizzas consumed in the United States every year is a measurement. Simple enough.

Where metrics differ is that metrics are measures that have a value assigned to them. Metrics are used to tell us whether things are improving or getting worse. Metrics have an objective. Getting an A on the exam is better than getting a D. Increasing profits of a company is good. Metrics are simply measures with a goal in mind. While there are differences between measures and metrics, it is rare that we measure something without assigning some sort of objective with that measure. As Youngme Moon says, "The minute we choose to measure something, we are essentially choosing to aspire to it. A metric, in other words, creates a pointer in a direction."[2]

We are drowning in data. The digital revolution has unleashed a tidal wave of data upon the world, making all kinds of information effortlessly available to anyone with an Internet connection. No longer constrained by the tediousness of physical records and ledgers, we have more data than we know what to do with. Computers have not only exponentially increased our calculating power, they have also increased our ability to collect, store, and share information. The Internet expanded this amount of information and fundamentally changed the ease with which it is exchanged. This new information is being collected and utilized by governments, businesses, organizations, and individuals to inform policy, develop better products and marketing strategies, enhance productivity, address social problems, and satisfy personal interests.

This explosion of data has led to an explosion of our use of metrics. With more information available to us, there are more measures for us to track, more goals to achieve, and more evaluations to conduct. The revolution in data has had innumerable benefits for our world, no doubt. Better data means better decisions. More and better information means our healthcare system saves more lives, businesses deliver better products and services, and people make better choices about their health, wealth, and happiness.

Improvements in data are reinforcing a trend that has been growing since the nineteenth century: performance management. The idea is simple. In order to improve any system or process, you simply need to break the system into manageable, measurable components; establish standards for those measurements; and then create incentives for people in those systems to meet those measurements. With more data available for us to analyze, the allure of this strategy only grows. Improvements in data analysis, computing, and information storage have accelerated this trend. With more information available for companies, organizations, and governments, the more measures can be optimized and the more tasks, activities, and targets can be tracked.

If you want to improve a retail business, break it into its component parts: supply chain management, sales, accounting, and so on. Give those in charge of supply chain standards for delivery times, inventory, transportation time, and such. Provide salespeople with goals and targets for the amount of sales. Do the same for marketing, research, and development, accounting, and any other component of the business. Nearly every organization has been the target of performance management, from public school systems, to multinational corporations, the healthcare system, sports teams, social media strategies, small companies, cities, supply chains, and our environment. The use of data and metrics has infiltrated nearly every part of our lives.

Yet the digital revolution has created an information hubris. The brighter the light we have to shine on the measurable parts of our world, the more we believe that the parts we cannot measure no longer exist. With the new information we have, we forget about all the things we don't know, or have trouble knowing. We focus so intensely on the things that are seen in the light, that we forget that the keys to success might be found in the dark. The business that discovers considerable new information on its supply chain, production process, and transport to market shouldn't neglect the harder-to-obtain information on marketability, innovation, employee motivation or simply unknown and unpredictable changes in the market.

This abundance of information has downsides. Just as ants can be led astray by a pheromone that would ordinarily lead them to food, we too can be led astray by metrics we think help us. Not only do we have to be critical about the veracity and integrity of the information we consume (and there are great books to read on that topic), we also have to understand what the data mean, why they are important, and how they affect what we do.

There are many books, articles, and resources dedicated to data science. You need only search statistics, analytics, or actuarial sciences on Amazon or Google before you come across thousands of resources that will tell you everything you need to know about statistical significance, data analysis, risk assessment, and analyzing information. But that is not what this book is about. This book is about a fundamentally different question. The question this book wants to answer, and what books on data science miss, is not, How do we analyze or evaluate different data?

Instead it is, How does what we measure affect what we do and how we do it? How does the way we measure something change the way we think and act, what we value, and ultimately what we achieve?

This book is about using the right metrics: the measures we can use in every aspect of our lives to make life better. But more important, this book is about the pitfalls of using the wrong metrics and the harm in misunderstanding them. For there is a dark side to metrics. Misusing, misunderstanding, and misrepresenting metrics can lead to counterproductive efforts, wasteful activities, and sometimes outright destructive behavior. Those same tools we use to understand, evaluate, and analyze our world can also cloud our judgment, misdirect our focus, or deceive us of the truth.

David Manheim says there are three main reasons we use metrics.[3] The first reason we use metrics is to gain an understanding of the truth. Our intuition, while sometimes useful, can often be wrong. Using measurements allows us to determine exactly what is happening. If a salesperson says he is great at his job, there might be good reason to believe him, maybe he is great with customers and understands his product well. But without looking at his actual sales data, we don't know how good of a salesperson he really is.

The same could be said for most anything we measure. Does China have a bigger economy than Germany? What is the crime rate in Philadelphia? How many patients does a hospital treat in a year? Those are not things most of us would have a good sense of. By measuring them, we get closer to the truth than our intuition would suggest. Metrics provide us with certainty. When we measure something, we are replacing our intuition with fact. Even a little bit of information moves us closer to the truth and further away from uncertainty.

Second, measurement helps us simplify complex systems. A CEO can't and frankly doesn't want to know every detail of what every division, manager, or employee in their company is doing. Government officials can't monitor every single service they provide to every citizen. A hospital can't monitor every single action of every nurse, doctor, specialist, or administrative staff it employs. A city cannot understand the actions of every commuter, business, or garbage truck. Metrics help reduce these complex systems in legible and meaningful ways. Metrics provide us with simplicity.

Third, measurement addresses issues of trust. If you were to ask employees, managers, government administrators, or athletes whether they are better than their peers, most would say they are. But how do you know? When an employee says she is working hard and contributing to the company, how do you know that she is? When a company says it has the highest sales, or greatest earnings in its field, can you trust it at its word? Metrics can help address this issue of trust. They create separate criteria that can be used to verify any claims, independent of anybody's word. Metrics provide us with verification.

I would add a fourth reason, partially linked to the issues of certainty and trust: Metrics allow us to be objective. In many systems there are many differing perspectives on what is valued and what matters. Who is a better police officer? Which athlete is better at his or her sport? Which manager has a better performing team? The answer will change depending on who you talk to, and what aspects of performance he or she thinks are more valuable. If we were to just rely on personal perspectives of which is better, we would never be able to resolve these types of questions.

Metrics provide an objective, dispassionate, and consistent criteria that we can use to compare and evaluate performance. Metrics allow us to remove the messy, sometimes controversial and emotionally charged, discussions about what is important and why. Metrics can cut through the dialogue and provide a clear, agreed-upon standard that applies equally to everyone. Metrics provide us with objectivity.

Most metrics ultimately are used for a similar purpose: to improve what we do. We use tests in school with the goal of improving learning. We measure what we do at work to increase our productivity and the company's bottom line. We measure company performance to make better investments. We measure which products are more environmentally friendly to preserve our planet. In an ideal world we choose the best metrics and follow the path they suggest to success.

Yet just like pheromone trails, these metrics can lead us astray. Each of these purposes of metrics have a downside. Throughout this book we will find that each of these purposes can mislead, misconstrue, and misrepresent what is really happening and undermine the goals that the metrics were intended for in the first place. Our metrics can cause us to undertake counterproductive actions. They can draw our focus to things that in the end don't matter. We spend an inordinate amount of our time and resources on ineffective activities because we choose the wrong metrics. Our metrics can distort our views of the world. We can even become slaves to our metrics, like ants in a death spiral, focusing so much on how well we score on our measurement that we forget what we are actually trying to achieve.

But we are not ants. We do not have to blindly follow the trail laid out by our metrics. We have the ability to look up from the path and reassess where we are going. We can stop and figure out whether we are truly getting closer to our goal, or if we are just spinning our wheels. We get to choose which metrics we should follow, and even whether we should be following any metric at all.

I am an urban planner by profession, and the study and practice of how cities function is full of all kinds of metrics. Through my education and career, I have come across numerous examples of poor misunderstandings and misuse of metrics in the world of urban planning, along with some good ones. The ways we measure congestion or housing affordability, for example, are seriously flawed metrics, as we will see later in this book. However, once I started understanding the shortcomings of these metrics, I started to notice that urban planning wasn't alone in its flaws when it came to measurement. I started to notice flawed metrics in other areas: education, healthcare, business, economics, environment, and sports, to name a few.

When I researched other metrics, or talked to professionals in other fields, I started to notice that there were similarities in the flaws people were noticing. An error in understanding a metric in urban planning was similar to one about how environmentally friendly a product was. An error a doctor noticed in how health clinics were evaluated was similar to one occurring in the business world. A better way to evaluate players in basketball was related to the decision the Coca-Cola Company made to start using plastic bottles. These errors are recurring, and they cross subject lines. This book is my attempt to categorize, describe, and offer solutions to the most common errors of metrics.

There are many ways a metric can mislead us. Misunderstanding how people will respond to metrics, focusing on what we put into something rather than what we get out, prioritizing the short- over the long-term, misusing denominators, capturing only part of a whole, not qualifying our measurements, focusing on what can be measured, or simply failing to recognize we can't always measure what really matters are all ways that metrics can lead us astray.

Fortunately we can learn from these errors. We can learn that our guides are not infallible. We can learn how to choose better maps on our journey, or to rely less on those that we know are imperfect. We can learn to recognize how and why our metrics can mislead us so we don't fall into the traps they set for us. We can learn how to improve on the measurements we use in our lives, by following the examples set by others. Finally, we can step back from incessantly measuring ourselves and learn to focus on those things that we cannot measure, but that are the most important to us. We will examine each of these errors in a separate chapter in this book, look at some examples of each, and discover lessons about how to identify and address each one.

Starting with the first chapter, "Teaching to the Test," this book delves into the world of standardized testing in schools and shows how fanatical dedication to a measurement can lead to unproductive, unnecessary, and sometimes incredibly destructive habits. The chapter shows how an unhealthy emphasis on a single measurement of student performance has worsened the quality of education, forced teachers to dumb down their material, rewarded students for brute memorization rather than authentic understanding, punished students for thinking deeply, and even driven teachers to cheat. More important the chapter demonstrates that this phenomenon is not limited to the classroom. Any metric, when exclusively and intensively pursued, can lead to perverse results, whether in business, healthcare, economics, sports, or any endeavor we pursue. The chapter shows that teaching to the test isn't just about schools, it is about the ability of any metric to alter the way we behave in radical, and often contradictory, ways.

The next chapter, "The Ins and Outs," explains how mismeasuring inputs, outputs, and outcomes can result in counterproductive efforts. The chapter tells the story of several women who, in their own way, discovered the difference among what you put into a task, what you do with that effort, and ultimately what you achieve. The chapter introduces Dr. Aufricht, who felt the healthcare system encouraged doctors to see more patients, rather than focus on improving their health; Heather White, who saw nonprofit organizations focus more on highlighting their efforts rather than their impacts; and Kali Ressler and Jodi Thompson, who, while working at Best Buy, found out that the world of business measured workers by how long they worked rather than what they actually achieved. Through all these stories, this chapter shows how metrics that focus on efforts are misguided and distract from the real goal of improving achievements.

The next chapter, "The Long and Short of It," examines how metrics can distort long-term versus short-term priorities. Through two examples, executive pay in corporations and research performance in academia, the chapter demonstrates how metrics cause us to overvalue short-term results at the expense of the long-term value. Metrics, founded on the certainty of quantification, deal poorly with the uncertain future and overvalue the short-term.

Next, is "The Problem of Per," our tendency to neglect, misuse, or even overuse the denominator (or the "per") in our measurements. The chapter shows how, by using the right denominator, New York is actually a much safer place for pedestrians than most US cities, even though it has the most pedestrian deaths of any city in America. It also discusses how using the wrong denominator can make a killer disease look good and how manipulating a denominator can make one of the highest energy-intensive countries look like the least.

The dangers of measuring just a small part of a complex whole is discussed in the next chapter, "The Forest and the Trees." This chapter shows how measuring just a small part of a complex system leads us to believe that paying less for a house farther away from work is cheaper (it isn't), that eating food from far away uses more energy than food closer to home (it doesn't), why plastic bottles can be more environmentally friendly than glass, why energy efficient lightbulbs can increase carbon emissions, and why the athlete who scores the most points isn't always the best player on the team.

The next chapter, "Apples and Oranges," discusses how lumping different things together into a single measurement can deceive us. For example, it shows how being outnumbered in war doesn't mean being at a disadvantage, how measuring diseases by the number of people they kill misses a big part of the picture (and why increases in cancer rates is actually a good thing), and how putting information on maps often leads to misunderstanding what is going on.

Next, "Not Everything That Can Be Counted Counts" looks at examples of where an obsession with measurement led to drastic consequences. In many organizations, measurement becomes an end in and of itself, and the real purpose of the organization is lost in the numbers game. The chapter shows how ultimately many leaders chose to focus on the numbers, not because they have an attentive focus on details, but because they are unable, or unwilling, to deal with the messy world outside of what can be quantified The chapter looks at two examples where organizations devolved into numbers games with terrible consequences: the New York Police Department in the 1990s and 2000s and the US military in Vietnam.

After that, "Not Everything That Counts Can Be Counted" gets to the root of the issue by taking a critical look at the fundamental driving forces behind metrics. First, the chapter examines the idea that metrics drive change and motivate people. The foundational theories of Taylorism, performance management, scientific management, key performance indicators, and most current organizational fads are built on the same assumption: If you measure people and provide incentives, you will get results. Using examples from business, motivation theory, and organizational psychology, the chapter examines how metrics and incentives, when used improperly, can in fact demotivate people and lead to counterproductive outcomes.

Subsequently, "Not Everything That Counts" examines one of the most used, and most criticized, metrics today: Gross Domestic Product (GDP). By examining the critiques of GDP, this chapter shows that the flaws of metrics are never in the metrics themselves, but in how people use them. Like GDP many metrics are used in ways never originally intended. More important, there is a lesson to be learned from the creator of GDP, one that speaks to every metric we deal with: Just because we can measure something, does not mean that it matters.

The penultimate chapter, "The Measure of Metrics," revisits the reasons we use metrics. The chapter reflects on the issues of complexity, objectivity, certainty, and trust that drive us to use metrics and how each of those motivations, in its own way, undermines the very purpose it intends to serve. The chapter examines how our desires for simplicity, objectivity, certainty, and trust can distort metrics from a useful tool into a terrible chimera. The second part of the chapter provides fourteen lessons about metrics that readers can use when dealing with them.

Finally, "Gateways Not Yardsticks" looks at how one organization, the Khan Academy, was able to rethink metrics and effectively turn them on their head. The chapter tells of how Salman Khan was able to develop a whole new approach to education by reexamining a simple idea: Why we test students in school. The chapter uses the lessons of the Khan Academy to draw broader lessons about how and why we use metrics in our lives and to remind us that metrics are not our masters.

This is not a book about statistics, analytics, or math (many of you are probably and understandably relieved). This book is not concerned with statistical validity, or the measure of the representativeness of a number. The book does not delve into the math behind regression analysis, probability, or other such statistical tools. There are great books on these topics, such as Nate Silver's *The Signal and the Noise*, which explores the science behind prediction and probability; Charles Wheelan's *Naked Statistics*, which provides a great overview of statistics in general; Daniel Kahneman's *Thinking Fast and Slow*, which delves into the psychology behind our understanding of probability, among other things; or Daniel Levitin's *A Field Guide to Lies*, which explains how statistics and other techniques can be used to mislead people.

This book doesn't discuss math at all, other than simple multiplication and division. Nor does this book discuss how accurate the things we measure are. It does not discuss data collection methods, statistical relevance, or bias in data.

Not that these things are not important. They most definitely are. Rather this book examines what conventional statistics and data science have mostly failed to. Conventional statistics is mostly concerned with whether the data being analyzed in our measurements are accurate or true. This book is concerned with another question altogether: whether the data being analyzed matters. Whether they are the right things to measure. Even if a measure is entirely true and accurate, that doesn't mean it properly captures the full picture of what you are trying to measure. Nor does it mean that the measure doesn't conflate efforts with results, nor intensity with size. An accurate measurement isn't the same thing as a good one. Too often that is forgotten.

This book seeks to answer a simple question: Are we measuring the right thing? Or, in the spirit of William Bruce Cameron's quote: Does what we are counting really count?

CHAPTER 1

TEACHING TO THE TEST

Goodhart's Law and the Paradox of Metrics

On April 27, 2015, Jeanene Worrell-Breeden waited for her train on the New York City subway. Worrell-Breeden, a primary school principal, was described as a "tireless champion for all," and praised for creating a "culture of academic excellence" at all schools where she taught (often where many students were poor).[1] She was the founding principal at the Teachers College Community School in Harlem, a school described as a "runaway success" by New York City Councilman Mark Levine.[2] Her school was the pride of the community, everyone in the neighborhood wanted his or her children to go to Teachers College Community School. In 2015, over 464 applications were received for students to enroll for just fifty spots at the school.

Two weeks before that day, the third-grade students of Teachers College Community School had completed an exam. Worrell-Breeden had spent the morning of the exam day serving breakfast to the students and holding a pep rally to raise the students' spirits.[3] Pep rallies are not normal for schools to hold prior to exams. But there was a lot riding on that particular one.

In 2013, New York, along with forty-two other states, adopted the Common Core program, an educational standard developed by the Obama administration as part of the Race to the Top initiative and intended to be applied across the United States. The program set out standards for what students needed to learn in English and math at the end of each grade, developed tests to evaluate students against those standards, and implemented an educational grant program where those test results played an important role in determining eligibility.[4] The first year of the assessment was to take place in the 2014–2015 school year and third-grade students would be the youngest to take the exams.

The tests themselves were developed by two consortia, the Smarter Balanced Assessment Consortium (SBAC) and partnership for Assessment of Readiness for College (PARCC), who were given 360 million dollars to create the new tests. Those tests would be highly influential in evaluating teachers and principals and in determining funding eligibility for the school for Race to the Top grants. How the students performed on the exam didn't just matter to the students, their parents, or their teachers. Thousands of dollars of grant money were on the line. The stakes were high.

On April 27, 2017, hours before Worrell-Breeden stood waiting for the B train near 135th Street and St. Nicholas Avenue, an unnamed colleague of Worrell-Breeden's had made a complaint to the New York City Education Department against Worrell-Breeden. The complainant alleged that Worrell-Breeden had admitted to forging test scores for several of her third-grade students on the Common Core exam.

As the B train approached, Jeanene Worrell-Breeden—educator, mentor, wife, and inspiration to hundreds of students—jumped in front of it. She was rushed to the Harlem Hospital Center. A week later she died.

▐▐▐▐▐▐▐▐▐▐

Every year, high school seniors all over the world prepare for their final exams. For the students this test is important. Extremely important. In many countries final tests determine half of high school students' final grades, if not more. Those grades will be used to determine what universities they can be admitted to, affecting the quality of education they receive, what relationships they will make during their time at university, and ultimately their future career path. Those grades will also determine their eligibility for thousands of dollars of scholarships, which will affect whether they have to take a part-time job to help pay for tuition, taking up precious studying time or time spent on extracurricular activities, which will influence their future employers' evaluation of them. To say there is a lot riding on these exams would be an understatement.

Take the math final exam, for example: a three-hour marathon of mathematical problem-solving. Most students will write their exam in the high school gymnasium, alongside hundreds of other students who are feeling varying degrees of anxiety. The exam itself will consist of a mix of questions covering subject matter the students learned throughout the year, the majority of which will be in multiple-choice format. The same will be the case for the other exams: social studies, English, and science.

The test isn't just important to the students. Teachers, principals, and school boards also have a lot riding on how well the students do on the exam. As the test will be used for university admissions, parents will be putting pressure on teachers to ensure their children do well on the exam so they can get into a good school.[5]

Principals also feel the pressure of the exam—in many jurisdictions the school's test scores will be published in the local paper. How well the school does could affect the future enrollment and reputation of the school as parents choose "better-performing schools" for their children. The test scores determine the amount of funding the school receives if the school is in a state that has adopted the Common Core program and the grant funding that goes along with it, or in a country that has adopted similar standards. The school board feels the pressure too as the performance of schools in their district will too affect how they attract students and funding. The pressure goes even higher up. State legislators, secretaries of education, governors, and even presidents have all felt the pressure to improve education. This often translates to the simplistic call: "Test scores are low, make them go up."[6]

This situation is all too familiar for anyone who has gone through high school, as most who are reading this book have done. Sadly, it is becoming familiar too to those in much younger grade levels; standardized tests are now part of the curriculum for students as early as third grade in Common Core states.

But there is a problem.

The problem isn't that we shouldn't demand our students work hard, or that teachers, principals, and school boards shouldn't do the best to teach our children. It isn't a problem because we shouldn't demand to know how our students, teachers, and schools are performing. It is a problem because standardized tests, especially exams that are heavily multiple-choice, timed, and heavily weighted, are a poor measurement of a student's understanding or ability. And they hurt learning.

Let's start with the questions themselves, specifically those that are multiple-choice. Multiple-choice questions are often used, as they are an efficient way to administer a test. They have several advantages: objective, simple to mark, easy for students to fill out, and determining correct answers doesn't depend on teachers trying to decipher the illegible scrawl of a high school senior. The problem with all of these advantages is they have everything to do with the ease of marking the exam and nothing to do with whether the test method is a good reflection of learning. As Bruce C. Bowers has said:

> The main purpose of standardized testing is to sort large numbers of students in as efficient a manner as possible. This limited goal, quite naturally, gives rise to short-answer, multiple-choice questions. When tests are constructed in this manner, active skills, such as writing, speaking, acting, drawing, constructing, repairing, or any number of other skills that can and should be taught in schools are automatically relegated to second-class status.[7]

Bowers's point is that multiple-choice tests discriminate against the kinds of questions, and therefore the kinds of thinking, that operate on a higher level than crude memorization. Simply selecting the correct answer leaves a lot to be desired. Multiple-choice tests lead students to the belief that being smart is simply a matter of knowing a lot of facts and being able to remember things quickly. Multiple-choice tests are often little more than a measurement of a student's performance of short-term memory.

Multiple-choice questions also lack an important component of a good test: requiring students to generate answers themselves. Such questions, termed free-response, not only require students to think more critically, but prevent them from short-cutting on a test. Imagine you were given the following question on a test:

Who was the twenty-seventh president of the United States?

> *a) George Washington*
> *b) Abraham Lincoln*
> *c) William Howard Taft*
> *d) Winston Churchill*

The answer of course is William Howard Taft. George Washington was the first president, Lincoln was the sixteenth, and Churchill was of course not a president of the United States at all. To know the answer to the above question, you don't need to know anything about William Howard Taft at all. You don't need to know he was the twenty-seventh president, or even a president at all. As long as you can disqualify the other answers, you will get the correct answer. In this question, answers a, b, and d might as well be Scooby Doo, RoboCop, and Conan the Barbarian.

Another flaw of multiple-choice questions is that a subset of students have particular trouble with them. These students don't struggle because they don't know the material. Nor is it that they suffer from test anxiety. In fact, many students who have trouble on multiple-choice tests are seen as some of the strongest students by their teachers. The reason these students have trouble on multiple-choice questions is because they are too smart.

Students with a greater depth of understanding approach the subject matter with greater appreciation for complexity and nuance, so they will ponder over questions for much longer than the examiners have planned for, causing them to rush through large parts near the end of the exam. They will select an answer, only to second-guess themselves a minute later. Often, talented students will approach a multiple-choice question and think "it can't be this easy, they must be trying to trick us." Because of this, many talented students will not do as well as their classroom performance nor their understanding of the material, would suggest.

These students are not demonstrating a lack of conviction or confidence. They aren't taking a long time on questions because they don't understand them. Many of these students understand the material with more subtlety and nuance than other students in the class. These students are thinking on a higher level. They have a deep understanding of the topic, knowing that phenomena are complex and have multiple causes. They think on a level that we would want our managers, leaders, politicians, and, well, everyone to think. But when they are faced with a multiple-choice question on a test that simplifies a complex problem, they hesitate:

> *Our beliefs and values about our world are expressed through our actions and interactions with the world around us, which in turn most wholly reflect our:*
>
> *a) ideology*
> *b) culture*
> *c) society*
> *d) individualism*

The above problem, taken from a twelfth-grade social studies practice diploma exam, is the kind of question that is difficult for a gifted student. In fact, it would pose difficulty for any person approaching the subject with a nuanced understanding. I have an undergraduate degree in political science with a minor in history, and I couldn't answer the question with any confidence. The answer is a) ideology.

The question takes an incredibly complicated phenomena involving the degree to which culture, ideology, personal beliefs, and societal norms influence our actions and interactions with the world around us and reduces it to a single statement. That is frustratingly simplistic. Political philosophers could debate the question for years, if not decades. Likely, "ideology" is the answer to the question simply because somewhere in the student's textbook there was a sentence that read "Ideology is the beliefs and values we have about our world that influence our actions and interactions with the world around us." The student was just expected to memorize it.

The question is not really about whether the student understands what ideology is, it is about whether he or she remembers reading a particular excerpt in the textbook. No wonder so many children are disillusioned and confused with the education system when so much of the evaluation comes down to whether they remember a particular phrase in a textbook.

That is another reason why multiple-choice questions are not good representations of ability of understanding. The more knowledgeable and sophisticated a student is, the more difficult the answers become and the more time he or she has to spend on them. In a timed exam environment, that will likely mean the student will do worse than those who choose the easy answer.[8]

Questions such as these can be found in all different courses and throughout all different subject matters. Multiple-choice questions inherently require subjects to be dumbed down in order to make answers cleaner. In the process they lose any sense of nuance, complexity, creativity, or diversity. Subjects that should be the subject of debate, personal differences, and context are reduced to a standardized answer. Here is an example from the writing and language section of an online practice SAT, produced by the College Board (the creator of the SAT):[9]

> *Paleontologists are using modern technology to gain a greater under-standing of the distant past. With the aid of computed tomography (CT) scanning and 3-D printing, researchers are able to create accurate models of prehistoric fossils.*
>
> *At this point, the writer is considering adding the following sentence.*
>
> *Fossils provide paleontologists with a convenient way of estimating the age of the rock in which the fossils are found.*
>
> *Should the writer make this addition here?*
>
> *a) Yes, because it supports the paragraph's argument with an impor-tant detail.*
>
> *b) Yes, because it provides a logical transition from the preceding sentence.*
>
> *c) No, because it is not directly related to the main point of the paragraph.*
>
> *d) No, because it undermines the main claim of the paragraph.*

The problem with the question is that it reduces an incredibly compli-cated, subjective, and, honestly, personal process—writing and editing—into a standardized formula. Depending on the audience for the writing (who the test taker isn't given information about in the exam), the per-sonal style and voice of the author, and the publication he or she is writing for, as well as the social climate he or she is writing in, the answer could be different. How does the student know if the audience even knows what fossils are? That might be useful information to provide depending on the audience.

I imagine those in the writing profession—writers, editors, market-ers, agents, publishers—not only will have varying opinions on how to best structure a piece of writing, the choice of words, paragraph struc-ture, and voice, but I can guarantee none of them would state that there is only one "correct" way to write. Writers, editors, and everyone involved in the writing process have continual discussions and back-and-forth about writing. No one has a "right" answer. Yet the question on the SAT practice exam assumes exactly that: There is only one correct answer. It is

c. Here are three questions from a chemistry practice diploma exam from my home province:

The symbol "Ga" represents what element?
What is the symbol for vanadium?
The symbol "Cm" represents what element?

While there are definitive answers to each of these questions, the response to all of these questions should be either: "Who cares?" or, if you are a chemist, "If you forgot, look at the periodic table on your desk for the answer." That is another downside of standardized tests: They often include questions with no discernible usefulness only because they are very easy to mark. It is memorization for the sake of memorization.

Question such as these are a poor evaluation of understanding or preparedness. How ridiculous would it be for your employer to ask you: "Quick, what is the symbol for vanadium?" and then to fire you for not knowing the answer? None of these questions are testing any kind of useful knowledge. They are simply asking you to memorize the periodic table of the elements. For what reason, other than to be able to test you on it, is entirely unclear.

Standardized tests are also generally biased against women. Tests such as the SAT tend to have a lot of multiple-choice questions, which women do not do as well as men on. A study in Ireland compared the results of similar subjects using multiple-choice tests and free-response tests. Men did better on the multiple-choice questions, and women did better on the free response.[10] Why is this?

First, men tend to use more of the shortcuts and tricks in answering multiple-choice tests than women, who tend to be more methodical in their process. Second, more women tend to suffer from test anxiety, and are more comfortable answering free-response questions, where they can express their fulsome understanding of a question, than multiple-choice, where they are more prone to second-guess themselves, furthering their anxiety.[11] Such test questions skew educational evaluations, discouraging smart and talented women from succeeding in school and adding to their frustrations with the education system. Apart from being heavily reliant on multiple-choice questions, nearly every standardized test written in our schools is timed. The countdown of the exam clock is perhaps the most anxiety-inducing aspect of the test experience. Every moment spent on a question is a moment you don't get to work on other questions. As the clock counts down, anxiety climbs.

The test stops being about answering questions correctly and becomes an exercise in answering quickly. Timed tests assume that knowledge and learning are about memorization and quick recall. In a world where Internet access is available on many people's phones, let alone their computers, and information on virtually anything is readily available almost anywhere, the usefulness of memorization is questionable. Even without access to information-rich Web resources, real-life situations rarely require people to remember facts, formulas, or processes on the spot. Other than trauma surgeons and athletes, how many professions require immediate reaction to a problem? How many workplaces prevent people from planning and strategizing about a problem before formulating a plan of action? As Alfie Kohn asks: How often are people forbidden to ask their coworkers for help?[12] Similarly, how many jobs prevent workers from having access to information relevant to their work? A company that removed manuals from the workplace would be a silly place to work.

Standardized tests are multiple-choice, so it is difficult to design the questions for higher-level thinking. Designing a multiple-choice test to sort students on their ability to apply creative thinking and problem-solving is incredibly difficult. So what happens? Students are tested on minutiae and memorization of irrelevant facts. They are tested on whether they remember the correct spelling of Neville Chamberlain's name, rather than the reason he was succeeded by Churchill. Complex concepts are dumbed down to simplistic definitions and categorizations. Higher-level learning is sacrificed for the desire for test questions that some children will get wrong, regardless of the reason why they are getting the question wrong. As Alfie Kohn points out, it is "easier to get agreement on whether a semi-colon has been used correctly than on whether an essay represents clear thinking."[13]

Multiple-choice, timed tests aim for objectivity and simplicity. But rarely is learning, or at least learning that is important, objective or simple. There are no doubt elements of learning that are objective or simple, or both; but those elements do not constitute the core of our learning, which is to understand. Memorizing a formula does not mean you understand it. Objectivity in tests is sacrificed in order to sort students, so questions are written to be biased, confusing, or just plain stupid.[14]

All of these shortcomings of how we test lead us to ask: What good are they? If timed, multiple-choice, norm-referenced tests are not useful at evaluating students' abilities to think creatively, critically analyze problems, or understand the material they are learning on a deep level, what are they useful for? Tests, despite their name, are not really designed to evaluate students' knowledge of subject material. What they are truly designed for, their real underlying purpose, is to sort and rank students. The primary purposes of standardized tests—the SATs, GREs, GMATs, MCATs, and LSATs—is to rank students in order to determine who gets admitted into which programs. A standardized test is a criterion for almost every postsecondary institution. Schools can only admit so many students each year, so a selection method is needed to facilitate this sorting. The most cost-effective (in other words, the cheapest) way to sort students is to use tests. Tests are not tools for authentic evaluation of the abilities and potential of students, but the "labelling of children; squeezing them into categories and limiting their futures."[15]

A test where each student scores 100 percent, even if each student excels at understanding the subject matter, is not a very good test for the purpose of admittance into college. (The question of how many people should be able to go to college, whether we should limit people's ability to attend a postsecondary institution altogether and how much funding is provided for them, and how that affects our society, is another debate altogether.) If everyone gets 100 percent on the test, the test must not be hard enough, nor discerning enough to weed out the unsuccessful students. Yet shouldn't we expect all of our students to get 100 percent on every test? Isn't that the purpose of education, to learn the subject matter? Knowing something 70 percent just doesn't seem right. So, tests are made harder. Or at least that is what test creators tell us. Too often rather, tests are simply made more arbitrary by including a lot more memorization and more questions that are deliberately vague.

The purpose of standardized admissions tests, in theory, is to determine which students will perform the best in school. Colleges and universities want to admit the students who will most likely perform the best in their classes and subsequently be more successful in their future careers. The idea is that the resources we put into higher education should be used on the students for whom it will have the greatest effect, which, in our test-happy society, means those students who do the best on tests. This is the message that testing companies, school administrators, and politicians who promote standardized tests have repeated again and again.

The problem, which may come as a shock, is that standardized tests have little, if any, correlation with success in college, when controlling for other factors.[16] Tests such as the MCAT (the medical college admission test) do little to predict how well students do on the practical aspects of medical school, such as clinical rotations, internships, or residencies.[17] The SAT is no better. One university, Bates College, decided to drop the SAT requirement for admission altogether due to its poor ability to predict college performance. Bates still allowed students to voluntarily submit SAT scores for consideration for admissions, and those who opted out submitted their scores only for the purposes of research (they weren't used in evaluating their admissions requirements). Researchers then compared the performance of those who submitted their SAT scores (which were generally higher) to those who didn't (generally lower) at the college. They found no statistical significance between the grades of students who did submit their grades and those who didn't, despite the fact that those who didn't on average scored 160 points less than those who did.[18]

Students who do well on standardized tests don't do any better after school either. There is little correlation between test scores and success in the workplace. This isn't surprising given the fact that tests are heavily weighted toward memorization and quick thinking rather than complex problem-solving and thorough analysis. Nor do tests evaluate motivation, social skills, or work ethic, which are often much more important traits to have in the workplace. In many workplaces the most useful workers are not the ones who can remember the most facts the quickest, but those who can make the best decisions. Memorizing a particular fact in a set amount of time is pretty useless when people have easy access to information.

So if those who do well on the SAT, LSAT, MCAT, GRE, and other standardized tests seem to do no better than others in undergraduate, law, medical, or graduate school, what are they better at? What exactly does high achievement on these tests predict? As Peter Sacks puts it, "Scoring high on standardized tests is a good predictor of one's ability to score high on standardized tests."[19]

In the drive to create "objective" criteria that could be used to separate students for college admissions, scholarship qualifications, or future jobs, we lost the objective of actually learning. Schools became test-preparation centers, focused intently on teaching children how to write tests well, and not to authentically understand what they were learning. Standardized tests send students the wrong message. Multiple-choice, timed tests tell students that education should be arduous work memorizing facts and figures. It sends the message to students that the most important criteria for evaluation is who can cram the hardest to fit as much irrelevant information into their heads before the exam. It removes all the wonder, awe, and curiosity involved in learning new ideas, discovering ways to solve problems, and understanding how our world works and fits together. Learning about math, science, social studies, and language should include activities filled with fascination, wonder, curiosity, and a desire to learn. Instead it is an arduous labor of memorization. No wonder most students hate school.

It is not just that tests are poor evaluators of learning, or that they focus on irrelevant information or dumbed down material. When the pressure to perform on tests grows, the classroom changes. Teachers, under pressure to have their students perform better on standardized tests, begin to focus less on learning and more on how to write tests well. They begin "teaching to the test."

First, teachers begin to focus less on material that may not be on the test. They spend more time drilling students on material that they believe (or sometimes nefariously already know) will be on the test, and less on engaging class discussions.[20] A particularly keen student, wanting to learn more about the subject, asks a question about material that is not on the test, and the teacher blows her off, not wanting to spend time on something that will not be evaluated, even though doing so would reinforce the student's desire to understand. Tests turn classrooms from places of inquiry and wonder into workhouses and turn teachers from learning facilitators into drill sergeants. It's not just the classroom that suffers. The other parts of school that make learning so rich and complete—playing on a sports team, acting in the school play, joining a club—are all potential victims to the relentless drive for better test scores. How many school athletes are told they can't play for the school team unless they increase their test scores?

Second, high-stakes tests cause teachers to dumb down the material. Focusing on tests shifts the focus in the classroom from understanding concepts to memorizing facts and figures. It may sound counterintuitive, but the shallower their thinking, the better students do on a test. Students who copy answers, guess a lot, and skip the hard parts of tests generally do better than those who review parts they do not understand, ask themselves questions as they read and try to connect what they are doing with what they learned. Those who are inquisitive are beaten on tests by those who have very little interest in actual learning. Knowing how flawed multiple-choice, timed tests can be, this isn't shocking. Those who answer as many unambiguous, simple questions in as short a time as possible will do better than those who spend more of their time deeply contemplating more ambiguous questions. But who is learning more? Tests teach children that school isn't about finding solutions to problems, gaining an understanding of a new concept, or discovering a facet of the wonderful world we live in. Tests teach children that school is about memorizing useless facts, cramming for tests, and trying not to be tricked by confusing questions. All the wonder, experimentation, and discovery of learning are replaced with the stress, inanity, and uselessness of memorization.

Third, teachers in test-oriented schools focus more on improving testing skills, rather than learning. Students are taught tricks and strategies for how to take tests, especially multiple-choice tests in a short time period. Guessing answers and reading answers before the questions are just two strategies that teachers teach. And they are taught at the expense of genuine learning. A study in the Canadian province of British Columbia by Thomas O'Shea and Marvin Wideen found that standardized tests caused teachers to spend more time lecturing in the classroom and less time leading classroom discussions.[21] The opposite is found in Japan, where schools typically have less of an emphasis on standardized tests. Compared to their American counterparts, Japanese teachers ask their students to come up with their own approaches to solving a problem and working them out,[22] while in the United States, students are simply instructed on the "correct" method to solve a problem and then practice implementing it. They have no idea why the method is correct. They are just told it is.

Fourth, teachers start to manipulate the composition of the classroom to ensure high test scores. Students having difficulty with the material are strategically removed from the classroom. Sometimes they are deemed to have learning disabilities, or simply excluded from tests in order to keep average scores high. Students who tend to do poorly on tests, in a relentless drive to improve average test scores, are put into remedial classes to remove them from the score calculations. Sometimes these exclusions are political. In 2015, New York education officials faced the dilemma where large numbers of students had chosen to opt out of standardized tests. That year, nearly 20 percent of students choose not to take standardized tests.[23]

Those students are not necessarily any less able than the others. In fact, they might exhibit higher levels of thinking. But because tests simplify concepts, punish creative and nuanced thinking, and reward speed, students who are more contemplative, thorough, and complex are told in fact that they are not as smart as the other students.

What have standardized tests done for schools? For starters, they have shifted the focus of the classroom from genuine learning to rote memorization. By doing so they have alienated and ostracized students who think on a deeper level than their peers. Standardized tests have brought a ruthless and unrelenting system of ranking into our schools, ensuring only a select few are able to advance. The problem is that those few are not necessarily any smarter or more able than the rest. They are just good at taking tests.

In all of these things that tests do to our schools, there is a common theme: They hurt real learning. With such an intense focus on sorting students, our tests become a perverted tool, rewarding simplistic ways of thinking and eroding authentic understanding. Tests have become the antithesis to learning.

The use of multiple-choice tests in schools is a result of choosing a metric based on the ease of use and implementation rather than its ability to accurately reflect the phenomena we are trying to measure. We shouldn't use a metric just because it is easy. Sure, it is easy to write multiple-choice questions that test students' memorization of mundane facts and figures, but that doesn't mean we should. Measuring how much time employees spend at work is easy, too, but that doesn't mean that's how we should measure their performance. Ease of measurement does not make the measurement relevant, important, or useful.

Standardized tests do not measure creative problem-solving well. That does not mean creative problem-solving is not important. Nor does it mean that we should do away with multiple-choice, timed tests completely. It simply means that we need to ensure that standardized tests do not dominate the classroom, nor become a substitute for what we deem important. Tests change schools. But they don't have to.

What standardized tests have done to our schools should be a warning of how blind adherence and deference to a metric can distort efforts, bringing about the opposite of what was intended. This phenomenon isn't restricted to schools. Any measurement, when followed with such blind devotion, separates us from the ultimate purpose and meaning behind anything we do. Just like the ants following the pheromone trail, blind adherence to standardized tests has led our education system down a perverse path, where learning is sacrificed for the ability to test well. Don't be an ant.

"Teaching to the test" may be a phrase ascribed to our education system, but "working out the clock," "looks good on paper," and "scores well" are just as familiar. All of them point to a situation where something may measure well, but in reality may be failing miserably. But the emphasis on test scores doesn't just change the way teachers operate in the classroom. Sometimes, in an environment of high-stakes testing, teachers will even begin to cheat.

||||||||||

In 2008, Heather Vogell and John Perry noticed something unusual about Atherton Elementary School in DeKalb County, Georgia. In the spring of that year, nearly half of the thirty-two fifth graders in the school had failed their yearly state education test. The students placed in the 10th percentile among elementary schools in the state, meaning that 90 percent of schools performed better on the test. However, when the students retook the test in the fall, under a provision recently implemented by federal authorities to allow schools to use updated test scores to meet requirements for federal funding, not only did the majority of students pass the exam, every single student did. On top of that, twenty-six of those students scored at the highest level possible on the exam. The school moved from the 10th percentile in the state to the 77th.

The improved test results meant the school achieved the status of "adequate yearly progress" as defined by the federal education program known as No Child Left Behind. Meeting the requirement meant the school would be eligible for further federal funding, and more important, would avoid punitive measures for failing to meet the standard. The principal of the school attributed the meteoric rise in the students' grades to intense tutoring that occurred over the summer, as well as increased attention paid by teachers to focus on the test.

Several other schools in Georgia had similarly unusual results. Adamsville Elementary and Parklane Elementary in Atlanta and two other schools in Glynn County and Gainesville also had achieved nearly impossible increases to test results.[24] Vogell and Perry, two journalists from the *Atlanta Journal Constitution*, published their findings in the paper.

Something was up.

Pittsburgh is a poor, predominantly black, working-class neighborhood in south Atlanta, about three miles from downtown. Situated adjacent to the Pegram rail shops in Atlanta, its name is a homage to the steel mills of Pittsburgh, Pennsylvania. Starting in the 1960s, wealthier black families began moving out of the neighborhood in search of wealthier areas in the city. From 1970 to 1990 the population decreased by half. By 2014 nearly half of the homes in the neighborhood were vacant. Prostitution and burglaries were endemic in the neighborhood. In the school district Pittsburgh belonged to, three-quarters of the students were living near or below the poverty line. Ninety percent were either black or Latino. Fewer than 40 percent graduated high school.[25] Pittsburgh was the kind of neighborhood people wanted to escape from, and many did. For those living in Pittsburgh, hope was rare. It was also home to Parks Middle School.

When Christopher Waller arrived at the school in 2005 as the new principal, he found a school that was on the verge of failure. His predecessor, while improving the school with renovations and hiring guidance counselors, had resigned amid accusations of sexual misconduct from his previous job.[26] Morale among the teachers was low. Students were struggling to keep up with the increasingly difficult standards set for them and often couldn't maintain the progress they had made in elementary school. Waller, the son of a teacher, had grown up in a small rural town in Georgia. As a child, he enjoyed playing "school" with his siblings (he played the teacher) or playing church (he played the preacher). He graduated with an education degree from college and, like his mother, his experience with education was primarily one working with low-income children.

At his first job he once had to remove a weapon from a student. Before arriving at Parks, Waller taught at various rural schools throughout Georgia as a science teacher, assistant football coach, administrative assistant, and assistant principal, and at night and on weekends he was a pastor at his church.[27]

Many students at Parks Middle didn't have a father at home; some had no parents at all. Many were raised by their grandparents, others were on the brink of being sent to juvenile detention. Others had parents who were on drugs or otherwise absent. Often during his time at Parks Middle, Waller found himself at court, pleading with judges not to send his students to jail.[28] Teachers' and parents' cars were stolen from the school. Break-ins at the school were common; one time the stolen equipment was recovered from the home of one of the parents. Some students were sexually assaulted walking home from school. Waller even had to testify against a man who had sexually abused and confined one of his students.[29]

Waller had an immense task in front of him. Parks Middle had done poorly on its tests over the last few years, putting its status in jeopardy. Waller had to turn around a school that was on the brink to ensure it met its performance targets, otherwise the school could lose funding, or worse, be closed. It was an incredible task. At age thirty-two, Waller was the youngest principal in the entire Atlanta Public School system.[30]

Four years earlier, in 2001, President George W. Bush had signed the No Child Left Behind Act. The act would drastically increase federal funding for education in the country, but would require schools to meet certain standards in order to qualify for the money. Federal support for education would increase by over 25 percent from 2001 to 2004. The program was based on an educational philosophy called standards-based education reform. Standards-based education reform posits that if you set high standards for education, establish measurable performance goals, and hold teachers and administrators to account for those goals, you will improve individual student performance. The system is heavily reliant on the use of standardized tests to determine the level of student performance and to track progress.

No Child Left Behind granted states funding based on the implementation of standardized tests. In order to qualify for funding, schools would have to demonstrate improved performance year over year. However, the standards for performance were left up to each state. In Georgia, those performance standards were implemented through standardized tests called the Criterion Referenced Competency Tests (CRCT). The tests focused on five areas: reading, math, English/language arts, science, and social studies.[31] Schools were classified as either meeting "Adequate Yearly Progress," meaning that the school's test scores were improving, or as "In Need of Improvement," meaning they were failing. For schools that did achieve Adequate Yearly Progress, federal funds would provide additional support. Those schools that didn't meet the Adequate Yearly Progress requirement would have to develop plans to improve performance over the next two years. Once a school was classified as "In Need of Improvement," students could choose to move to another school (and take associated funding with them). If schools didn't improve after the two-year performance plan, the school would be forced to offer free tutoring to students, putting further strain on resources. If the fourth year was missed, the school could have measures implemented against its will, possibly including the wholesale replacement of staff or introduction of a new curriculum. If performance doesn't improve by the sixth year, drastic measures were imposed on the school, such as a take-over by the state or the closure and disbandment of the school entirely.

This was the dilemma that Christopher Waller found himself in during the 2006 school year. Parks Middle had shown poor results in previous years and was classified as a school "In Need of Improvement." Fifty-eight percent of the students in the school needed to pass the math CRCT and 67 percent had to pass language CRCT that year, or the school could face shutdown.[32] As Waller put it: "It didn't matter how much the child was taught or how much the child learned, if we didn't keep up with the targets, we would not be there to help the children continue the learning process. If we did not meet AYP then the school would close."[33]

‖‖‖‖‖‖‖

In 1999 Beverly Hall became the superintendent of Atlanta Public Schools. Hall had considerable experience in serving disadvantaged and underperforming schools. Born in Montego Bay, Jamaica, Hall graduated from Brooklyn College and then received her master's from the City University of New York and her education degree from Fordham

University.[34] She worked in Fort Greene in Brooklyn and in Newark, where she worked as the superintendent since 1995.[35] When she came to Atlanta, she brought with her not only a passion for educating disadvantaged students, but also a knack for fund-raising. But more than anything, Hall believed in accountability.[36]

In addition to the incentives and punitive measures that the federal No Child Left Behind Act implemented on the school, under Beverly Hall Atlanta Public Schools devised additional measures tied to test performance. A wing of the school board, called the Department of Research, Planning and Accountability, set out yearly targets for each school to meet. Subsuperintendents from the school board would monitor performance by individual schools and hold principals to account.[37]

If schools met their performance targets, Hall would reward them with grant money secured by donors. Teachers, principals, support staff, and even bus drivers would receive up to two thousand dollars in cash as a bonus if the school met its target. Otherwise, if principals did not meet performance targets within three years, they would be fired.[38] No exceptions, no excuses.[39] Hall followed up on her threats. In her ten years as the superintendent, 90 percent of principals were replaced.[40]

Test results were everything at Atlanta Public Schools. Every fall the district would hold a convocation ceremony at the Georgia Dome, the home of the Atlanta Falcons. Schools that met their performance targets would be recognized by being sat on the field itself, while underperforming schools were relegated to the bleachers. The seating arrangement was so important that there was even a term created for it: "making the floor."[41]

For Waller the focus on testing at Atlanta Public Schools, in the form of CRCT results, was unlike anything he had every experienced before. In his experience in rural counties the focus was on instruction, or performance, or in one rural county, just trying to get the kids to come to class and not get into fights.[42] But in Atlanta Public Schools it was testing, testing, and more testing. Not only were the standards that schools were required to meet greater than what No Child Left Behind established, they were constantly increasing, with the idea that progress should be continual. Hall had implemented a system whereby each year the number of students who met the standard had to increase by 3 percent.[43] As Waller put it, "Even though the kids who performed at one level moved on to another grade level, they set the standard for the grade level behind them. It became increasingly more difficult to meet that target of kids exceeding the standard from year to year."[44]

In Atlanta Public Schools under Beverly Hall, there were no excuses. Meet the standard or suffer the consequences. Hall made it clear to Waller, as she did with every other principal in the system, what was expected of people in his position: "The way people keep their jobs in Atlanta is they make targets."[45] When principals would meet with Hall, in groups of ten or twelve, she would display each school's scores in large graphs in the room and would ask each principal whether they would meet their targets that year. No one dared to say no.[46]

In addition to the funding from the federal government through the No Child Left Behind Act, Hall was able to secure millions in private donations for Atlanta Public Schools, which were distributed throughout the system. Hall would use the money from philanthropists to pay for tutors and help schools set up after-school programs. Advocating for the role of education in lifting people out of poverty, Hall was able to raise over forty million dollars for the school district from the GE Foundation and the Bill and Melinda Gates Foundation alone.[47]

The results achieved across Atlanta were nothing short of astonishing. When she began as superintendent, fewer than 50 percent of eighth graders met the state's language arts standards. By 2009 that number had risen to 90 percent. Schools were turned around. Students were given hope. Beverly Hall had proven that the educational reform movement and performance targets worked. By setting rigorous targets and holding teachers, principals, and administrators accountable, Hall had created a turnaround for Atlanta Public Schools. Her work at Atlanta Public

Schools caught the attention of the American Association of School Administrators, who named her the National Superintendent of the Year in 2009. The results that Beverly Hall achieved with Atlanta Public Schools were so incredible that the city council had declared that September 8, 2009, be Dr. Beverly L. Hall Day. A ceremony was held in her honor.[48]

||||||||||

When Waller began his tenure as principal at Parks Middle, he noticed something very unusual. The students entering Parks Middle from the elementary schools that fed Parks Middle had done well on the CRCT exams in language arts. Yet, when they showed up for class at Parks Middle, they struggled to read even at a first-grade level. There was no explanation why students would lose four grade levels of reading comprehensive over the summer. Waller suspected there was only one explanation for the discrepancy: The elementary schools were cheating.[49]

Waller tried to bring the situation up with the subsuperintendent responsible for the district Parks Middle School belonged to, Michael Pitts, but he was brushed off. Instead, Pitts responded to Waller's concern by threatening that if Waller continued to complain, he would receive only the "lowest performing" students from those schools, further exacerbating the scale of the task he had.[50]

Overwhelmed by his situation Waller brought up the conundrum with several teachers at his school, and the predicament the test results put them in. One teacher told him that she had heard about an elementary school where teachers would change students' tests by erasing the answers after the children had written the exam. Gregory Reid, the vice principal, told Waller he had heard of schools where teachers were able to obtain the test questions in advance.[51]

Waller was in a difficult position. He was in charge of a school that was on the verge of being closed down, required to meet standards that were unrealistic. The punishment for not meeting those targets wouldn't just be felt by Waller himself—teachers would be relocated, or potentially dismissed. More important the students could lose their school. For many, it was the only source of stability in their lives. So, in order to keep up with what was happening in the elementary schools feeding into Parks Middle, and to keep his school operating, Waller decided to do what dozens of principals in the Atlanta Public Schools system were already doing: cheat.[52]

Waller knew he had to only work with teachers who he could trust. So he built a small, but dedicated, inner circle of teachers who would help him ensure the school would meet their yearly performance targets. The first teacher he recruited, after months of pressure, was Damany Lewis, a math teacher at the school. Lewis was in his late twenties, born in East Oakland to a bank-teller mother and crack-addict father. He had worked at Parks since 2000. He was the football coach and soccer coach and had started the chess club. Lewis was, by all accounts, a superstar. Knowing that many students didn't have the means to do so, Lewis would wash their clothes for them. For others, he offered a place to sleep when their parents were absent or high on drugs.[53] Waller was only able to persuade Lewis to help cheat after convincing him that if the students failed the test, the school would close, students would be separated, and the role that Parks Middle played in the community would end. Lewis yielded.

The cheating system at Parks Middle centered around the two strategies that Waller learned of earlier: obtaining tests before they were administered and distributing them to trusted teachers, and physically changing students' test answers after the tests were handed in but before they were graded. Obtaining the tests was not too difficult. Lewis would sneak into the office where tests were kept, open the test packages with a razor, obtain a couple copies of the test, and reseal the plastic on the package using a lighter. The tests were then given to trusted teachers who would review the questions and then teach them to the students. In order to change the tests themselves, Waller would distract the testing coordinator, Alfred Kiel, by taking him out for long lunches downtown during testing days. When all was clear, a group of teachers would enter Kiel's office and alter the tests.[54] Teachers would review the students' answers to make sure they answered the questions correctly.

Where the students didn't, the teachers would erase the wrong answers and write in correct ones. Waller was cautious though; he made sure teachers didn't change more than about a fifth of questions, and only enough answers were changed to make sure the students passed the tests by a few percentage points, nothing more.[55]

Test scores in Parks Middle under Waller increased dramatically. In 2005, 86 percent of eighth graders scored proficient in math. In the year before, it was 24 percent. Reading went from 35 percent proficiency to 78 percent.[56] The system of cheating was never implicitly condoned by Beverly Hall or the Atlanta Public Schools, but everyone knew what was going on. Waller, recounting the scandal years later, said that there were ways that Hall made it clear that cheating was acceptable, if not encouraged, but without ever directly stating so. Hall would use code words like "reform at high levels" to describe the measures schools took to obtain results without directly instructing anyone to act improperly.[57] Yet Hall made sure the principals in her system knew exactly what was required of them. She had staff demonstrate to principals exactly how many students needed to pass exams and how many correct answers were required to meet the standards.[58] Hall also protected teachers and principals who cheated. When Tameka Grant, a teacher at Parks Middle, wrote to Hall, stating that Waller was persuading teachers to cheat on tests, the response she got from Hall was, "Waller is not going anywhere." Soon after she lodged her complaint, Grant was transferred to one of the most dangerous schools in the district.[59] Hall made it clear, whistleblowers get punished. That was the system. Principals would form inner circles of teachers they could trust to help the school cheat on the tests. The superintendent and the upper echelons of Atlanta Public Schools would protect and reward those principals with bonuses. If anyone complained, they were shut out, repositioned, or otherwise ostracized. Any claims of cheating by anyone inside or outside the organization would be summarily dismissed or ignored.

After several years the cheating system at Parks Middle was almost automatic. Waller trusted his inner circle of teachers would take care of the manipulation of test results and would obtain the tests prior to the test day. He never directly instructed teachers to manipulate the test results, but it was understood. Teachers who could be trusted would participate either by directly manipulating the students' test results themselves by erasing wrong answers and replacing them with right ones, or they would obtain and review the CRCT exams in advance and make sure their students knew the questions. Nobody talked openly about the cheating happening at the school, but many knew about it. As Waller described it, cheating had become a "well-oiled machine" at Parks Middle.[60]

In 2009 everything would come apart.

Heather Vogell and John Perry's article about Atherton and the questionable test improvements at three other elementary schools was published in December 2008. The two had used a statistical technique called regression analysis to compare test scores from a few select schools that had taken a retest.[61] The two followed up their December article with another in October 2009, one month after the city had celebrated Beverly Hall Day.[62] This time, the duo had examined CRCT scores between 2008 and 2009 and compared the results from year to year. Again, the two pointed out some incredibly improbable test results from schools across the state. West Manor and Peyton Elementary Schools went from among the bottom performing schools one year, to among the best the next. Vogell and Perry found numerous cases where grades from one year to the next improved astronomically, but also cases where results deteriorated sharply.[63] Given how widespread cheating was in Atlanta Public Schools, and across the state, this made sense. Students writing exams where teachers were cheating would have inflated scores one year, and if they moved to a class where the teachers weren't cheating, their scores would plummet, and vice versa.

Some results were truly unbelievable. In West Manor Elementary in 2008, fourth graders ranked 830th in the state, but in 2009 those children, now in fifth grade, scored at the very top statewide. Peyton Elementary was among the lowest in math in 2008, but fourth in 2009. This was despite the fact that on practice exams 94 percent of students scored at the lowest of four levels.

The results couldn't be ignored. Something very strange, probably inappropriate and possibly criminal, was happening in Georgia schools. The journalists were confident that something would have to be done. The article stated in clear terms "statistically unlikely test scores are showing up in more classrooms, suggesting the cheating investigation that has engulfed four schools might be about to widen."[64] They were right. The articles had got the attention of not only the Atlanta Public School Board, but the office of Governor Sonny Perdue. The governor's office did a quick investigation and found that abnormal results were found in about one in five schools in the district. Parks Middle itself was found to have suspicious marks on tests from 75 percent of classrooms.[65]

Atlanta Public Schools promised to look into the suspicious results and launched a blue-ribbon commission to investigate. The commission, organized and staffed by Atlanta Public Schools, would find that there was no coordinated effort to manipulate test scores.[66] Governor Perdue was not convinced. So in August 2010 he authorized an executive order that gave the former state attorney general, Michael Bowers, along with a former district attorney, Robert E. Wilson, and a special investigator, Richard Hyde, authority to conduct a thorough investigation into the questionable test results. They were given subpoena powers and the budget to hire more than fifty investigators.[67]

The investigators initially came up against considerable opposition from the school board and teachers. Nobody seemed to want to cooperate. But the investigators persisted. In the fall of that year, the fifty or so Georgia Bureau of Investigation agents spent the month visiting various schools throughout the state, including Parks Middle.[68] Investigators sat in cafeterias, teachers' lounges, hallways, and classrooms. They approached teachers in order to get them to aid the investigation. Eventually, they succeeded. The investigators convinced numerous teachers to agree to become witnesses in the case, some agreeing to wear wires to record conversations with fellow teachers.[69] The full investigation would span two and a half years. Beverly Hall and many others would retire during the investigation. Many others were fired or lost their teaching licenses during the investigation.

On top of the interviews, the Governor's Office for Student Achievement contracted CTB McGraw Hill to investigate wrong-to-right (WTR) answer changes on tests. The analysis CTB McGraw Hill conducted involved identifying where answers on a multiple-choice test had been erased and counting the number of those changes that were changed from wrong to right. By comparing the number of those changes to a typical test, the investigators would be able to identify if the tests had been tampered with. CTB McGraw Hill found that in Atlanta and thirty-four other school districts, there were "a significant number of classes that had WTR erasures that were dramatically and disconcertingly higher than the state average." Parks Middle had the highest incidence of the changes.[70] Gregory Cizek, a professor of educational measurement hired by the investigators, described the probability of the erasures being random as likely as filling the Georgia Dome to capacity and "every person in the dome being over seven feet tall."[71]

The investigation involved over two thousand interviews with various educational staff throughout the state. Cheating was occurring in over forty-four schools in Atlanta alone. The culture of cheating became so prominent that it was estimated that cheating was occurring at 83 percent of Atlanta Public Schools.[72] Just ten months after the special investigation began, on June 20, 2011, the investigators issued a report implicating 178 teachers and principals in the scandal. Eighty-two of those implicated had already confessed.[73]

The initial charges in the case resulted in 110 teachers being placed on administrative leave after confessing to cheating or being suspected of doing so.[74] Damany Lewis was one of the first teachers to agree to cooperate in return for immunity from charges.[75] The jig was up. The investigators also gave a scathing indictment of Atlanta Public Schools, and directly of Beverly Hall, saying that a "culture of fear, intimidation and retaliation had infested the district, allowing cheating at all levels to go unchecked for years." They also indicated that test results within the school system had been "used as an abusive and cruel weapon to embarrass and punish."[76]

The investigators concluded that the immense pressure to meet targets led teachers to cheat. Targets were implemented by Atlanta Public Schools in such a way that the teachers and administrators believed they had to choose between cheating to meet targets or failing to meet targets and losing their jobs.[77]

As time went on, the increasing standards, the fact that each successive class of students was expected to constantly improve, combined with the fact that cheating was already widespread meant that it was nearly impossible for teachers to meet the standards expected of them without cheating. The report provided by the investigators stated: "Multiple years of test misconduct in the district compounded the level of cheating that was required annually to not only match the prior year's false scores, but also to surpass them. The gap between where the students were academically and the targets they were trying to reach grew larger."[78]

Cheating wasn't an option for principals and teachers in Atlanta. It was the only way to survive.

For many teachers at Parks Middle, cheating on the tests was just a means to an end. To them it was the students who mattered. For Damany

Lewis, what mattered was that students at Parks Middle actually believed they could escape their zip code. Lewis justified the cheating in his own mind because, for him, if the school closed, and if the students were reassigned, it would be like ripping the heart out of the community. The leadership and guidance the students received at Parks Middle, and the belief that they could accomplish something, was more than enough reason to fudge a few answers. That the students believed they could do better than what was expected of them was justification enough. "I'm going to do everything I can to prevent the why-try spirit," Lewis said.[79] For Waller, the changes at the school were having a positive effect on the students. They "started seeing things differently. They saw a way out."[80]

All in all, over 170 teachers, principals, and senior administrators in Atlanta and other parts of Georgia would be charged with various crimes, many of the principals and senior administrators tried under the Racketeer Influenced and Corrupt Organizations (RICO) Statute, the same legal provision used to indict members of organized crime. Damany Lewis would be the first teacher fired as a result of the scandal, after he refused to resign. The statement he read in his termination hearing in March 2012 simply said: "I think the evidence will prove that there was a systemic problem in Atlanta public schools. That's my statement"[81]

On March 22, 2013, Christopher Waller, Beverly Hall, and thirty-three other administrators were indicted by a grand jury under the RICO Statute. Beverly Hall's charges included racketeering, making false statements, theft, influencing witnesses, and conspiracy. It wasn't until April 1, 2015, that eleven of those educators in the Atlanta region were convicted of racketeering and several other crimes in connection to cheating on standardized tests. Hall was not one of them; she died a month earlier of cancer. But the indictment didn't shy away from attributing much of the blame for the scandal on Hall:

> *Over time, the unreasonable pressure to meet annual APS (Atlanta Public Schools) targets led some employees to cheat. The refusal of Beverly Hall*

and her top administrators to accept anything other than satisfying targets
created an environment where achieving the desired end result was more
important than the students' education.[82]

Waller would serve five years of probation and pay forty thousand
dollars in restitution.[83] Parks Middle School would close in 2014 and
would be merged with Sylvan Hills Middle School.

All for a test.

||||||||||

What happened in the Atlanta Public Schools wasn't an anomaly. Widespread cheating had been reported in other cities such as Philadelphia,
Toledo, El Paso, Baltimore, Cincinnati, Houston, and St. Louis, just to
name a few.[84] In some cases cheating can have tragic results. Although we
can never know what was going through Jeanene Worrell-Breeden's (the
New York school principal who had jumped in front of a train after being
reported for cheating on her grade three's tests) mind that tragic April
day—her grandmother had recently passed away and she was reported
to be having marriage troubles—we can only speculate that the pressure
of the third-grade tests, and the investigation into her cheating on the
exams, had contributed to her decision to take her life.

But it isn't just schools where people respond to performance metrics
in unanticipated, perverse, and sometimes dishonest ways. In fact, people
respond in the ways that teachers did in the Atlanta Public Schools in
nearly every facet of life. While the response may not involve cheating or
other immoral or illegal actions, people will find ways to meet a goal. The
phenomenon is so prevalent it even has a name: Goodhart's Law.[85]

Charles Goodhart was an economist who studied monetary policy. What Goodhart found was that when governments try to regulate
the financial system, investors will anticipate the effects of that regulation and profit from it. What Goodhart concluded was that once any

measure is tied to incentives, people will find ways to maximize that measure, whether or not their actions help achieve the original intent of the metric. The best paraphrase of his law is, "When a measure becomes a target, it ceases to be a good measure." This is what happened in Atlanta. Tests were not just methods of evaluating student progress, there were incentives tied to them. Large ones. Principals and teachers could lose their jobs if test targets were not met. Not only that, but the schools may be forced to close, or be taken over and restructured. If they were met, teachers would receive bonuses. The incentives for achieving high test scores were powerful.

Examples of people responding to metrics and incentives in perverse ways can be found everywhere. In the nineteenth century, paleontologists working in China were interested in collecting dinosaur bones to study the prehistoric animals found there. Complete fossils are rare, as geological forces over millennia will break apart skeletons and other remains, and often, paleontologists have to deal with fragments of bones or otherwise incomplete fossils. So paleontologists, seeking help from local peasants, offered to pay people for each fragment of a dinosaur bone they turned in. The peasants were quick to learn how to game the system: Since they were paid per "fragment," the peasants started smashing the dinosaur bones they found so they could turn in multiple "fragments."[86] In 1992, Sears starting paying commissions to their mechanics to undertake repairs on equipment, which resulted in the mechanics undertaking unnecessary repairs in order to earn the commissions.[87]

In Australia, train conductors were penalized for arriving late on their schedule. So they began to completely skip over stations, leaving passengers at the platform wondering why their train just blew by. In the United Kingdom an emergency department began measuring the time it took for patients to see a doctor upon arriving at the emergency room. Admissions staff began to refuse to allow ambulances to unload patients until doctors were ready to see them. The result was that ambulances were left waiting until a doctor was ready, tying up valuable paramedic resources and decreasing response times to emergencies.[88] During the 1990s in New York and Pennsylvania, the states began publishing mortality data on hospitals and individual surgeons with the intention of implementing a system of accountability in healthcare. The idea was that patients would be able to select better-performing hospitals or surgeons, and doctors and medical administrators would have an incentive to improve their care. What happened instead was that surgeons began to turn away patients with complicated problems in order to improve their success rates.[89]

When the British colonized India, they had a concern in the capital city of Delhi: cobras. There were a large number of the poisonous snakes inhabiting the city, creating a dangerous situation for both the colonial government and the local population. The colonial government had an idea: They would put a bounty on the snakes. Every person who turned in a dead cobra would be paid a fee. The program appeared to be quite successful, as numerous snakes were killed and their bounties paid. But soon the colonial government discovered why so many snakes were able to be captured and killed: Locals had started to breed the snakes in order to sell their corpses to the government! Upon realizing that the Indians were gaming the system, the British canceled the bounty on the snakes. Now that the cobras were valueless, those who were raising them set them free. The result was an order of magnitude increase to the cobra population of the city. The British, through their efforts to contain the cobra population in the city, only made the situation worse. Horst Siebert, a German economist who studied the phenomenon, called it "Der Kobra-Effekt": the Cobra Effect.[90]

This phenomenon, where people respond to metrics in perverse and counterproductive ways, whether called the Cobra Effect or Goodhart's Law, will be found throughout this book. What we will see is that when a metric is used, people will find a way to achieve it, whether or not their actions achieve the objectives behind the metric.

The Atlanta Public Schools scandal may be an extreme example of Goodhart's Law, but it is a useful one. The greater the pressure to meet standards, the more that is on the line, the greater the likelihood that people will push the limits of what is acceptable to meet them, and the more creative they will get with finding ways to achieve those standards. They just won't do so in the way that you would anticipate.

The Atlanta Public School scandal also introduces an important distinction that will occur throughout this book. In response to pressure to achieve test scores, teachers responded in two very different ways. In the first case teachers simply changed the way they taught. They focused more on material they believed would be on the test, they dedicated more time to test preparation and teaching test skills, and they eliminated components of the classroom, whether they were part of the curriculum or not, that were not going to be on the test. This is "teaching to the test." The other response they took was to cheat.

The important distinction between these two responses is that the first one involves a real change to what is happening. Teaching to the test means that students are taught how to take a test at the expense of other aspects of learning. Subject matter not on the test is ignored, deeper understanding is sacrificed to simpler ways of thinking that are easier to test, and aspects of learning that are not captured in multiple-choice tests, such as creativity and inquiry, are lost. Cheating, as immoral and illegal it is, doesn't necessarily require that any changes to the classroom take place. Students may still learn to be creative, cover subjects not on the test, and explore a deeper and longer-lasting connection to the material. Cheating simply involves a manipulation of the measurement itself.

Goodhart's Law doesn't make this distinction, but it is an important one, and one that will occur throughout this book. Goodhart simply stated that any measure, when made into a metric, will cease to be useful, because people will eventually learn to game the system. But Goodhart never expanded on how people would game the system. People can either fundamentally change their behavior, often in perverse ways, to maximize the metric on which they are being measured, or they can simply find ways to change the reporting of the metric without changing their behavior at all. Often both of these strategies will occur at the same time, but it is important to understand that they are different but not necessarily separate. Teachers who were cheating on the tests were also changing what they were teaching in the classroom, but they didn't necessarily have to.

The other lesson from this chapter, introduced with the discussion on standardized tests, is that often metrics are chosen not because they are good indicators of what needs to be measured, but because they are easy to measure. When combined with incentives to perform to certain standards, easy measures distort behavior so that people focus on what is easy and measurable, rather than what is hard yet important.

∎∎∎∎∎∎∎∎∎∎∎

Metrics affect what we do, how we behave, and what we ultimately choose to value. Hauser and Katz put it: "You are what you measure."[91] Dan Ariely said it differently: "What you measure is what you get."[92] There is a caution in that statement. Once you start measuring something, and the more emphasis you put on it, the more people will find ways to do exactly that. And they will find all kinds of ways to achieve what you are measuring. If you choose the wrong measure, people will start to do the wrong things. What you measure may be what you get. But it's all you get.

What the emphasis on testing has done to our schools serves as a cautionary tale of the perversion that any metric can have on our society. Few metrics are designed well, or are even relevant, fewer are useful, and none are perfect. If we let a metric dominate the way we operate anything in our lives, from our schools, to work, to our society, we will be blinded to everything the metric fails to represent. Treating a metric as infallible, incontestable, or sacred never leads anywhere good. Failing to understand how the powerful incentives behind metrics can lead to counterproductive behavior leads to places much worse.

The harm in any metric doesn't come from the metric itself, but how it is used and rewarded. A measurement does not change our thinking, behavior, or environment by itself. Yet the purpose of a metric is to do exactly those things: We measure things so that we change. Why measure something if it will not change the way you look at, do, or influence something? It is in the way in which metrics are used that they can lead to good or harm. And they can be used in different ways. In this book we will criticize a lot of metrics for a variety of reasons. Ultimately we are not criticizing the metric, but how we use it. Teaching to the test is a case study in putting too much emphasis on a metric. Placing blind faith in any metric and tying powerful incentives to it will only lead to failure. No metric should prevent us from questioning what we are trying to achieve and how to measure it. Measurement is not a substitute for understanding, and no metric can replace our need to think about what we are ultimately trying to achieve.

There are many ways that metrics are imperfect, many which we will explore in this book. When we place all of our effort on the metric, rather than what we are truly trying to achieve, we pursue counterproductive measures, distort our efforts, or just do things inefficiently. This book will explore many other ways metrics fail. But, let's start with the "Ins and Outs," or how we confuse resources, efforts, yields, and results.

CHAPTER 2
THE INS AND OUTS
The Logic Model and Program Evaluation

After seven years of working as a family doctor, Dr. Margaret Aufricht was frustrated. "It just seemed . . . ," Dr. Aufricht pauses, searching for the appropriate word, "stupid." She leans forward slightly. "It was inefficient."[1]

For those seven years, Dr. Aufricht worked as a partner in a clinic in the community. In Canada's public health system, many doctors work independently, operating their own clinics, sometimes alone, other times with several colleagues. In Canada, the system is publicly funded: The government pays the bills (well, mostly), though many components of the health system are operated privately. These private clinics charge the government for their services. One method of charging the government, the dominant method in the province of Alberta, is to use a fee-for-service model. (Health care in Canada falls under provincial government responsibility and so there are slight variations between provinces on how healthcare is provided.) This is the system under which Dr. Aufricht worked.

Fee-for-service operates much like it sounds. For each "service unit" a doctor performs—seeing a patient, making a diagnosis, providing counselling or administering a treatment—they are paid a set fee. Surgeons were paid per surgery (a combination of the type of procedure and the length of time), psychiatrists are paid for each session, dermatologists are paid for treating a rash, your family doctor is paid to hit you on the knee with that weird hammer to test your reflexes. Many doctors working in hospitals and those working in a private practice are paid through a similar system. Both are responsible for paying for support. In a private clinic, the doctors pool their money to pay for their support staff and overhead. Essentially, in Canada, many doctors act as independent contractors.

Each billing period, doctors submit their billing claims to the government, who then evaluate the submissions and pay the doctors for their work. A peculiar aspect of the fee-for-service model is that it almost exclusively applies to doctors. Nursing staff, administration, health-care specialists, and others are not necessarily paid under a fee-for-service model. If they work at a hospital, they are paid a salary by the government. In a private primary health clinic (publicly funded, but privately run), the support staff are typically paid using the doctors' fees. The problem with this system, especially in private clinics, is that the only money coming in is for things the doctors can bill for. For Dr. Aufricht, this resulted in an emphasis on billing, with little discernment of the effectiveness of what she was doing. "You had to see a lot of people in a half a day to pay your rent," she says. "Some days you would see a half day of super-easy patients, and you wouldn't really use your skills. Other days you would see really difficult patients, and you wouldn't have enough time." The focus of the clinic was to get the doctors to bill as much as possible.

"Patients would just be asked come in for every problem. If a patient wanted test results, under fee-for-service, they come in. We don't get paid for providing test results over the phone. Why would we give telephone advice? We are paid zero for that. You don't get paid for a follow-up telephone call. You just have everyone come in," Dr. Aufricht sighs. That is what her clinic, and many other fee-for-service clinics, did. They shifted their focus to maximize things that are billable and minimize things that are not. "There were all kinds of false obstacles," says Dr. Aufricht. Under fee-for-service there is no reason or incentive to provide what she calls "comprehensive service." "You didn't have the people around you to help you provide the support to the patient," she says. Because the payment model worked such that the only revenue came from a doctor seeing a patient; work done by nurses or other healthcare specialists was undervalued. Why have a nurse practitioner provide support service, when all they were was a drain on resources? Therefore, many fee-for-service clinics ran bare-bones operations. Dr. Aufricht decided to do something different.

||||||||||

Heather White encountered a very similar problem working for Family and Childhood Support Services (FCSS) at the City of Calgary, a department that provides funding to nongovernmental agencies trying to promote positive change in the community. She found similar shortcomings in how the service measured their performance.

"A few years ago," she explains, "FCSS reported that our programs and services reached four million Calgarians." She laughs. "How did we do that when there were less than one million people living in Calgary at the time?

"Often agencies were thinking that more was better. They would think anytime they had contact with a person, that was to be counted. An agency who delivered thirty-thousand newsletters would say, 'Oh, that's thirty thousand people.' If they went to an event and made a speech, they would count another two hundred people," Heather laughs.

Much of the push for organizations to report in this way came from donors, who wanted solid numbers reported. The easiest way to report those hard numbers was to simply count the things an organization did. The more they could count, the better. Donors in turn could point to those numbers and say, "This is how many people were reached."

But something struck Heather a few years before, when she was working in an agency that provided transitional housing. Clients would enter the program, be provided services and housing they required, and then, if successful, would leave the program. "If the numbers went down, that was seen as good. It meant more people were starting the program and then leaving," says Heather.

"But then one year, we had three suicides . . . ," Heather shakes her head, "and it was good for the books." For Heather, how things were measured was a wake-up call. "For me," she says, "that was, it was . . . we gotta get on this thing." If a suicide looked good on the books, then there was a serious problem with how things were being measured. Getting the measurement right became paramount to Heather's work. Heather wanted to change that.

||||||||||

Both Dr. Aufricht and Heather White were battling with a common mistake of metrics: the output. At the fee-for-service clinic, the output Dr. Aufricht was evaluated on was the number of patients she saw. Heather White dealt with organizations that would measure themselves by the number of people reached, regardless of how that interaction changed the target population or even if it resulted in change at all. In both cases the focus was on what was done, but not what was accomplished. These mistakes are not rare. Many organizations confuse what they do with what they are trying to accomplish. Charities confuse the funds they raise for the change they are trying to make. Companies confuse hours worked with value. Business Web strategies confuse clicks and web views with effective marketing and sales. Effort is confused with effect, investment is confused with return, the means are confused with the ends.

These problems have long plagued the nonprofit world, and it is there where some solutions can be found. For decades many nonprofit organizations suffered from the same problem: focusing on inputs and outputs. Charities, aid organizations, and similar groups tended (and many still tend) to spend their efforts measuring how much effort they were putting into addressing a problem, rather than measuring and understanding the change they effect.

Since the 1970s, more and more nonprofits have started to adopt program-evaluation techniques to change the way they approach their work. One popular technique is called the logic model. Some of these first models were developed by Carol Weiss, Michael Fullan, and Huey Chen in the 1970s, but the process really didn't gain attention until the mid-1990s, when the United Way of America published their report "Measuring Program Outcomes."[2]

The logic model divides any program into four components: inputs (or resources), activities, outputs, and outcomes (and impacts). Inputs are what go into a program. This can be anything from financial inputs (money) but also includes volunteer time, equipment, land, and other hard resources. Activities (which are sometimes grouped into outputs) are the things that a program does. This could be the number of pamphlets printed, the number of speeches given, or the number of billable hours for a doctor. Outputs are what are produced by the activities undertaken. These can be things like the number of people who attend a class or the number of patients who are treated. Finally, outcomes are changes in awareness, skills, knowledge, situation, condition, or behavior, and impacts are these changes over long periods of time.[3]

Outcomes, the ultimate and most important part of the logic model, are those things which any program is trying to achieve. Outcomes are the entire point of the exercise. They are the hardest to define, understand, and measure, which is why they are neglected so often when it comes to measurement. Many organizations, hesitant to deal with such complicated objectives, fall back to use inputs or outputs, often with counterproductive results.

Let's look at an example to help understand the logic model. Imagine you are a highway patrol division captain whose jurisdiction includes a particularly dangerous stretch of road. This highway has three times more fatal accidents per year than any other in the state, with an average of twenty fatal accidents per year (obviously an exaggeration, but bear with me). You have been tasked with improving the safety of the road. The department of highways gives you a budget of two million dollars per year to improve the highway and reduce the number of fatal accidents. You get to work. You take a multifaceted approach. You increase patrols and set up speed traps along the highway at strategic locations to catch speeders, while also launching a multimedia campaign to warn against the dangers of speeding. You hire five new officers to patrol the highway, with a specific focus on catching speeders. You spend money on television and radio advertisements and electronic signs warning against the dangers of speeding.

In the first year of the program, you are able to run over two hundred TV and radio advertisements, reaching over six million viewers and listeners. Four highway sign displays are installed, and messages are seen by over two million drivers. The five officers put in over five thousand patrol hours, issuing over eight thousand tickets and violation notices. It is a tremendous undertaking. At the end of the year you prepare a report on the program. What can you report?

If you were to focus on inputs, you would report the four million dollars spent and the five new officers hired. A focus on activities would look at the number of hours those officers spent patrolling the highway, the amount of TV and radio ads broadcast, and the number of highway signs installed. Outputs would look at the number of speeders caught or ticketed, the number of viewers who saw the TV and radio ads, and how many people passed by the warning signs cautioning against speeding on the highway.

However, none of these measurements actually tells us the most important aspect of all: Did the highway become safer? Did the number of fatal accidents decrease? Without that crucial bit of information, all the other data reported are meaningless. Sure, if five officers were hired and they gave out an average of one hundred tickets a week each, that is probably a pretty productive team. But if during that time, the number of fatal accidents on the highway increased, that doesn't say much for the effectiveness of giving out speeding tickets.

The outcome measurement for the highway program should be aligned with the goal of what the task was in the first place: making the highway safer. But what does *safer* mean? Does it mean that cars are driving at slower speeds? In that case, should we look at average speeds, or perhaps the percentage of people driving at "dangerous speeds"? Should the police efforts be evaluated in terms of the effect on average speeds? Perhaps. But speed doesn't necessarily mean the road is safer. Even slow drivers can be dangerous. Maybe the road itself is dangerous, with poor visibility, sharp turns, and poor driving surfaces. In that case, would visibility analysis and assessments of the road surface quality be a better metric to measure the safety of the road?

The ultimate outcome should be about safety. And measuring safety isn't so easy. Does it mean fewer fatal accidents? Or just accidents in general? Do we measure impacts on human health and mortality, or do we include property damage as well? All of these have different implications, and all are arguably good outcome measurements. The tough part is that there is no one correct measure. This book will discuss several lessons of what to look for in a good metric. Measuring an outcome is just the beginning.

As difficult as this is and as complicated as it might've seemed in the preceding example, the safety of a highway is a fairly simple outcome to measure comparatively. Imagine trying to determine what the outcome of an education system should be (hopefully the previous chapter convinced you that just good test scores, an output, should not be it). What about a healthcare system? We know that doctor visits (another output) are not a good measure either, but what do we measure instead? How do we measure how healthy people are? What about our economy? What should be the outcome of that, and how should we measure it? Outcomes are complex, vague, difficult to define and measure, and often changing. It is no wonder they are often underemphasized, undermeasured, and often neglected. But as in the highway example, that does not mean they are not important. In fact, they are often the only thing that is important.

A highway patrol captain who brags about how many tickets her division gave out while fatal accidents tripled is no better than the teacher whose test scores increased while his students' understanding suffered. The hospital that provides more treatments while patient health plummets is not a role model, despite the numbers it reports.

Inputs, outputs, and outcomes are abused and misconstrued all too often. Organizations that are doing a terrible job highlight metrics that make them look good. Others who are doing great work may have little understanding about how to prove it. Inefficiency is rewarded, counterproductive efforts are applauded, and ineffective programs are made to look good when evaluators, administrators, and the public have a poor understanding of the difference between inputs, outputs, and outcomes. Knowing what these are, what they do, and when they should be used will go a long way to improving our understanding of what we do.

Heather White and Dr. Aufricht's cases both involved a problem with outputs. But it is not only outputs that are misused. Inputs also can be misunderstood, with similar results. Two such ways are "the input-inflation fallacy" and "the input-reduction fallacy." Input inflation is where an organization will either highlight, increase, or focus on an input with the aim of demonstrating that a cause or effort is being taken seriously. Charities are notorious for this. How often is the first thing a charity advertises on their websites, pamphlets, and other media the amount of money they have raised? How many "fund-raising meters" are displayed in lobbies, at kick-off events, and galas? How many speeches by politicians, charity organizers, and the like highlight the total amount of money raised? This is not to say that increasing the funds raised is not a laudable goal, nor that it shouldn't be celebrated. But it should never be confused for what is actually accomplished. Governments are just as complicit in input inflation. Politicians will highlight the amount of money invested in a particular piece of infrastructure, a government program, or hiring more people. Yet, lacking from that conversation is the evaluation of what that investment will accomplish. Input inflation, when not balanced with an understanding of the outcomes achieved, only encourages inefficiency. Flooring the gas pedal isn't a good thing if you are spinning your wheels. Governments often emphasize inputs because citizens confuse effort with results. Infrastructure programs are infamous for emphasizing how many jobs are created with the project. "This bridge construction will create two hundred jobs" or "construction of this building will employ five hundred tradespeople" are the type of tropes that politicians love to dish out. But wait, wouldn't it be more effective if the bridge only created one hundred jobs or the building was built with only two hundred tradespeople? Wouldn't that mean that the bridge and building are being built more efficiently? Don't more jobs, created with the same amount of money, mean that wages are lower? Of course program evaluation is not as simple as this, but simply stating one project or program creates more jobs than another does little to tell us how efficiently the work is being done, whether the jobs are high paying or low paying, or what the effect of the program or project ultimately is. The idea is that people like jobs, and the more jobs the better.

The other input fallacy works in the opposite way. Input-reduction fallacies occur when the reduction of an input is highlighted, with little to no regard to the impact on outcomes. This is evident in business when costs are cut, wages reduced, or benefits slashed in the name of cost saving. Input-reduction is also seen in government, where so-called fiscal conservatives will aim to cut budgets in the same way. But efficiency cannot be accomplished simply by reducing an input if you do not also understand what is happening to the outcome. In some cases reducing inputs decreases efficiency, as the effect on outcomes is greater than the reduction in inputs. Doing something cheaper does not mean doing something cost effectively.

||||||||||

Heather White began to implement a program where all the social agencies her organization provided funding for would use a standardized system of measurement. Different agencies of course had different goals and mandates, but the methods of measurement would be the same across the board. Two different organizations both working on reducing family violence would no longer self-identify goals and create their own evaluations (under what was called the Holmes System) but would have to adopt standard evaluation criteria. Most important, these metrics were aimed at measuring the change in the clients' lives, in one way or another, and not how much work was put into achieving that goal.

The standard used for the measurements was a long list of survey questions, broken down into different subject areas, that participants have to complete both prior to beginning a program and after. Before she became involved "there was almost no pretesting happening," Heather says in disbelief. Oddly, many organizations did not have a clear picture of their clients' lives coming into their programs. It would be terribly difficult to understand how a client's life has changed if you didn't have a grasp on his or her initial condition. In order to measure outcomes, Heather knew that baseline evaluations had to be taken.

The questions that formed the baseline evaluation not only were standardized in FCSS, they came from the national long-form census: a longer, more detailed version of the mandatory census every Canadian would have to complete every five years, but only distributed to a smaller random sampling of the population. Using census questions meant that the organizations could not only evaluate the change in their participant's lives, but they could compare that to a national average and evaluate how their programs were faring against a valid benchmark. More important, those measurements focused on the outcomes of a program.

"We didn't believe that agencies were trying to trick us," Heather says, "but we had an obligation to build their capacities. Now everyone uses our tools, and they can't pick and choose what survey questions to use." But the surveys do more than just allow for comparisons against an established benchmark, they also let Heather know how much of an impact their funding is having. That was the biggest change that Heather implemented: Instead of focusing on how much the organization did, or how many clients they reached, Heather shifted the focus onto how much of an impact the work had.

||||||||||

Dr. Aufricht and her partners decided to take a jump to rethink their funding model. "All we asked for was a change in the funding model. Instead of fee-for-service we would get paid for taking care of the patient over the year." Dr. Aufricht and her partners wanted to do things differently.

Luckily the timing was right, as the federal government was funding primary healthcare pilot projects and the Calgary Health Region (the local funding body) was looking at new methods to provide primary healthcare within the province with a desire to integrate more health services into primary care. So when Dr. Aufricht and her partners approached them with a new way to fund her clinic, the Health Region was receptive. After two years of working out the details, they transitioned the Crowfoot Village Family Practice (CVFP) to a new funding model.

Instead of being paid each time a doctor saw a patient, Dr. Aufricht and her colleagues would get paid a yearly stipend (paid out in two-week increments) for each patient they had registered in their clinic, under what is called a capitation system. The arrangement negotiated with the government was that each patient had to be formally rostered, and each had to sign an agreement that he or she would make his or her best attempt to go to the clinic for healthcare. If a patient went somewhere else, CVFP would be on the hook for the bill in order to avoid double dipping (what are called negations). All but 6 of their 10,500 existing patients signed up for the new model.

The way CVFP was paid meant they could do things differently. Unlike a typical primary health clinic in Alberta, CVFP integrated a robust roster of healthcare professionals, much more than what would be found in a typical clinic. Apart from doctors, CVFP now had pharmacists, diabetic educators, respiratory therapists, chronic disease nurses, registered nurses, psychologists, social workers, dieticians, and nurse practitioners, in addition to the family physicians found in a primary health clinic. On top of those other health professionals, they had two and a half support staff for every physician. In 2011 they hired Shauna Thome as executive director to manage operations in the clinic and to act as an advocate for the model they run to the government (and pretty much anyone who would listen).

They could add all these services in large part due to the change in how CVFP collected revenue.

Almost immediately, the perversity and inefficiency of the fee-for service model became evident. Shauna Thome calls it "the whites of the eyes" billing. Under fee-for-service, the doctor had to physically see a patient in person in order to bill for the service. The doctor couldn't delegate the service to another healthcare professional, use e-mail, or even speak to the patient on the phone (this has now changed). This led to all kinds of strange practices. Patients would have to come into the clinic for routine things such as prescription renewals or normal test results.[4]

The other problem with fee-for-service billing was that it only allowed doctors to bill for a single service for each visit. It is common practice to find signs in fee-for-service clinics that read "one issue per visit," which means that doctors require patients to return multiple times to discuss various issues. Given that doctors only got paid every time they saw a patient, it was in their best interest to have patients come back for as many things as possible. This would mean that some issues would have to wait until the doctor was available again, delaying the patient's access to healthcare. Sometimes this meant that patients would wait too long and might go to an urgent care center or emergency room, which is much more expensive, for services that could have been dealt with easily by their family physician.

The fee-for-service system also allowed only doctors to bill for services; it didn't recognize the services of other healthcare providers, such as nurse practitioners, respiratory therapists, dieticians, or diabetes specialists. Shauna Thome calls this "doorknob medicine." A doctor would literally open the door to the patient room only to introduce another healthcare professional to the patient. The nurse might provide the service, but because the doctor needs to see the patient in order to bill the service, he or she has to be there, at least for part of the visit. Sometimes, the doctor didn't even take his or her hand off the doorknob.

When the clinic started with the new funding model in 1999, CVFP received about two hundred dollars per patient per year on average. That payment varied quite significantly depending on the patients, who were divided by gender and age groups of five-year cohorts, the rates being based on provincial averages for healthcare provision.

"The most you get paid for is old patients who are healthy. The 90-year-old who comes in once per year for a physical . . . you're laughing," Dr. Aufricht says. "Teenage boys are hard to get paid anything for. It's like fifty dollars a year." (There are very understandable concerns with the patient-based funding model. "Patient skimming," where clinics choose only healthy patients that they get a lot of money for, is something that needs to be prevented. Clinics running a patient-based funding model, such as CVFP, should not be able to interview patients or otherwise screen them. As Dr. Aufricht explains: "Either the clinic is 'open' for new patients, or it is 'closed.'" There is no opportunity to select only certain types of patients. The clinic decided that any patient who contacted the clinic but decided against rostering would be voluntarily reported to the provincial health authorities by CVFP in the interest of full disclosure. Often the reason is simply because the clinic isn't located conveniently for that patient.)

But that simple change in the way they got paid changed everything for CVFP. "A lot of the things we ended up doing we didn't anticipate at the beginning," says Dr. Aufricht. They began to look at every process in the clinic, examine what everyone did, always with the goal of finding efficiencies and promoting their patients' health in the most efficient manner.

Dr. Aufricht immediately began to see changes in her clinic when they shifted away from the fee-for-service model. The change in the way they were paid for services caused CVFP to allocate resources more effectively. Many patient interactions at CVFP started with a phone call. When a patient called in, clerical staff would refer the call to a triage nurse for several problems. The triage nurse spoke with the patient and determined what resources the patient needed. "The guy with the first day of a cold doesn't need to come in," explains Dr. Aufricht. "That same guy would likely have seen the doctor under the fee-for-service model."

CVFP found more efficient ways to deal with what would normally constitute a visit, either by dealing with patients over the phone with a registered nurse, delegating the task to another staff member, or simply determining that the patient did not need to come in at all. "Like a patient with a sore throat for a day or two" explains Dr. Aufricht, "Now the nurse takes the history following a protocol and if there is anything questionable, the doc would see them, otherwise they are counselled on how to manage their symptoms at home and to come in if things haven't settled within a few days for a throat swab." The physicians still knew what was going on, as the nurses kept them informed, but now the doctors' time was better spent on tasks that would better utilize their skills. Under a fee-for-service model, the clinic would not be paid for any of that. The old system rewarded inefficiency.

The system also allowed the clinic to do things a lot quicker than in a typical clinic. Because they weren't paid every time a patient visited them, there was no incentive for CVFP to require patients to come in for every problem. Take for example an adult female patient who suspects she has a urinary tract infection. Normally, this would require a multistep, multiday process. The patient would book an appointment with her doctor, then go see the doctor in person, possibly after waiting a couple of days. The doctor would give her a requisition for a test, then the patient would visit a lab, get the test, get the results, and then go back to the doctor, who writes a prescription. Finally, the patient would go to the pharmacy to get the prescription. The entire process could take a few days and cost the patient a lot of lost time.

At CVFP the process took a fraction of the time. If an adult female patient called in with a suspected urinary tract infection, a nurse would review the symptoms and rule out worrisome features by asking standardized questions. Then the nurse would fax a requisition into a lab. The patient would still have to go to the lab (that, you do have to do in person), but then the lab could electronically send the results to the clinic, and the nurse could then send a prescription by physician protocol to the pharmacy. The patient never had to go in to the clinic at all. Usually, this could all be done in a single day.

CVFP started providing more patient communication and services over the phone, like protocols for urinary tract infections or yeast infections in women. "It really changed the pattern of care," says Dr. Aufricht. "We had the nurses do a lot more: take histories and teach home blood pressure monitoring, that kind of thing." They also started doing things to maximize the effectiveness of patient visits. If a patient came in with a cold, and hadn't been in to see the doctor for two years, the nurse would record his or her blood pressure. In contrast to the one issue per visit practice of fee-for-service clinics, CVFP would take the opposite approach. CVFP performed what they call "max-packing" of appointments. They tried to get as many healthcare services into a single appointment as they could, knowing their patients' time was valuable. There was even a staff member, called a proactive coordinator, that was responsible for maximizing the services for each patient visit. The proactive coordinator looked a week in advance and proactively booked tests and services that the patient had coming up, such as a mammogram, pap smear, colonoscopy, or diabetic screening. As a result, patients had to visit the clinic about 25 percent less than typical, saving their time.

The model that CVFP ran also allowed physicians to manage 30 percent more patients than a typical doctor, as they were able to better utilize the resources of the health professionals they worked with, and because their appointments were simply more efficient. The motto for CVFP was, "The right care, by the right provider, at the right time." The other important piece was a focus on patient self-education. "If a mom had a kid with a fever, the nurse would spend time going through what the parent had to know. After four or five call-ins, she would get really good at self-managing."

The practice at CVFP wasn't just about using resources more efficiently or reducing costs. Dr. Aufricht also wanted to improve the overall health of her patients. This was not just because she was a caring doctor. With patients who would be clients of the clinic for over fifteen years, keeping patients healthy was good business. As Shauna Thome says, "The healthier the patients, the less they come in, the more patients we can serve."

If CVFP was going to be paid the same amount for a patient in their sixties whether they came in ten times a year with numerous complications or came in once for a routine checkup, it was in the interest of the clinic to keep patients as healthy as possible. Perversely, under a fee-for-service model, doctors would be paid more the unhealthier their patients were and the more care they needed. Healthy patients don't require as many visits, and so there are fewer services for the doctor to bill. The CVFP flipped that model on its head.

This focus on prevention, monitoring, and health promotion didn't just mean that patients would, in the long run, cost less to the clinic, it also meant they had a much lower burden on the healthcare system as a whole. A study done by the Alberta Health Quality Council on the CVFP found that the number of hospitalizations and emergency room visits from CVFP patients decreased significantly compared to similar patients. Emergency room visits that resulted in the patient being discharged to home dropped by 13 percent, and visits that resulted in a hospitalization dropped by 17 percent against the standard. The average hospital stay for CVFP patients was a stunning 45 percent shorter than similar patients. The percentage of emergency room visits for upper respiratory tract infections among CVFP patients dropped from 14.3 percent in 1997–1998 to 7.5 percent in 2001–2002, much faster than it did for the population as a whole (19.3 percent to 16.3 percent).[5] The savings in acute care for the original 10,500 patients alone was calculated to between five million and six million dollars every year, almost as much as the clinic was receiving in capitation payments.

More significant, visits to the family doctor at CVFP dropped by 28 percent.[6] This didn't necessarily mean that patients were not receiving fewer healthcare services. It simply meant that CVFP had found ways to provide patients with the same level of care without requiring them to come into the clinic as often. Freed from the absurd requirement that they would only be paid if they saw a patient directly, Dr. Aufricht and her colleagues began running their clinic more effectively. Routine tasks, even some complicated ones, were given to the other medical staff in the clinic. Nurses and nurse practitioners were given the power to use their training and not have to constantly defer to the doctors. Consequently, the doctors could use their time more effectively. Instead of spending time telling patients routine test results, the doctors would spend their time dealing with more complicated cases, evaluating and treating cases where their skills were best put to use.

What Dr. Aufricht did at CVFP, quite deliberately, was to inverse the relationship of inputs, outputs, and outcomes. In the fee-for-service model, the system was incentivized toward outputs (doctors undertaking various tasks and procedures). Inputs (how much doctors were paid) were at the mercy of those outputs. Outcomes were strangely left out of the equation, or at least were not paid much attention to. It was no surprise that healthcare costs easily escalated: When you only pay doctors for each task they do, they are incentivized to find ways to do as many of those tasks as possible, whether or not they have a useful impact on patient health. Perversely, unhealthy patients are great for a fee-for-service model; the sicker they are, the more they need to come in, and the more the services can be billed for them.

But CVFP flipped that around. Instead of paying for outputs, it instead fixed inputs (the cost per patient) and let the clinic figure out the best way to deliver healthcare within those fixed costs. It was in the clinic's interest to not only eliminate as many redundancies and efficiencies as possible, but also deliver the most effective healthcare it could. Because patients would stay with them for long periods of time (and the clinic got dinged each time a patient went for care elsewhere), the clinic was incentivized to maximize the output: patient health. The unhealthier the patients, the more resources the clinic would have to spend on them, and the less money it would make. So not only did CVFP do away with redundancies like calling patients in for routine test results, it also put more resources into preventive healthcare, patient education, and fostering healthy lifestyles among clients.

Yet, capitation has its drawbacks. Capitation programs need to mitigate what is called "cream skimming." Because capitation pays for each patient per year, no matter what level of healthcare is required, it is in a clinic's interest to find patients who are healthier than average. The best determinant of health is wealth and education. The more educated and wealthier patients are, the less they cost in healthcare. So costs should take into account age, gender, complexity, and income (the model that CVFP worked under only included age and gender). The per-patient fees paid to a clinic in a higher-income area of the city shouldn't apply to a clinic in a lower-income area. A capitation model that doesn't take this into account can create its own perverse incentives. The province of Ontario, for example, has an incentive that rewards physicians for positive health outcomes for their patients, but this only creates competition between clinics to attract high-income patients and avoid taking on low-income patients, who need the care the most.

Furthermore, if the clinic is being paid for each patient in its roster whether or not it sees those patients means that the clinic can cut back services in order to maximize profit. That is why things like negations (when the clinic is billed if the patient seeks health services elsewhere) are important; they give an incentive for the clinic to ensure it is providing the right amount of care so that the patient feels his or her needs are being met. The fact that patients may also stay with their family doctor for years creates an incentive for the clinic to focus on long-term prevention and healthy lifestyles. If a patient will be with you for a decade, it only makes sense to instill healthy lifestyles and habits in the patient, because it saves the clinic money in the long run.

This brings up an important aspect of healthcare that goes beyond just the payment model. What matters most in healthcare seems not to be the techniques used or the equipment physicians have at their disposal (although those are important), but something much less tangible: trust. When patients trusts their doctor, they listen to the advice the doctor gives and follow his or her instructions. When patients trust their doctor, they go to him or her for the care they require rather than to an urgent care clinic or the emergency room (sometimes they do need to go to the ER though!). Trust, or more appropriately, a lack of trust, costs healthcare systems an incredible amount of money.

Take for instance the phenomenon of unnecessary testing. Unnecessary testing happens when a doctor does not feel a test (an X-ray, CT scan, mammogram, and such) is not medically necessary, but orders one anyway. This may be because the doctor simply does not fully know a patient's full medical history (contrary to popular opinion, a doctor cannot simply pull up your entire medical history at the click of a button), but more often it is because patients insist on it. It is a massive problem. In 2014, 73 percent of physicians said the frequency of unnecessary tests was a very serious or somewhat serious problem.[7] Unnecessary testing is estimated to cost over two hundred billion dollars (yes, billion!) a year in the United States,[8] and sixty billion dollars in Canada.

This is both a doctor problem and a patient problem. As Shauna Thome says, "For most patients, a visit is only successful if they leave with a piece of paper." Many patients feel that their medical care should have a tangible result, a test, a prescription, an X-ray. But often, these tests are just placebos and don't tell doctors any more than they already know. Yet, it is hard for doctors to tell patients that they just need to wait it out, or that nothing can really be done, or that a test won't tell them anything new. Sometimes when patients see a doctor they are looking for some sort of outcome, but more often than not, they just want to be heard and feel as though someone is listening to them. While there are all sorts of factors contributing to the unnecessary testing problem, such as the fear of malpractice insurance, the rise of what Shauna Thome calls "Dr. Google," or aggressive marketing by pharmaceutical companies, a major factor is trust. Patients who don't fully trust their doctor will insist on some sort of confirmation in the form of a test or a prescription.

That same issue of trust is experienced by each and every one of us, and it happens at work.

||||||||||

"Why I am in this meeting?" "I am at work, but I am not really doing anything, I should go home, but if I do, others will think I am not showing commitment." "John is always the first to arrive at the office and always the last to leave, but he really doesn't contribute."

No doubt you have had similar thoughts at work at some point in your career. That feeling of being ineffective, of wasting time, of facing false obstacles is something that many of us have felt at one time or another at our jobs.

Spending too much time focused on "billable hours" rather than focusing on the actual objective of your job is probably the way you have felt about your job at one time or another (if you haven't, your employer is doing something right). The reason you feel this way is that almost all of us are evaluated primarily on one thing at work: time. Time is something we are measured on every single day. If you don't think so, try coming in three hours late without prior approval. Or take a day off without management's consent. Or think about how much office gossip is focused on how much everyone works. The amount of time you are at work—not how much time you are doing effective work, not the effort you put into your work—but the time you are physically at your job rules how employees are viewed in the modern corporate world. Cali Ressler and Jody Thompson felt this way too.

The pair met while working together at Best Buy in 2001. The company had recently embarked upon a mission to become one of the top places to work in America, and Ressler and Thompson were part of a team that was tasked with making that happen. The team undertook an internal survey of employees asking them what they wanted the most from work. If you are going to be one of the best places to work, it is best to start with asking employees what they actually care about.

The overwhelming response from the survey was "trust me with my time."[9] Many employers simply don't trust their employees with their time. They require a prescribed set of hours to be worked each day, require employees to ask for permission to get time off, give them a lecture when they show up late, and often pay and evaluate them based on how many hours they work. Employees wanted this to change, and Best Buy was going to lead the way in making that change.

The way Ressler and Thompson saw it, modern work culture assumes that physical presence multiplied by time equals effort. This leads to all sorts of shortcomings. As they put it, "We go to work and watch someone who isn't very good at their job get promoted because they got in earlier and stayed later than anyone else."[10]

The idea is similar to how students are treated in high school compared to how they are treated in college. In high school, attendance is taken and missing class, coming in late, or leaving early can result in harsh stares, a phone call home, or a reprimand. In college, most professors couldn't care less if you attend a lecture. This isn't because professors don't care if you learn the material, it is that they treat you like an adult and trust you to make decisions on how to manage your time. If you don't come to class, that is your decision, and it is you who suffers the consequences if you do poorly in the class as a result. Yet when you leave college and enter the workforce, you are back to being treated like an adolescent. Your time is strictly controlled, and you are monitored on how much time you spend at work.

In a modern-knowledge economy, productivity simply doesn't work like this. If your job is to solve problems, create something, or come up with a new way of doing things, the time you are working is less important than how productive you are when you are working. Ideas are fluid, they don't only occur during working hours. Creativity requires your brain to put together disparate ideas, make connections that are not obvious, and understand problems in novel ways. Simply sitting at a desk is not a guarantee that your brain will accomplish any of that. Ideas require creativity, not just physical presence.[11]

If you wake up from a dream with a realization of a solution to a problem you have been working on, is that not work? If you are thinking about how to solve a work problem when going for a run, is that not work? If you are at your desk looking at the screen and thinking about surfing, or the latest episode of the show you are binge-watching, is that work?

What Ressler and Thompson found during their time at Best Buy was that time had come to dominate every aspect of work culture. Their plan was to create the anathema to a time-focused work environment. It was called the ROWE, the Results-Only Work Environment, and is the inspiration behind their book *Why Work Sucks and How to Fix It: The Results-Only Revolution*.

What the ROWE did was flip the workplace on its head. Rather than the focus of work culture, time was to be entirely eliminated from all aspects of work. Employees would no longer be required to show up at work at certain hours of the day. They wouldn't even be expected to show up for any day during a week. Vacation time was virtually unlimited. All meetings were declared nonmandatory. Employees could take off from work anytime they wanted; in fact they could work entirely from home if they wanted. What was expected of them was that they got their work done.

This wasn't flextime. It was the complete removal of time. The transition was not easy. Many workers were not used to a results-only work culture. The first thing Ressler and Thompson identified in the workplace that had to go for a ROWE to work was what they called Sludge. Sludge was all the gossip, judgment, and criticism that was created out of the old perception of time. It was the comments about how unmotivated Julia must be because she showed up an hour late. The unspoken judgment of Phil because he left work to go take a sick kid home. The view that Fred was one of the best workers because he was the first to come in and the last to leave, despite the fact the quality and quantity of his work didn't reflect it. The perception that for an employee to be productive, he or she had to be sitting in a chair. The loathing an employee had for another who didn't spend as much time at work as he or she did. Sludge is evident in all workplaces, and it becomes more pronounced when transitioning to a ROWE. But for any ROWE to work, Sludge needs to be eliminated.

Ressler and Thompson attacked sludge head-on. They first had to educate workers on what it was and show them how prevalent and counterproductive it was. Like any problem, you need to acknowledge it before you can address it. Then they helped workers eliminate it. Next they had to change the way workers thought about time. They had to teach them to completely eliminate the notion of time from work and shift the focus to productivity. This meant that showing up at two in the afternoon was acceptable. That work schedules were obsolete, paid vacation was unlimited, no meeting was mandatory. and nobody was allowed to talk about how much they worked. But more important it meant that managers had to be much clearer on roles, expectations, and deadlines; nobody on a project could demand last-minute requests from anyone; and workers had to learn to be efficient with their time, and to do so, they had to eliminate unnecessary work. But the transition was made. Workers learned to trust each other. If one took an afternoon off to take care of a sick kid, the other workers knew they would support their coworker when they took a long weekend to go skiing.

More important they learned to be productive with their time. No longer worried about showing up at the right time, sitting in their desks until everyone else went home, or attending meetings that they had no reason to be at, employees could focus on what they needed to do. With all that wasted time eliminated, not only did employees find more freedom, they became more productive in their jobs.

Trey, part of a team at Best Buy that produces online courses, began working in a ROWE environment. Soon Trey found himself spending his mornings watching *South Park* and his afternoons working while watching ESPN.[12] In any other workplace culture someone who watches *South Park* and works while ESPN is on would quickly be ostracized if not fired. It's hard not to react to Trey's situation with judgment, condescension, or loathing. From the outside it looks like Trey is slacking off and doesn't care about work. Yet his team went from producing ten to twelve courses a month to almost forty. When all you care about is results, what someone does with his or her time is not important. You just care about what he or she gets done, and a near quadrupling of productivity is something any manager would desire.

Ressler and Thompson completely eliminated the concept of the input of time from the workplace and forced the workplace to focus on what really mattered: outcomes. Their program saw productivity increase, while employees felt more trusted and valued at work. Plus, they got a lot of amazing vacations.

A ROWE doesn't work for all types of work. Some industries depend on workers being present throughout their shift: retail salespeople, paramedics, emergency room staff, lifeguards, security guards, and other such workers. In these industries, telling workers they can show up whenever they like is a recipe for disaster. Yet all these industries can take inspiration from the idea behind a ROWE. While salespeople need to be in the store for their entire shift, their job entails more than just being around. A security guard who watches a robbery take place without doing anything shouldn't be rewarded just because she or he showed up for work that day. In these cases, time is a necessary component of work, but it isn't the goal.

What Ressler and Thompson had discovered was that time was being used as a substitute for measuring productive work. Instead of measuring real productivity, Best Buy, like many other companies, measured time instead. The thinking was that if someone worked longer, that meant he or she was more productive.

||||||||||

The CVFP has been operating for nearly twenty years. During that entire time, it has always been a pilot program. The model that CVFP uses, despite its benefits, is still rare in Alberta, one other clinic in the province started at the same time.

The patients who use the clinic have lower rates of hospitalizations and urgent care visits than similar patients in the area. According to Shauna Thome if every clinic in the province adopted their model, there would be nearly three billion dollars in savings every year. The model still remains a speck of dust in the system.

Yet, when the government reviews the model, they compare how CVFP would perform under the fee-for-service model. CVFP, while being under a different payment model, still has to "shadow bill" in order to be compared to other clinics. It looks bad. Because they can only "shadow bill" for services normally offered under a fee-for-service model, all the additional services they offer—the respiratory therapists, dieticians, diabetes educators, and so on—aren't counted. Not only that, but the fact that doctors do not require unnecessary visits, such as the patient with a urinary tract infection who can get a prescription without seeing the doctor, means that the clinic records fewer services that they provide.

All that means is that the clinic provides less billable "services" for the money it is paid. But that's the entire point. The clinic offers more health-care, just not the type that is normally counted, and it makes things more efficient for patients and the clinic itself. It's maddening.

You can sense Shauna Thome's frustration when she talks about being evaluated as a fee-for-service clinic. But it is easy to understand when you see how easily metrics confuse what is measured and what matters. Thome sums it up nicely: "We are an outcome focused entity in an activity-focused world."

‖‖‖‖‖‖‖‖‖‖

Understanding inputs, activities, outputs, and outcomes does not mean we should abandon any metric that measures inputs or outputs in a rush to embrace the outcome as the be-all and end-all of measurement. Input and output metrics will, and should, continue to be used. In some cases, as we will see later in this book, they are actually preferable. But they shouldn't be confused with an outcome metric, and they shouldn't be used as the default evaluation in any endeavor. We should be aware of how each can mislead us and the common ways that they are misused.

Input metrics can be misused by emphasizing how large they are, like the money spent per patient. They can also be misused when emphasizing how small they are, like when companies or governments slash budgets without any understanding of the effects of those cuts. Both errors occur because there is a lack of understanding of the impact or outcome of the activity. Input errors result in inefficiency either because they seek to increase the input (the numerator in the efficiency equation) with little regard to the resulting increase in the outcome, or because the input is reduced with little regard to the resulting decrease in the outcome. Output metrics usually lead to inefficiency due to counterproductivity. Without a clear link to the desired outcome, maximizing outputs leads to either wasted effort or efforts that actually undermine the goal.

CHAPTER 3
THE LONG AND SHORT OF IT

Intertemporal Problems and Undervaluing Time

There is a tyrant terrorizing nearly every public company in the US—it's called the quarterly earnings report. It dominates and distorts the decisions of executives, analysts and auditors. Yet it says almost nothing about a business's health. How did a single number come to loom so large?
—Harris Collingwood in *The Earnings Game: Everyone Plays, Nobody Wins*

There was a problem in corporate America in the 1980s. At least those in corporate America believed there was a problem.

The problem was that there was no tie between the performance of the company and the compensation of the executives. CEOs and other executives were largely paid on a salary system, sometimes topped off with various bonuses. The problem was that there was no tie to the performance of the company to the compensation of the executives. The CEO would receive his or her salary regardless of whether the company raked in record profits or completely tanked. While bonuses did offer some incentive for the executives to pursue the best interests of the company, many felt there was a disconnect between what executives were paid and how they performed.

Shareholders, economists, boards of directors, academics, and others pondered the problem. It was given a name: the agency problem. To put it succinctly, corporations had two components: principals (shareholders) and agents (management). The principals were interested in making profits from their investments, and they delegated duties to the agents to act in their best interest to maximize their investments. That's what an executive is supposed to do: make money for the shareholders by managing the company. The problem is that agents are self-interested; that is, they may undertake actions for their own benefit, which may be detrimental to the interests of shareholders.[1]

The problem is exacerbated by the fact that managers know a lot more about the companies they run than shareholders do. It's not like fund managers or individual shareholders are reviewing weekly reports, sitting in on strategy meetings, or making decisions in boardrooms. There is an information gap between management and shareholders. What a CEO does day-to-day can't be monitored. So how can a board of directors or shareholders be sure the executives they hired to run the company aren't just sitting around playing golf and taking three-hour lunches, let alone working to maximize the company's share value? The objective of the agency problem is to find ways for the agents to work in the interests of the principals. How can we ensure management acts in the interest of shareholders?

The answer to this problem, as many academics, boards of directors, businesspeople, and executives themselves came to, was simple: tie executive compensation to the performance of the corporation. The idea was known as "shareholder value."[2] If executives were paid based on how well the company did, they would do their best to ensure the company did well and make investors money. The exact way to do this was, and still is, the subject of rigorous debate, but by-and-large a consensus settled on one measure: earnings per share. There were several ways to tie executive compensation to earnings, one being through bonuses provided if certain earnings targets were met. The other, which came to dominate executive compensation schemes, was stock options.

Through the 1990s the emphasis by corporate boards on shareholder value coalesced around the idea that stock options should be a large component of executive compensation. By 1998, stock options made up 45 percent of the median pay package for CEOs.[3] A standard option plan would give the executive the option to purchase a defined amount of shares in the company at any time within ten years at the current market price of the stock. So if the stock price rose, the CEO could purchase stock at the lower price and sell for a profit (or keep them). Over the 1980s and 1990s, earnings per share, and its counterpart, stock options, came to dominate how executives were paid. By 2012, earnings per share was the most popular metric of corporate performance, being used by half of all companies.[4]

At the same time, earnings per share and stock price became almost synonymous. The greater the earnings per share, the higher the stock price. More correctly, the more the earnings per share matched, or exceeded, *expectations* of shareholders, the higher the stock price. Whenever the earnings realized did not meet the expectations of the market, the stock price would fall. Perhaps more than anything, a company's earnings drive the stock price.[5] Thus, the symbiosis between earnings and share price became the driving factor behind executive actions. In order to reap higher rewards, executives had to improve their company's earnings, thus improving the stock price and subsequently earning them greater profits when it came time to cash in on their stock options.

But there is a problem with earnings. They are myopic. A company's value, ideally, is based on its long-term prospects. Being able to generate profits not just today, but into the future, is what gives a company its real value.[6] The connection between the amount of earnings per share generated quarter to quarter has a relationship to the long-term value creation of a company that is tenuous at best.

An ideal investor would undertake a complex analysis on a company, called a discounted cash flow, to determine its true value. The analysis would consider things such as market share, profit growth, competitive advantages, research and development, marketing potential, quality of the executive team, risk factors such as competition, resource availability, and political volatility of markets, just to name a few. But doing a discounted cash flow is expensive, time-consuming, and incredibly speculative. Doing this type of analysis involves making numerous assumptions about future productivity, market share, competitive advantage, competency of management, capital allocation, labor resources—the list goes on. Cash flow analysis is tedious, complex, and often feels more like divination than science. So instead of undertaking the fundamental research necessary to evaluate a company's prospects, many investors simply resort to using earnings as their benchmark to evaluate a company.[7]

The short-term focus of using earnings as a way to evaluate a company is further exacerbated by the fact that the stock market itself is shortsighted. Currently the average stock is held by a shareholder for a period of less than a year. This short investment horizon means that stockholders are looking to realize returns over short periods and do not have the patience to wait out business decisions that may take years, or even decades, to come to fruition.[8] These shortsighted stockholders will put pressure on executives to actualize these earnings by pressuring the board of directors to reward managers who perform in the short-term and punish ones who don't. As John Coffee describes them, investors are "primarily financial engineers interested in the largest possible profit in the shortest period of time" who maintain a "laser beam focus on quarter-to-quarter earnings."[9]

Furthermore, given this short time period of investment, many stockholders base their decisions on the beliefs and opinions of others, as they often do not have the time or the patience to properly research a company's position, and so often they just follow the herd. And so an unmet earnings report can ripple through the investment world, creating a self-reinforcing spiral of disinvestment and decline in value.

Not only are earnings used by many to evaluate stock value, fund managers who stray from the pack and evaluate companies differently and invest their clients' money against the earnings tide may find themselves with fewer clients, or worse, faced with dismissal due to investor pressure. Many fund managers are evaluated against some benchmark, the S&P 500, or against an index of their peers. As the performance of those stock indices is driven by short-term earnings performance, a fund manager who strays too far from conventional wisdom by investing in companies with great long-term prospects but currently poor short-term performance, may soon find themselves out of a job. The power of the herd is strong, and that herd is shortsighted.[10]

This emphasis on earnings, their role in determining stock prices, the pressure from investment managers to produce them, the use of them for executive bonuses, and, more important, how they indirectly determine the value of executives' stock options is a self-reinforcing cycle. Investment managers, not wanting to stray too far from the herd, forgo fundamental research to make their investment decisions and instead rely on earnings as the benchmark for evaluating a company; executives in turn point to this emphasis by the investors to justify their own obsession with earnings. The result is that executives focus on earnings. A lot. But this focus on earnings gets CEOs to do some funny things. And sometimes illegal things.

There are several ways executives respond to pressure on short-term earnings. The first is that they find ways to manipulate the numbers to make things seem like they are good in the short-term, without having to fundamentally change anything about the business. This practice is known as "earnings management." Earnings management is one of those phrases that has a range of meaning. On the one end of the spectrum, earnings management is an innocuous method of "emphasizing" a company's positive attributes and downplaying its shortcomings. On the other end of the spectrum, earnings management is known by another word: *fraud*.

In accounting, there are ways to emphasize profits or losses in any given period depending on how you present the information, changing the earnings you can report. At its most basic, earnings management involves reporting revenues earlier and deferring the reporting of expenses to a later date. In accounting, earnings are a combination of realized cash flows (the actual money you receive and spend in a given period) and assumptions about future income and expenses (called accruals). Things like the depreciation of assets, machinery or buildings, the amortization of an expense, receivables, long-term contracts, employee pension plans, stock options for management and staff, warranties, supplier payables, taxes, and environmental obligations are accruals. They will impact the earnings of a company, but only in the future. So accountants have to make various assumptions about how to count those future costs and revenues, and managers can manipulate how those accruals will be realized, through restructuring of pensions or stock option grants, even revenues.[11]

There is little doubt that earnings management happens in a lot of companies. Studies have shown that companies are more likely to report earnings that exactly match, or are just slightly above or below, what analysts predicted rather than what would normally be expected.[12] Given the influence of meeting earnings expectations on stock prices, and the incentives managers have to meet certain stock price targets, it isn't any surprise that those reports just happen to meet expectations! In fact, the greater the share of a CEO's pay is stock options or consists of bonuses tied to stock prices, the more likely they are to engage in earnings management and inflate reported earnings.[13] This is Goodhart's Law once again.

Accruals are a huge part of a company's value. On average, existing sales of a company account for only about 5 percent of its share value. So manipulating how accruals are reported can have a substantial impact on a company's share value.[14] Earnings management is what happens when those assumptions are stretched. If you have a contract to sell your product to a purchaser with a delivery date six months from now, but have a supplier who you owe now, technically you are operating at a current loss. But report that purchase order right now and defer reporting the costs until a few months from now, and you just made your company look like it is a profit-producing machine! The problem with earnings management is that much of what a company does, and how it reports its assets, revenues, and costs, isn't available to investors.

There are of course regulations to prevent the worst abuses of earnings management. Institutions such as the Financial Accounting Standards Board (FASB) and the Generally Accepted Accounting Practices (GAAP) regulate how earnings can be reported. While smaller manipulation of earnings accounting is a widespread phenomenon, companies get into trouble when those standards are pushed and exceeded. You can only push off expenses and count profits early for so long until the accounting catches up with you. Eventually there are no more profits to account for and only expenses left to report. When the accounting game eventually catches up to the company, the result is a crash of stock prices and, sometimes, prison. The Enron, Worldcom, Nortel, and eToys scandals were all examples of companies pushing the limits of accounting practices beyond acceptable limits.[15]

Yet the other way executives can manipulate earnings may not be as shocking as outright accounting fraud, but it is just as destructive. In order to get earnings up, managers can undertake actions that will increase the short-term profitability of the company, while sacrificing its long-term value. In academia this is called "short-termism."

Short-termism, in the simplest of terms, is when companies undertake decisions that are beneficial for them in the short-term but detrimental in the long-term.[16] Short-termism is what is referred to as an "intertemporal problem." Intertemporal problems arise where decisions have to be made where the costs and benefits of a decision are spread out over time. If you lend someone money and that someone promises to repay you a few months later, you are faced with an intertemporal problem. While you are certain about lending the money now, you can never be certain that you will be repaid, as the future is never certain. The reason why lenders charge interest (in addition to wanting to make a profit on their investment) is that they can't predict the future and so want some insurance against an unknown future event. As Prelec and Lowenstein said, "Anything that is delayed is almost by definition uncertain."[17] Humans, by their nature, are biased to things that are immediate and certain, even if the alternative, which may be more distant and uncertain, is better.[18]

This is the dilemma all executives face when making decisions that will affect the long-term viability of their company. They can choose to invest in the development of a new product, but there is no certainty that the research will create results. Nor is there certainty that the market will not have changed by the time the new product is rolled out. The history of business is strewn with the wreckage of companies that developed products only to find that either consumers no longer wanted what they were selling, or that a competitor had developed something better. Yet there are probably more companies that collapsed because they neglected to take risks and invest in new products, services, or markets.

Intertemporal problems are further exacerbated by the time periods that managers act within. Most executives are hired only for short periods of time. Not only is the future uncertain, managers may not be around to reap the benefits of a project or investment that may take years, if not decades, to be realized.[19] The effects of uncertainty of the intertemporal problems of long-term decisions for a company are further exacerbated by the compensation structure of bonuses and stock options that reward executives for short-term earnings. There is a fundamental clash between hiring executives for short periods of time, with compensation tied to short-term performance, incentivizing them to undertake high-risk and high-return ventures, and the debt holders of a company, who view such high-risk ventures as running ultimately against their interest, which is the long-term profitability of the company.[20]

As with earnings management, there are various ways executives can adjust how they manage their company in order to increase short-term earnings while sacrificing the long-term creation of value and competitive advantage. Executives may choose projects that offer faster paybacks, or projects that are successful in the short-term but poor in the long-term, in order to play the earnings game. Some executives may choose to sell high-value assets in order to increase short-term earnings, but with detrimental impacts on the company's long-term viability. A study by Graham, Harvey, and Raigopal found that a majority of companies were willing to sacrifice their long-term economic value in order to deliver short-term earnings.[21]

Short-termism is widespread, especially in the United States and United Kingdom. When compared to German or Japanese companies, US and UK companies are more heavily focused on short-term earnings, which is a product of the fact that rather than private individuals or investment funds, shareholders in German or Japanese firms tend to be banks, which tend to place greater value on long-term prospects.[22] This is tied to their incentives. Most executives believe that investing for the long-term in their companies is not rewarded with higher stock prices. As with earnings management, executives are able to engage in short-termism largely because there are large parts of the operations of a business that aren't easily observable to shareholders. To understand why, we need to learn about the lemon problem.

In 1970 George Akerlof published an article about an observation he had about how the quality of goods is reflected in the price of those goods. Most of us believe, with good reason, that the price of something is a reflection of its quality. The better quality something is, the more valuable it is. A better-quality knife is worth more than a poor-quality one. A better-performing computer is more valuable than one that can barely run Word. Sounds pretty simple. But there is a catch.

What Akerlof observed is that what matters is not the quality of an individual product, but the average quality of any *type* of product. This is known as the Lemon Law.[23] Akerlof used the example of used cars. Everyone knows the experience. Cheesy and often sleazy salespeople trying to do a sales job on you to sell you a car that is worth far less than the sticker price. When you go to buy a used car, there is an information mismatch between you, who knows very little about the car you are about to buy, and the used-car agent, who knows a lot more. You don't know if the Mazda you are about to buy has had numerous engine issues in the past. Nor do you know if the Ford you have your eye on has trouble with its alternator. More important you don't know if the Honda you want to purchase is actually an impeccable automobile with absolutely no problems and will require very little maintenance over many years to come. Not knowing any of this, you, like most people, assume that most of the cars you will look at will probably have at least some problems. You assume that most of the cars are lemons, or at least somewhere between a lemon and a "peach."

But the car salespeople know this. They know that you are going to figure that any car they try to sell you is at least a little suspect. So they focus on selling you cars that are in fact lemons, knowing that they can at least make a profit on them. What they won't do is try to sell you a good car, because even if it is in great condition, they know you will suspect that it isn't, so they can't get good value for it. The lemon problem is not that the salespeople will sell you lemons, it is that, because of the asymmetry of information, they could never sell you a peach. What this means is that good cars actually have to be sold at a discount in order to "match" the assumed quality of the other used cars, if they get sold at all. This is why, even when selling a good car to a used-car dealership, you won't get your money's worth; the salespeople know that no one will believe the car is good quality, so they have to sell it at roughly the same price as cars in far worse condition.

Lemon problems affect all kinds of markets where consumers are not able to trust the quality of the products due to an information mismatch. If there is no way to accurately discern between high-quality and low-quality products, consumers will simply assume all the products are of low-quality. Markets in developing countries struggle with this information mismatch. Where consumers can't tell the difference, it is high-quality products that suffer. They can't command a higher price, because people don't trust that the product is actually as good as it claims to be. Lemon problems mean that product quality remains low.

That is the problem with executive performance. Many shareholders do not have a lot of information about the company the executives are managing. The executives could attempt to focus on long-term profitability by undertaking various investments and actions that would lead them there, but more likely than not shareholders wouldn't recognize that. This is further exacerbated by the fact that most investors just follow earnings. Investments in the long-term profitability of a company are like high-quality cars in a used-car dealership. Investors can't tell if it is a lemon or a peach. Instead what they see are earnings. Because many in the stock market are so focused on earnings, it is tough for executives to try to sell their company as a peach. Instead they settle for selling a lemon.

For example, US firms did little to enter into the markets for machine tools, consumer electronics, copiers, or semiconductors, because those industries had fairly low profit margins and therefore wouldn't show strong earnings reports. But those industries had very high growth potential. One example was Cincinnati Milacron, a manufacturer of industrial robots. After several years of designing and building the robots, the company had to leave the industry, as it could no longer justify investments in advanced technology given the focus on short-term earnings.[24] The focus on short-term earnings meant that US firms missed out on being competitive in very lucrative industries, simply because those industries required long-term investment.

As Peter Drucker, the famous management expert once commented, "the quest for higher earnings every quarter has pushed managers into decisions they know are costly, if not suicidal, mistakes."[25] Short-termism resulting from pressure to improve quarterly earnings is often characterized by excessive risk taking and the neglect of investments that yield long-term results. Two popular options to improve short-term profits at the expense of long-term growth are cuts in research and development and marketing.

Research and development and marketing are fundamental to the success of a business. Investment in research and development and advertising are arguably the two main drivers that lead to the growth of a business and have incredible influence on a firm's performance and value.[26] Yet marketing is often treated as a discretionary expense by executives. When cuts need to be made, marketing is frequently the first item on the chopping block.[27] This is despite the fact that marketing has immense value for companies. It helps create brand equity, reinforces customer loyalty, and helps a company enter new markets and sell new products, which are fundamental to its long-term growth and viability. But marketing is soft: Its benefits are largely intangible and often long-term.

The problem with both research and development and advertising and marketing in general is that they are quintessential intertemporal problems. Investment in research and development and advertising are costs that are borne immediately, but their returns are not realized until long after the investment has been spent, and those returns are never guaranteed. In fact, accounting practices require that research and development costs be expensed in the current period, while their benefits aren't accrued until the future. As Johnson and Kaplan argued, accounting measures performance over "too brief a period, before long-term consequences from making short-term decisions become apparent."[28] This is a fundamental problem with the accounting model: It is shortsighted.

When faced with pressure to demonstrate short-term earnings, combined with the fact that research and development and advertising are certain costs in the current period while their benefits are uncertain and in the future, executives do what only makes sense given the situation: They cut those things most fundamental to their business.[29] They want to sell peaches, but they know that they can only sell lemons. And many of them admit to it. A survey of nearly four thousand corporate managers by the researchers Graham, Harvey and Raigopal found that nearly 80 percent of them would decrease spending on research and development, advertising, maintenance, or hiring in order to meet short-term earnings targets.[30] A study by Currim, Lim, and Kim found that a greater emphasis on long-term compensation (as opposed to short-term earnings bonuses or stock options exercised in the short-term) led to increased research and development spending as well as spending in advertising.[31] The same goes for companies that have more institutional investors, such as banks: They are less likely to reduce research and development spending, because their investors are a lot more involved in monitoring and researching the decisions of the business. A study by Bushee showed that firms with large institutional investors show a lower probability of cutting research and development spending.[32]

Managers know that research and development and marketing are valuable, and the more their compensation is tied to long-term performance, the more they invest in these categories. This is especially evident when we look at when a manager will cut research and development spending. As Natalie Mizik points out, the closer a manager nears retirement, the greater the desire for them to take actions to bolster the stock price, at the expense of long-term profitability. She cites a study done by Dechow and Sloan that found executives tend to cut research and development spending in their final year before retirement.[33] Another researcher found the same: The closer to retirement a CEO is or when a company experiences short-term earnings decline, the more likely he or she is to cut research and development spending.[34] Managers will invest in research and marketing early in their terms, as they understand the long-term value of those investments, but also realize that nearer to the end of their term, they can cut those things because they won't be around long enough to experience the downside of those decisions.

The effect of these short-term decisions focused on earnings is ultimately the loss of competitive advantage in the long-term. In a 1986 survey of one hundred CEOs of major corporations, eighty-two said that the attention to quarterly earnings contributed to a decline in long-term investment.[35] A study by Larney et al. showed that national brands often lose market share during recessions, due to cuts to marketing, and that original market share is never recovered when the economy picks back up.[36] In order to keep costs low during tough times, companies sacrifice their long-term viability.

These two strategies—earnings management and short-termism—are much like the way teachers respond to pressure to increase test results: You can either manipulate the data or you can focus on achieving the metric at the expense of the students' learning. Managers who practice earnings management are like teachers who cheat on their students' tests; they are more concerned with what *appears* to be happening and manipulate the information to fit the narrative. On the other hand, managers who undertake short-term management decisions are like teachers who teach to the test; they shift priorities to what is measured (test scores or earnings), and in the process, change the fundamentals of their companies or their students' learning. But it seems that the second strategy is more destructive. Mizik notes that firms that cut marketing and research and development have lower future stock market evaluations, and those firms underperform compared to those that undertake earnings management.[37]

There are ways to temper the effect of the emphasis on short-term earnings in companies. In terms of compensation schemes, there are a few changes that boards, shareholders, and others invested in a company can advocate for. Executive compensation is a combination of a base salary, cash bonuses for achieving certain outcomes, stock options, restricted stock awards, incentive plan payouts as well as other annual forms of compensation.[38] While salaries do not reward executives for performance, cash bonuses typically reward for short-term outcomes, and stock options may become useless if they are underwater. Restricted stocks, especially those with long vesting periods (the period that must pass before the stock can be exercised), can incentivize executives to make better long-term decisions. Placing these periods farther into the future can discourage executives from making decisions, such as cutting research and development, that will lower the value of the company into the future.

Another option is to structure stock options so that they are "indexed" to a blend of the company's competitors. Two problems arise with providing regular stock options to executives due to changes in the market. The first is that you reward executives for actions that they are not responsible for. As much as CEOs hate to admit it, a lot of the success of a company has little to do with the actions of the executives themselves, and a lot to do with market factors beyond their control. You didn't have to do a lot in the mid-2000s to make money as an oil and gas company, when the price of oil was exceeding one hundred dollars a barrel. By that same token, an executive in that same industry shouldn't be blamed when the price falls through the floor.

The second downside occurs in a scenario when stocks are "underwater." This occurs when the current price of a stock is far below the exercise price of the stock option. When stocks are underwater, managers are faced with a dilemma: They can either take drastic and often risky action to get the stock price back up, so that their option has at least some value, or they can throw in the towel altogether. Managers hoping to increase their stock price can undertake risky projects such as acquisitions (which more often than not, hurt the long-term profitability of a company) or divestitures. Selling assets is a good way to increase earnings in the short-term, but may have serious long-term impacts. Both options carry a lot of risk, and often a risk that is too high for the company. But when the executive has nothing to lose and everything to gain from such ventures, either option is bound to occur.

The idea behind indexing stock options is to tie the compensation of an executive to the *relative* performance of the company, rather than the absolute performance. Should CEOs really be rewarded for high earnings performance when, despite that performance, they are the lowest performer in their industry? They are just being rewarded for being part of a wave. By the same token, if an executive manages to keep a company afloat in an industry that is suffering major loses, shouldn't he or she be rewarded for his or her actions?

Companies should also be wary of hiring executives for short periods of time and offering incentives for quick fixes. A company struggling to increase its earnings may hire a CEO for only a couple of years to turn the situation around. But this strategy can be destructive. The new executive may cut essential value-creating services (such as research and development and marketing) or sell off valuable assets in order to increase earnings in the short-term, receiving healthy bonuses for doing so. But after the CEO has left with a considerable bonus, the company may find itself gutted and unable to stay competitive. Managers who are hired for longer duration have a lower chance of pursing short-term profits.[39]

Companies can also improve their accounting practices in order to mitigate the overemphasis on short-term earnings. Alfred Rappaport suggests that companies should separate their short-term cash flows from their long-term accruals, classify their accruals by levels of uncertainty, provide a range and likely estimate for each accrual category, exclude arbitrary value-irrelevant accruals, and provide details on the assumptions and risks for each accrual.[40] In short, by disclosing more of their assumptions, it makes it much more difficult for companies to hide the impact of their decisions from their shareholders.

Another strategy companies should undertake is to measure and monitor other, nonfinancial performances, such as product quality, workplace safety, customer loyalty, and customer satisfaction.[41] Understanding how decisions affect various aspects of a company's core services can mitigate the tendency to increase earnings at the expense of long-term value.

A study by Ittner and Larcker found that companies that measured these nonfinancial aspects and verified whether those aspects had an effect on the company's value, had returns on average one and a half times greater than those who didn't.[42]

Changing the nature of who invests in a company can also change the emphasis on short-term versus long-term decisions. As noted, companies whose investors are large institutions such as banks, are less likely to pursue risky short-term endeavors that hurt the long-term profitability of the company. A good strategy for individual investors is to stay away from the shortsighted herd and find more stability with the slow-moving, but risk-averse institutional investors, such as banks.

Finally, shareholders, boards of directors, and others can just stop paying CEOs as much as they do. CEOs are highly paid in part because boards of directors generally consist of highly paid individuals themselves, and they just expect the CEO should be highly paid. As Edward Lazear notes, much of the literature in economics suggests that CEO pay is inflated. There doesn't seem to be a lot of evidence to suggest that the high levels of CEO pay have actually resulted in increased performance of the companies they manage. Counterintuitively, the larger the share of pay the CEO has compared to the top five executives in a company, the lower the profit and efficiency of a company. In short, absurdly high pay for CEOs is inefficient.[43]

||||||||||

In 2013 Randy Schekman wrote an article in the *Guardian* lambasting three journals in the world of scientific research: *Nature, Cell,* and *Science.*[44] These are not just any journals. *Nature, Cell,* and *Science* are *the* journals. Nearly every scientist aspires to have an article published in one of these publications. *Nature* is one of the oldest scientific journals in the world, with its first publication in 1869. *Science* began publishing in 1880 and has a current subscriber base of 130,000, including numerous academic institutions, bringing its estimated readership to about 570,000 people. *Nature* and *Science* publish articles from the broadest spectrum of scientific research. If a scientist wants to reach a broad audience and be widely known and respected, publishing in *Nature* or *Science* is a good way to get there.

So when Randy Schekman criticized the journals in his 2013 article, it created quite a stir. It wasn't just because someone was criticizing the most respected, prestigious, widely read, and impactful journals in the world. It was because of who was doing it. Earlier that year Randy Schekman had won the Nobel Prize in Medicine.

Research universities are one of the greatest achievements of the twentieth century. The basic idea behind the research university is that scientific discovery is a public good and that the training, discovery, and innovation that these universities provide benefit society as a whole.[45] University level research is one of the best long-term investments that can be made.[46] Publicly funded research has provided society with the benefits of discoveries as varied as Braille, RNA splicing, aspirin, cell division, the science of climate change, magnetic resonance imaging (MRI), vitamins, the discovery of electrons, the nuclear reactor, radiocarbon dating, chemical bonding, radar, GPS, penicillin, the discovery of DNA, the Internet, and the computer,[47] just to name a very small fraction. Even many of the innovations we think of as having been developed in the private sector, were in fact the result of public research: Google's algorithms were first developed at Stanford University.

Public research expanded massively after World War II, promoted enthusiastically by Vannevar Bush, the chief scientist and policy maker under both Presidents Roosevelt and Truman. Bush encouraged scientific research and development, arguing that its benefit was more than validated during World War II with numerous military and communications advances helping the Allies win the war.[48] Bush also argued that because the benefits were widespread, there was little need for systematic evaluation of the research.[49] However, as time went on, a need (or at least the perception of a need) to provide rigorous evaluation of how to fund and incentivize the right type of research developed. With limited research funding to go around, government departments, nonprofit granting agencies, and other organizations had to figure out a way to evaluate scientific research.

The debate on establishing criteria for evaluating scientific research eventually settled on one idea: The greater the reach of a research article and the more times it is cited by other researchers, the more impactful it is.[50] This system of rating academics on their publications is called *bibliometrics*.

First, as not everyone is familiar with how academic research works, a quick summary of what journals, articles, and citations are and what they do is useful. Whenever academics or researchers want to share the results of their research, they typically publish their study in an academic journal. Each journal has a committee (or several committees) that reviews articles that researchers submitted for publication and chooses which articles to publish in the most current volume of the journal. Journals cover all kinds of subjects, with vastly different levels of distribution, readership, and prestige. They can be as broad as *Science*, which publishes in nearly every scientific field, to the *American Journal of Potato Research*, which, as its name suggests, has a pretty narrow scope of what it publishes and, consequently, how widely it is read. There are nearly fifty thousand academic journals in circulation. (Academia Obscura created a list of "5 Super Specific Academic Journals," the *American Journal of Potato Research* topped the list. The others included *Rangifer: Research, Management and Husbandry of Reindeer and Other Northern Ungulates*, which publishes articles about, well, reindeer; *Journal of Near-Death Studies*, which is exactly as it sounds; *Answers Research Journal*, which only publishes articles demonstrating Earth is younger than the scientific consensus; and the *Journal of Negative Results in BioMedicine*, which, rather importantly, publishes studies where the negative results of hypotheses were discovered. More on that later.)[51]

When scientists write a research paper, in addition to explaining the methods and results of their research, they often cite previous work that informed, inspired, or otherwise was used in their research. These citations are tracked and recorded with each publication.

There are two dominant metrics that constitute bibliometrics: impact factor and the h-index. Journal impact factor (or JIF) is simply the average number of citations an article receives in any particular journal over the past two years. Impact factor has been calculated in the *Web of Science Journal Citation Reports* since 1975. A large number of journals are evaluated in the reports, providing an assessment of the scope of a journal's reach and influence. *Science* and *Nature* have very high-impact factors, as the articles published in those journals typically go on to be cited in further research, while some journals, especially those covering incredibly niche fields of science, typically have low-impact factors. For example, the impact factor of *Nature* was 41.577 in 2018, while the impact factor of the *Romanian Journal of Information of Science and Technology* was 0.288.[52]

H-index is a measure of an individual researcher's impact, again using citations. Described as "an index to quantify an individual's scientific research output," the h-index is calculated by determining the lowest number of articles that a researcher has published that have been cited that same number of times.[53] So if a researcher publishes fifteen articles that were all cited at least fifteen times, her h-index is fifteen. If a researcher publishes one thousand articles, but only twenty of them were cited at least twenty times, then his h-index is twenty. It is a fairly widespread metric among scientific disciplines, with promotions, financial incentives, and other perks awarded to researchers who achieve high h-indices.[54]

Taken together these two metrics are used to evaluate, reward, and incentivize academics. Grant reviewers will look at the h-index of researchers applying for grants to inform their decisions on rewarding funding. Researchers are given financial incentives if they achieve certain impact factors with their research.[55] Aside from impact factor and h-index, professors are also provided bonuses, better salaries, promotions, and all sorts of other rewards for bringing in research dollars to their institution. A survey (in *Nature* no less) found that a majority of scientists believed that bibliometrics were used in hiring decisions, tenure decisions, promotions, salary and bonuses, and performance reviews.[56]

Bibliometrics are not immune to Goodhart's Law. The emphasis on publishing and citations creates an environment of "hyper-competition" among academics and researchers.[57] The focus on quantitative bibliometrics and research dollars raised shifts the objective of research away from socially relevant outcomes and quality to merely obtaining citations. Expensive research that results in articles published in a widely read journal are emphasized over everything else.[58] And researchers know how to manipulate the stats. Seventy-one percent of respondents to the survey in *Nature* believed it was possible for them to "game" or "cheat" their way into better evaluations.[59]

Researchers and universities find ways to increase their citations in all sorts of ways. Some universities will contact researchers in one field and offer compensation for that researcher to include the university as an "affiliated body" when the research is published, artificially increasing the research output of that institution. This practice allows smaller institutions, that do not have the resources to properly fund research themselves, appear as if they do, enhancing their prestige.[60] Reviewers sometimes will even request that the papers they review include their own work to be cited as part of the paper.[61]

The emphasis on bibliometrics, like nearly every other metric discussed in this book, has created an entire ecosystem of journals, researchers, and publishing practices that exist simply to "up" the citation count of an article. The number of citations in academia has doubled every nine years since World War II, resulting in "busier academics, shorter and less comprehensive papers."[62] In order to demonstrate the absurdity of citation metrics and their susceptibility to inflation, Cyril Labb, a computer scientist, created a fictional character named Ike Antkare who was able to publish 102 computer-generated fake papers and achieve an h-index on Google Scholar greater than Albert Einstein.[63]

The emphasis on citations has led to what Edwards and Roy describe as an "avalanche of substandard incremental papers."[64] Researchers have responded to demands of increasing their citations and number of publications by cranking out vast quantities of marginal, dubious, or simply nonimpactful studies instead of publishing significant, useful, or replicable research. The number of journals has also skyrocketed, with numerous journals publishing dubious studies simply to up a researcher's citation count. In 2004 in the Czech Republic, the government introduced a points-based funding system for research outputs, which led to a short-term increase in publications in lower impact journals simply to earn more points.[65] A similar situation occurred in Australia, where incentives for the number of publications by researchers led to a greater number of papers being published, but the overall impact of that research actually declined in that same period.[66] This erosion of the quality of research in favor of quantity has resulted in numerous retractions from journals. Since 1975 the percentage of retracted articles in life science and biomedical research has increased tenfold. Two-thirds of these retractions were due to misconduct by the researchers. The costs for investigations into that scientific misconduct have risen to nearly one hundred million dollars a year.[67]

Another drawback of impact factor is simply that some fields of science publish more, are read more, and are cited more than others. Sometimes this is simply a function of how many people are working in a field. Medicine is a field where thousands of researchers, doctors, and other practitioners are constantly researching, publishing, and reading each other's work. Compare that to something like theoretical physics.[68] How many doctors do you know? Now, how many theoretical physicists do you know?

Bibliometrics also are skewed toward emphasizing scholarship and publication output. What isn't considered is whether the research developed is socially impactful or relevant. As Rekhi and Lane note, the true value of scientific research cannot be "monetized, packed, and fit neatly into dollars and cents." What monetary value can you give to biodiversity? How can you express clean oceans in terms of jobs or income?[69]

This explosion of research papers, citations, and dubious journals hurts the reputation of science. As more questionable studies are published, as more retractions are made and results falsified, the more the public loses trust in the institutions of research.[70] The emphasis on increasing grant funding itself has many perverse outcomes. Researchers spend more time writing grant proposals and less time researching, and they spend less time teaching and more time researching. In one example from the Netherlands, applying for a €40M grant required researchers to spend €9.3M. In 2012, Australian scientists spent the equivalent of 550 working years just on writing grant proposals.[71]

This results in untenured or adjunct faculty having to take up the role of teaching, while more senior academics spend more time researching, or rather writing, grants.[72] Universities shift into becoming "profit centers" focused on creating new products or patents, rather than providing science as a public good, or making discoveries that may not have a commercial application, but provide benefit to the public.[73]

This was Schekman's critique: The scientific world had become distorted in how it views and rewards scientific research. There is an entire ecosystem in the research community centered around one thing: What journal you publish in and how many citations you receive. Publishing an article in a journal such as *Nature* or *Science* is given more weight and more prestige than say, the *Journal of Biological Chemistry*. *Nature* and *Science* have a higher readership and reach more people after all. The obsession with which journal your research is published in has repercussions throughout the scientific and research system. Panels that determine grant funding will look at where a researcher has published previous work as a method to determine the importance of research. Professorships are awarded based on where an academic publishes.

There is a deeper flaw about bibliometrics beyond the issues of citation inflation, dubious journals, increasing rates of retraction, and the incentives behind bibliometrics that emphasize on publishing, publishing often, and publishing big in academia. The problem is that the idea that the more wide-read and more cited an article is, the more important it is to advancing science is simply not how science works.

There are two ways to think about scientific research. The first is that research is incremental, predictable, low-risk, and continual. Advances are made in incremental steps, with each step being the logical extension of what came before it. Research can be counted on to produce results and to produce results in a specified time period. The iPhone 5 was followed by the iPhone 6 and then the 7 and so on, each being a slight improvement upon the last.

The other way to think about scientific research is that it is intermittent, unpredictable, high-risk, and sporadic. Research doesn't proceed at a predictable pace, but rather moves forward in leaps and bounds, or can stall for long periods. The path that research follows is unpredictable and can go off in directions that were entirely unanticipated. Often paths of research result in dead-ends, but they can also lead to groundbreaking discoveries. This is more like going from a book to radio to the Internet.

Both of these views are correct. Scientific discovery can be slow and incremental, yet predictable. Or it can be unpredictable and often unfruitful, yet potentially groundbreaking. It is this difference in these two ways of how scientific progress is made that bibliometrics has such an impact, for it is good at evaluating the first and very poor at evaluating the second.

Real, groundbreaking scientific research isn't characterized by continual, regular, and frequent publication of results. Often initial results in fundamental research into new fields are characterized by repeated failure, unexpected results, numerous setbacks and roadblocks, changes of direction, and general uncertainty. As Holmstrom noted, the most innovative projects are risky, unpredictable, long-term, labor intensive, and idiosyncratic.[74] Yet, bibliometrics requires that researchers provide predictable publication of results. Fundamental research is inherently a long-term phenomenon. Research outcomes may not be delivered for many years, yet bibliometrics requires researchers to continually publish.[75]

Bibliometrics also is flawed in that it generally rewards the principal author or several authors of a study. As Ed Yong said, modern science is the "teamiest of team sports."[76] Research is rarely conducted by an individual. Rather entire teams of researchers, post-docs, students, technicians, and other collaborators undertake projects that span years. One of the largest research projects undertaken in recent years, the discovery of the Higgs boson, a particle that is fundamental to explaining why things have mass, is said to have over five thousand authors![77] When it comes to fundamental research, the groundbreaking kind that leads to entirely new technologies, processes, or ways of seeing the world, the initial proposal isn't characterized by a regular and continual schedule of anticipated results or even a clear idea of where the research might lead. Fundamental research is more likely to be described as: "Let's see what happens when we do X." Even those discoveries that do have potential for commercial applications may take decades for the results to be realized in the market.[78]

Additionally, groundbreaking science is often not popular. It is weird, and likely only understood by a few individuals when initial discoveries are published. The kinds of research that win Nobel Prizes are rarely published in big journals like *Nature* or *Science*. Rather they are published in obscure journals that have readership in the dozens, not hundreds, or thousands, or hundreds of thousands. The average number of people who first read many of the research papers that go on to win Nobel Prizes is probably less than one hundred. The number of people who understand the complex details and initial significance of ideas such as string theory or site-specific mutagenesis can often be counted on two hands. Many of the breakthroughs in modern science aren't well understood until several years, if not decades, after the initial research.

Finally, fundamental research is ultimately a risky endeavor. Not every project will yield results. The emphasis on certainty of results means that risky research isn't pursued. As Nobel Laureate Roger Krongberg said, "If the work you propose to do isn't virtually certain of success, then it won't get funded."[79]

Government has conventionally borne the burden of fundamental research, which is only natural given the high-risk and long-term nature of the task.[80] The lack of obvious and certain short-term results deters private industry from undertaking this type of high-risk, but high-reward research. But with the advent and spread of bibliometrics, the essential requirements of fundamental research are being undermined. The incentives to publish shift the focus to incremental research, where results are guaranteed, but impacts are low. Why try out an untested approach, when you can just build upon someone else's previous work?[81] Not only is the focus being shifted to lower-impact, incremental research, but funding into research and development in general has been in decline since the 1960s, when US federal funding consisted of 2 percent of total GDP, compared to around 0.78 percent in 2014.[82]

The way that science is funded and evaluated affects the results it produces. Pierre Azoulay, Joshua S. Graff, and Gustavo Manso compared two different institutions that fund scientific research in different ways—The National Institutes of Health (NIH) and the Howard Hughes Medical Institute (HHMI).[83] Both institutions fund medical research, but the way they do so is substantially different. While the NIH provides grants that last three years, the HHMI provides grants that last five years. But where the two institutions really differ is in how they assess the research they fund. The NIH is notoriously risk averse. The agency is not forgiving of failure, and grant applications are rarely renewed when results are not encouraging. The agency also requires applicants to provide clearly defined deliverables for their projects, and they often have to provide preliminary evidence prior to receiving funding for a project. Experiments have to be mapped out, and the course of the project cannot be changed easily.[84]

On the other hand, the HHMI is very adaptable and open to change. The institute encourages the researchers it funds to "take risks, explore unproven avenues and embrace the unknown, even if it means uncertainty or the chance of failure."[85] The institute funds "people, not projects," so if initial results from research are not fruitful, the researchers can change course and allocate resources to another direction. The HHMI also provides more in-depth and useful feedback to the researchers, with other scientists typically making up the panels that provide feedback on the grant process.[86] The HHMI researchers do not publish more articles than those funded by the NIH. In fact, HHMI researchers tend to experience more failures and dead-ends in research. But they also produce more innovative breakthroughs.[87]

Rather than provide powerful incentives to researchers, it is counterintuitively better to provide very low-powered incentives, such as basic salaries rather than bonuses, for research outcomes. Providing those incentives simply shifts the focus of researchers from long-term, risky projects to those that can be easily measured.[88] Instead of creating incentives for the production of results, with fundamental research it is actually better to ensure that the inputs into the research are optimized. (Recall in chapter 2 that sometimes measuring inputs is preferable? This is when.) Because fundamental research is long-term and high risk, trying to guarantee results just goes against what the research needs to thrive. Paying academics for "results" of exploratory, groundbreaking research is like not paying for fire insurance because you house is not currently on fire. Fundamental research is a probabilistic approach to discovery—not all research will yield results, but some will be groundbreaking.

Funding agencies should know that they cannot predict the outcomes nor the timing of fundamental research. They cannot know whether the research they fund will lead to a world-changing discovery or simply fall into a dead-end. But what agencies can do is ensure that the environments that the research is undertaken in is enabling. What grant agencies need to do is ensure that researchers have the right people, adequate resourcing, a proper method of defining goals, the proper allocation of time, and the right process to encourage research and foster a culture of collaboration.[89]

With fundamental research the goal shouldn't be for every project to produce results, but rather overall the most impactful results are achieved. If only 80 percent of research projects produce results, or even 5 percent of projects, the cost is worth it as long as the results produced are significant. This is like buying several lottery tickets. You don't need every ticket you buy to win, you just need one winner to hit the jackpot. (Note: Don't buy lottery tickets, unless it is for a charity; you will lose your money.) Simplistic quantitative metrics for research evaluations can also be replaced with more robust sets of quantitative and qualitative evaluations. For example, in 2008, Australia replaced its quantitative metrics for research assessment with a "Research Quality Framework," which included panels that assessed the impacts of the social, economic, and environmental benefits of research beyond just commercial application.[90]

There is a growing movement against bibliometrics in the research world. Randy Schekman's article in the *Guardian* is just one of a growing number of "Quit Lit" articles written by researchers who are leaving the profession, or refusing to be evaluated by citation metrics. One group of researchers started the *Declaration on Research Assessment* (DORA), which recognizes that the ways scientific research is evaluated needs to change. It had obtained 871 organizations and 12,788 individual signatories by August 2016.[91] Randy Schekman himself has advocated for open-access journals that focus on quality of research rather than just upping citations, and is currently the editor of *eLife*, a journal that deliberately doesn't promote its impact factor (although it was given one anyway). Until our governments, research organizations, and other funders of research recognize what fundamental research needs to thrive, there will be more Schekmans.

Bibliometrics tries to capture the complex phenomenon of fundamental research with a single number, and by doing so it distorts and damages the fundamental goal of scientific research: to discover novel ways of thinking and understanding the world. Scientific research needs to be able to fail and it needs to be able to pursue long-term goals. Asking research to provide results every step of the way, and to be popular while doing so, is simply wrong.

||||||||||

It isn't just executive pay and academic research that are susceptible to short-term biases. Short-term thinking is something that is ingrained in all of us. The struggle to obtain satisfaction in the short-term by sacrificing contentment in the long-term is a universal trait. Philosophers such as John Stuart Mill, David Hume, and Jeremy Bentham all commented on our tendency to undervalue the future and focus on the present. These struggles are found everywhere. Many people who go into advanced education have to make a decision to forgo current income for the prospects of higher income in the future, but that decision isn't always certain. Those suffering from drug addiction well know the struggle between short-term gratification and the long-term impacts of those decisions. In business these conflicts are encountered whenever a company makes a decision to invest in technology, train more workers, enter into new markets, or develop new products.[92]

Metrics, by their very nature, are intertemporal problems. We can know and measure what is happening in the present, or the recent past, but the same can't be said about the future. We can measure quarterly profits and the number of publications academics produce, as well as things such as test scores, short-term productivity targets, activities completed, or the number of patients a doctor sees. But the future is always unknown. We can't get detailed measurements about what will occur in the future. We don't know if investment in research and development will result in increased profits in the future, or if the work a researcher does will result in a groundbreaking discovery. Health professionals cannot know for certain if the habits and understanding they instill in their patients will lead to healthier lifestyles ten or fifty years into the future. A teacher cannot know for sure if the lessons he used to help students think creatively will result in those students solving complex problems in their work decades from now. So we measure executives on last quarter's earnings. We measure academics on the number of articles they published in the last year. We measure doctors by how many patients they see and how many procedures they perform. We measure teachers on how well their students do on an exam they will not remember in three months.

The more emphasis we put on metrics and only count the things that can be counted, the more we neglect to consider and plan for the future. Intertemporal problems are ultimately problems about information and certainty. We have information about today, but we don't have information about the future, so we base our decisions on what we know now, and not on what we can only guess about the future. We suffer for it.

CHAPTER 4
THE PROBLEM OF PER
Denominator Errors

Vancouver has the worst traffic congestion in Canada, perhaps North America. That was the message spread on headlines of local media in Vancouver in early March 2016. *Huffington Post*'s headline read "Vancouver traffic congestion is the worst in the country."[1] The next year it was the same. CTV ran an article in 2017 showing how Vancouver was seventy-first when measured against over a hundred cities.[2] In 2018, similar stories ran. "Vancouver nowhere near the top in global gridlock ranking" read the *CityNews* headline on February 6, 2018.[3] You get the point.

It has been the same story for years. In 2013 the average metro Vancouver resident, who had a thirty-minute commute, wasted ninety-three additional hours in traffic that year. The average commute in Vancouver, it is claimed, takes 36 percent longer in rush hour than it does when traffic is free-flowing. Evidently this means that Vancouver has the "worst" traffic congestion in North America.

Similar stories run in dozens upon dozens of newspapers throughout Canada and the United States every year, each with their own local interpretation. Every few months a new congestion report is published by one of the three large organizations that publish such studies: INRIX, TomTom, or the Texas A&M Transport Institute. And every few months, local media outlets report on the results of these studies, often using them to lambast or laud political inaction or action on the issue that is the focus of so much of our municipal government's time: traffic.

These articles are then shared on social media platforms like Twitter and Facebook. They are commented on, discussed, debated, and argued about over and over. Some will take the opportunity to disparage whichever politicians and their respective transportation policies, others will come to their defense. Some will use this as an opportunity to "trash talk" other cities and how bad their congestion is.

Few really understand what is going on. For over the last few decades, Vancouver was one of only a handful of major cities in North America in successfully reducing the average commuting time of its citizens. It was done by encouraging more growth in the downtown, allowing people to live closer to work, and investing in a convenient and efficient transit system. Yet the reports continually claim Vancouver is among the most congested cities in North America. How can a city that has reduced average commuting times be the worst for congestion on the continent?

Behind all the noisy data of these articles; the comparisons between cities, the number of hours spent commuting, the percentage delays, how much of your life you are wasting idling in traffic; there is a rather simple metric. And it is misleading.

Every year since 1982, the Texas Transportation Institute has provided this measure of congestion across the United States. According to their own report, "The Texas Transportation Institute is considered a national leader in providing congestion and mobility information. *The Urban Mobility Report* is the most widely quoted report on urban congestion and the associated costs in the nation." The measure they developed is the Time Travel Index.

The Time Travel Index (TTI) is a metric that is incredibly complex to compile data for, but the metric itself is stunningly simplistic. The TTI is simply a ratio of the time a trip takes during rush hour (also called peak period travel) to the time that same trip would take under congestion-free conditions. A commute that would take one hour under "free-flow" conditions that now takes an hour and a half during rush hour is given a time travel index of 1.5. The daily "time lost" in such a scenario would be one hour (half an hour each way). This same formula is used by TomTom and INRIX when they publish similar reports using data from vehicles equipped with their navigation systems, or by other organizations publishing similar congestion rankings. The collection of the data differs, but the concept is the same.

The TTI formula looks sensible at first glance. A trip that normally takes an hour but takes an hour and a half in rush hour is worse than a similar trip that takes only an hour and ten minutes in rush hour. But upon closer inspection, something is wrong. How could Vancouver reduce the amount of time people spent in traffic, yet be rated as worse by the measure? The reason is that due to the way it is measured, the TTI has the potential to be incredibly perverse. How else can a city that has reduced average commute times over the last decade score so badly?

Imagine two commuters both living in the same city, both working in the same office downtown, Monica and Richard. Monica lives close to the downtown and Richard lives farther away. Monica lives just one block off the route Richard takes to work, and so both of them use the exact same roads from downtown to Monica's house. Once past Monica's house, Richard has a lot more driving to do to get home.

Imagine that it takes ten minutes to get from Monica's house to downtown (and vice versa) when there is no traffic. From Richard's house it takes forty minutes. However, on the average work day, traffic is bad enough to make the trip between Monica's and downtown about twenty minutes, double the time it would take with no traffic. So both Richard and Monica spend the first twenty minutes of their commute going from work to Monica's house. Once past Monica's house, traffic lightens up a bit and Richard's remaining thirty-minute commute takes forty minutes instead. Richard spends an hour getting home, and Monica spends twenty minutes. However, according to the TTI, Monica's commute is worse.

Work it out. Monica has a time travel index of 2.0, her commute takes double the time than it would with no traffic. Richard's index is

1.5, his forty-minute commute takes an hour instead, yet Richard's total travel time is three times that of Monica's. In the perverse world on the time-travel index, Richard has a better commute than Monica.

Expand this idea to an entire city. Imagine millions of commuters and how their aggregate travel times would be evaluated with such a metric. Is it possible that the time travel index makes cities with longer average commutes look good, while those with short, yet congested commutes look bad? Does City A with a time travel index of 1.2 have better commutes than City B with a time travel index of 1.3, or is it just that those people living in City A drive longer to work each day? Is it just the case that their percentage of time spent in congested traffic is less than in City B, as their commutes are longer in general? To find out, one would have to dig into the numbers provided in these reports, working backward to calculate what the average commute times are in each city. That is exactly what Joe Cortright did.

Cortright, working under the nonprofit CEOs for Cities, published a scathing critique of the Time Travel Index and the *Urban Mobility Report* (the yearly report in which the results of the index are published) in 2010. The critique illustrates numerous flaws in how the TTI gathers data, the models it uses to determine average vehicle speeds and fuel consumption. But most important, Cortright's critique illustrates the perverse nature of the TTI itself. (I am going to ignore these numerous flaws that Cortright points out in the methodology and assume vehicle speed data used by the TTI are accurate and only focus on the critique of the metric itself for simplicity. If interested in Cortright's other critiques, find the report in the endnotes.)[4]

Cortright points out numerous instances where the TTI distorts the reality of commuting. Like Vancouver, the city of Portland, Oregon, looks bad in the eyes of the TTI. From 1982 to 2007 its TTI increased from 1.07 to 1.29 (congestion rankings would say its congestion went from 7 percent to 29 percent). However, due to better city planning and transportation policies, average commute times in Portland dropped in that same period from fifty-four minutes per day to forty-three. The main reason was the fact that average commuting distance dropped from 19.6 miles to 16 miles (more people began living closer to work, bringing down the average commute distance).[5]

The TTI emphasizes the number of hours of delay in each city, the point of which is that cities with more yearly hours of delay are somehow "worse" than those with fewer. But this too entirely distorts the reality of commuting. Cortright compares San Francisco and Kansas City to illustrate this absurdity. San Francisco had 55 hours of delay per commuter per year, while Kansas city only had 15. However, when it comes to total commuting time, San Francisco is by far a better place to commute, with only 186 hours spent commuting compared to Kansas' 229.[6]

In fact, when we examine the cities with the worst and best TTI scores and compare their average commute times, it is as if the TTI has completely inverted which cities are better and worse for commuting. Let's look at the worst cities according to the TTI: New York City has a TTI of 1.37 and 44 hours of delay per year; Chicago a score of 1.43 and 41 hours of delay; and San Francisco has a TTI of 1.42 and 55 hours of delay. Now let's look at some of the best cities according to the TTI: Buffalo has only 11 hours of delay a year (TTI score 1.07), Cleveland only 12 hours a year (TTI score 1.08), Kansas City has only 15 hours (TTI score of 1.07), and Rochester only 10 hours of delay a year (TTI of 1.06).

Now here is where things get interesting: The average commute times in Buffalo, Cleveland, Kansas, and Rochester are 168 hours, 162 hours, 229 hours, and 177 hours, respectively. The supposed "congested" cities of New York, Chicago, and San Francisco have average commute times of 163 hours, 136 hours, and 186 hours, respectively. Commuters in Chicago, with some of the worst TTI scores in the country, not only spend less time commuting on average than those living in Kansas City, with some of the best scores in the country, they spend a lot less. Almost 100 hours per year less. Yet, according to the TTI, Chicago is a much worse place for commuting than Kansas City. It is even more absurd considering Chicago had a population of 8.4 million while Kansas City had 1.5 million. A city that is almost five times as large that spends only 60 percent of the time in traffic is given a congestion score that is not only worse, but much worse.

The TTI distorts the relationship between the three aspects of commuting: speed, distance, and time. The TTI ignores the distance aspect of the equation, basing the metric entirely on the difference in speed. The measurement is blind to distance. Both those cities with lower and higher than average travel distances are distorted in the metric. As Cortright notes, "Some cities have managed to achieve shorter travel times and actually reduce peak hour travel times. The key is that some metropolitan areas have land use patterns and transportation systems that enable their residents to take *shorter trips and minimize the burden of peak hour travel*" (emphasis added).[7]

||||||||||

The TTI fails as a metric because it misuses a denominator. When it comes to getting to work, the goal should be making the journey take less time, not less time compared to some abstract (and unstandardized) ideal. Measuring only the additional time against some theoretical (and flawed) uncongested commute neglects most of the time people spend commuting. For the TTI, only certain types of time matter, but others don't. By measuring in such a way, it makes long commutes look better than short ones.

The TTI makes real solutions to the problem of commuting look like they are making things worse. The TTI focuses on moving fast, but it doesn't really care about how far or long you have to travel. Reaching maximum speed is what the measurement strives for, not reducing the total amount of time spent commuting. Cities where average commuting distances decrease (by more people choosing to live closer to work or their work moving closer to them) are seen as making congestion worse. But this is silly. The person who drives 2 miles to work contributes a lot less to congestion than the person traveling 20 miles to work, yet under the TTI, the former is seen as worse.

The error lies in the fact that the TTI uses a ratio to calculate its value: time spent commuting in rush hour versus time spent commuting in "free-flow" traffic. The assumption is that reducing congestion (time spent commuting in rush hour) will improve the measurement—that is, the numerator reduces the ratio. It neglects to take into account the other way to reduce the ratio, increasing the denominator, or increasing travel time in free-flow conditions (which essentially equates to increasing travel distance). Yet as Cortright points out, in many instances that is exactly what is happening. Commute distances (and therefore commute times) are increasing, but this looks like an improvement according to the TTI. It seems the best way to "reduce congestion" is to have people drive for hours after they get out of traffic.

‖‖‖‖‖‖‖‖‖

The problem with the TTI is that it counts only time against the ideal on congested commutes. It uses a denominator when it shouldn't. It gets the "per" wrong. If the average commute in a city is two hours every day, it really doesn't matter if that commute is all due to congestion or not. Two hours is a long time to spend driving, whether that time is spent moving along quickly or stuck at a light (although drivers do perceive time waiting as much longer than they perceive time moving). A better measure would be to simply report the average commute in each city, and perhaps the standard deviation, or some other representation of variance. (I am sure many would argue that longer commutes are justified in terms of housing quality, cost, or size. If that is the case, shouldn't we just measure housing satisfaction separately instead of assuming longer commutes mean higher satisfaction with housing?)

There may not be many metrics akin to the time travel index, as there are not many instances comparable to commuting in peak versus non-peak periods. But there is a lesson in the critique of the TTI that can be used with almost any metric, and is another lesson for metrics: Are you using the right "per" in your measure?

If so, you might be using a perverse metric, where improving the "score" on the measure actually worsens the condition you are measuring. The TTI introduces us to metrics that use ratios. While this type of ratio is unique, ratios in metrics are not. In fact they are quite common, and often misunderstood. That is the subject of this chapter.

||||||||||

Think about these two questions: Are millennials driving less than the generation before them? Is car ownership on the decline? Now, think about how you would measure these.

According to a 2015 article by *Bloomberg* Business[8] and the *Atlantic*,[9] the answer to both questions is a resounding no. According to these articles car ownership was in fact increasing among the younger generation. Both magazines stated that in 2014, millennials purchased 3.7 million cars, while Generation X purchasers only accounted for 3.3 million purchases. Clearly millennials were buying more cars than their older counterparts. Right?

The problem with this comparison is simple. There are a lot more millennials than there are Gen Xers: seventy-eight million compared to forty-nine million. This is mostly due to the method of delineating these groups: Millennials, as defined in the articles, were born between 1977 and 1994 and Gen Xers from 1965 to 1976. There are seventeen years of millennials and eleven years of Gen Xers, so the millennials group is larger simply due to the fact that it includes a larger age cohort. According to the data, millennials bought 47.5 cars per 1,000 persons, while Gen Xers bought 67.1 cars per 1,000 people.[10] *City Observatory*, a journal focused on cities and urban issues, caught on to this glaring error and published a retort. Their response: Those who wrote the *Bloomberg Business* and the *Atlantic* articles simply forgot to divide.

The problem was the opposite of the TTI. In this case, people forgot to use a denominator in the measure. What the question people were trying to answer wasn't if millennials bought more cars in total than Gen Xers, but whether they bought more per person. If it seems silly that someone simply forgot to divide, you'd be surprised at how many metrics you will encounter that make the same mistake. Simply neglecting to measure using a "per" is surprisingly common.

This story, while perhaps a bit wonky, raises an important issue about measurement: What is the measurement trying to say? Is it a question of intensity or raw size? Often these concepts are confused. We are often presented with measures that purport to say one thing, when really they say another. The example here was trying to use a metric to show that millennials are purchasing fewer cars than the generation before them. Instead, it showed that the millennial generation is simply larger than the generation before it.

This may seem to be a simple problem, and one that is rarely made, but if you look closely you will see that this error happens again and again and again. And it happens everywhere. Frequently metrics are chosen to represent a particular fact, when they really say something completely different. These problems are similar to what in scientific research are called unit of analysis errors—denominator neglect or denominator inflation. I like to call them the "problems of per." Often these errors are made because the denominator, or "per," is either neglected, poorly chosen, or sometimes manipulated. Other times denominators are simply forgotten. Sometimes deliberately to overemphasize the importance of the measure, to distort fair comparisons, or due to laziness (as in the *Bloomberg* article about millennials buying cars), but most often they are omitted because people don't even think about them. When presented with a metric, people often fail to ask the important question "Per what?"

I like to call this the "China fallacy." It is a frequent comparison made by political pundits, journalists, and everyday people: Compare whatever you want to China. Do you want to demonstrate that your country does not pollute very much? Compare your total amount of emissions to China; they will undoubtedly have more. Do you want to demonstrate that your country is not building enough roads, rail lines, or buildings? Or that your country doesn't invest enough in whatever area you are advocating for? Perhaps you want to compare the number of cell phones sold. China probably is doing more. In many of these comparisons, the advocate will neglect to compare how many of whatever per person each country has. He or she will simply state the total amount, neglecting to mention that China has over a billion people. He or she is just forgetting to divide.

Metrics that measure intensity or efficiency should use a denominator. In many cases the best denominator to use is the number of people, or per capita. Even this simple tool is often neglected. Cities are often compared on a gross measurement, whether it be the number of violent crimes (many news articles compare the total number of murders from one city to another rather than the murder rate per thousand people), the number of head offices, or things like the number of parks. We often compare countries by the raw size of their economies, number of Nobel Prize winners, or number of "famous people." If the point of the measurement is simply to state which country has the most of any of those things, then the measurement is fine, but if trying to see which country is the wealthiest, smartest, or most famous, one need look at per capita. But it isn't just neglecting a denominator that leads to problems. Using the wrong ones can be just as misleading.

||||||||||

New York City seems to be a dangerous place to be a pedestrian. On average, a pedestrian is killed just under every three days in the Big Apple. According to the National Highway Traffic Safety Administration, in

2012 New York City topped the list of number of pedestrians killed in US cities with over 500,000 people. With 127 pedestrians killed that year, New York surpassed cities like Los Angeles (99), Chicago (47), and San Francisco (14) along with more car-dependent cities like Houston (46) or Phoenix (39). But it is not just the total number of pedestrians killed in each city where New York tops the list. New York also has a higher percentage of pedestrians who are killed in all traffic fatalities. Looking at all traffic fatalities, pedestrians in New York are much more likely to be the victim of a collision than in other cities. Across the nation 14 percent of all traffic fatalities are pedestrians, in New York it is 47 percent.

Hold on. We know it isn't fair to compare a place like New York, with a population in 2012 of over 8.3 million, with a city like Phoenix, with a population of 1.5 million. Measuring pedestrian safety is a matter of intensity, and we should use a per capita measurement to reflect this. Somebody should not take comfort in the fact that they are walking in a town with one of the lowest total number of pedestrian fatalities in the nation, when the number of pedestrians killed as a ratio to the total population is one of the highest in the nation. Being in a town of 1,000 people where 5 pedestrians are killed every year would be a horrible place to live. Since we are measuring intensity, we should at least look at the per capita rates of pedestrian fatalities in each city.

Taking this into account, New York starts to look a lot better, but still not great. In New York, 1.52 pedestrians are killed each year for every 100,000 people. While places like Boston (0.79), Washington (1.11), San Jose (1.22), and Baltimore (0.97) do better, New York is not as bad for pedestrians as places such as Los Angeles (2.57), Dallas (3.22), Oklahoma (3.34), or, the worst on the list, Detroit, with 3.99 pedestrian fatalities per 100,000 people per year. New York is slightly worse than the national average (which includes all cities, towns, and rural areas under 500,000 people) of 1.51 pedestrians killed per 100,000 people.

Yet New York is in fact one of the safest places to be a pedestrian in America. Why? Simply because New York has a lot of pedestrians.

Using a per capita metric sometimes does not reflect the right intensity we are trying to measure. Pedestrian deaths are a case in point. While New York is roughly average for the number of pedestrians killed per 100,000 people, it has a far greater number of people walking (or cycling) than do most cities in America. In fact it has an incredibly greater number more.

With roughly 10 percent of people walking to work, New York has one of the highest percentages of pedestrian commuters in the United States (Boston at 14 percent and Washington, DC, at 11 percent are the only two cities higher).[11] If we add the number of transit users (as most transit trips start and end with a walking trip), New York skyrockets to first with a combined walk/transit share of 65 percent (Boston ends up with 49 percent and Washington with 48 percent).

So while you may take comfort in the fact that in your city, there are only 0.5 pedestrians killed per 100,000 people, if almost no one walks, you shouldn't feel so safe. What an analysis of pedestrian safety should look at is not the number of deaths per total population, but the number of pedestrians.

The city of Vancouver did in fact undertake this analysis. Vancouver recognized that in order to become the greenest city in the world by 2020, a goal they adopted in 2009, they would have to increase the number of people walking, cycling, and taking transit to work. To encourage more people to walk, they would have to make walking safer. So they undertook an exhaustive study to understand where, why, and how pedestrians were unsafe. More important, they understood that they couldn't measure safety as a ratio to the total population; they had to measure it as a ratio to the number of people walking.

While they do report that the total number of pedestrian collisions in Vancouver have been dropping fairly consistently since 1996, they also note that Vancouver has one of the lowest death rates per million walk-to-work trips. So does New York. For every million walk-to-work trips,

1.0 pedestrian in Vancouver is killed by a vehicle. In New York it is 1.5 pedestrians. In Los Angeles it is 5.2.

This is not meant to give anyone the impression that 1.0 pedestrian deaths per 1 million walk-to-work trips is acceptable, let alone 1.5. No pedestrian deaths should be acceptable. But if one is to focus on the safety of pedestrians, the safety of pedestrians should be measured, and it should not include people driving to work or staying at home. The fact that someone at home wasn't run over by a car shouldn't give us much comfort. To put it another way, if a million more New Yorkers started walking to work tomorrow, but the number of pedestrian deaths slightly increased, it would not be a sign of diminished pedestrian safety.

So is New York a dangerous place to walk? The answer, after looking deeper at the data, is very different than the answer that came from just looking at the raw number of fatalities. In fact when considering how many pedestrians and pedestrian trips are made within the city, New York is one of the safest places to be a pedestrian in the United States. In fact New Yorkers are 75 percent less likely to die in an automobile accident than Americans as a whole.[12] On an average walk through New York, you are much less likely to be the victim of a traffic collision than in, say, Dallas. That is not to say that pedestrian safety cannot be improved in New York (and it should), but to say it is more dangerous for a pedestrian in New York than Dallas is just false.

||||||||||

Another metric that is misunderstood due to how it is calculated has to do with disease. But this time it is not the denominator that leads to the distortion, but the numerator. There are three ways to measure a disease's effect on a population: prevalence, incidence, and mortality. Prevalence is the number of people in a given population who have a certain disease (or condition). For example, 50 people per 100,000 have the bubonic plague (let's hope not), 10 people per 100,000 have syphilis, or 120 people per 100,000 have glaucoma. (All of these numbers are made up. Please don't think that 50 people out of 100,000 have bubonic plague.) Incidence is how many people in a given population contract the disease in a given period. Ten people get avian flu out of 100,000 in a year. Sixty-five people get malaria per 100,000. Mortality is the number of people in a given population who die from the disease. One hundred people per 100,000 die from cancer. Obviously, decreasing each of these numbers is desirable. We want fewer people to contract the disease, fewer to live with it, and fewer to die from it. But the interesting thing about these measures is that positive changes in one of these measures can actually make another worse.

Say, for example, a treatment is discovered that extends the lifespan of people with malaria. Such an improvement, if incidence rates stay constant, can increase the prevalence of the disease. If people do not die as early from malaria, it means they live longer. If they live longer, more of them will be around to be counted as living with the disease each year. Therefore the prevalence rate of the disease will rise. The measurement tells a bad story, when in fact the burden of disease is decreasing. On the contrary, a disease that kills its victims very quickly will have a low prevalence rate, as few people live a long enough time with the disease to be counted as living with the disease year over year. Sometimes a decrease in prevalence of a disease is not due to a decrease in people contracting it, but that people are dying of it faster. An article celebrating the fact that fewer people are living with a certain disease than before may in fact not be good news. It might be because many of them are dying.

|||||||||||

Denominators not only have to be specific to the particular purpose or goal being measured, but that denominator has to make sense. It has to be reasonably connected to the purpose, impact, or influence of something.

If we were to measure educational costs by calculating the cost of our education system per textbook, it would seem silly. Or if we were to evaluate a company's labor costs per employee washroom, it would be absurd. These are of course ridiculous examples, but they illustrate that the "per" has to make sense. Unfortunately there are numerous instances where this doesn't happen.

One case of denominator misuse that offers several lessons comes from a *Toronto Sun* article from June 3, 2015, written by Barrie Goldstein.[13] In the article Goldstein defended the greenhouse gas emissions of Canada. Goldstein's argument basically was that criticisms of Canada's "per capita" emissions, which are among the highest in the world, are unfair. According to Goldstein, Canada is one of the lowest emitters of greenhouse gases. Why? Because it has some of the lowest emissions per square kilometer. Goldstein argues that emissions based on area, rather than per person, is a more valid measure of emission intensity. We will see why this is fallacious, and how to learn from it, but it is easy to see how Goldstein falls into this error, as many have done with problems of "per."

Canada does have some of the highest per capita emissions in the world. Goldstein mentioned that at 17.91 tonnes of carbon emitted per person per year, Canada was the second highest in the world, below only the United States at 19.74 tonnes. For comparison, Japan was 10.23, Germany was 10.22, Brazil was 1.94, Indonesia had 1.77, and India was 1.38. But for Goldstein, Canada's very high emissions are justified because it is very big and very cold. (Never mind that emissions for Russia, which is just as big and cold as Canada are 11.13 tonnes per person per year.)

Goldstein's main contention is that larger land areas justify higher greenhouse gas emissions, mostly through increased use of transportation. He points out that Germany has lower emissions per capita because it has 2.3 times the population of Canada yet has a land area one-third the size of one of Canada's larger provinces, Ontario. By using less energy to transport goods and people, Goldstein's argument goes, Germany has a distinctive advantage over Canada in terms of the amount of energy the country needs.

Goldstein may have a point here. Countries that are less dense do have to expend more energy transporting goods. But to understand if transport is what causes the difference in greenhouse gas emissions, we should investigate a few things. First, how much of a country's emissions is attributable to transportation, specifically long-distance freight transportation? Freight transportation would be affected by low population densities, or at least dense concentrations of population that are spread out from each other. If a country has a higher proportion of emissions attributable to transportation, it may be an indication that transporting goods long distances may contribute to the higher emission numbers.

Second, we should look at the number of ton-kilometers of freight transport per capita in either country (if a larger country does in fact require goods to be transported farther distances, than we should measure how many goods travel how far, per person). Perhaps the increased emissions from transportation are due to workers commuting long distances by car instead of using public transit, rather than shipping goods long distances between cities.

Third, we should look at the average emissions per ton-kilometer for freight transportation in each country. Perhaps the greater amount of emissions is not due to either the distance goods have to travel per person, or the distance people travel within cities, but simply because less efficient means of shipping goods are used. Transporting goods by ship or train is more efficient than transporting them by truck. Let's take a look.

First, let's look at the total carbon emission picture. According to Environment Canada, per capita emissions in 2014 were 20.6 tonnes per Canadian per year.[14] Of this, transportation accounts for 23 percent. Passenger cars and trucks make up to 50.1 percent of the transportation portion, while freight makes up 39.6 percent.[15] As for Germany, a PricewaterhouseCoopers report shows that the transport sector makes up about 28 percent of the energy consumption in the country, and freight accounts for about 28 percent of that.[16] For comparison, in the United States, transportation makes up 26 percent of emissions.[17]

Canada is definitely a large country, but its population is also concentrated in a few pockets that are fairly dense, such as southern Ontario. There is not a lot of freight transport headed to the far north contributing to greenhouse gas emissions. It could very well be the case that, although Canada is very large, its freight transportation is not that much greater per capita than other countries. If Goldstein wants to argue that Canada is a larger country, and therefore requires more energy to transport goods, he should compare the relative amounts of emissions attributable to transportation in each country, as we did above, then show how this is attributable to the number of ton-kilometers per capita rather than emissions per ton-kilometer.

Again, there is some data to help here. According to the Railway Association of Canada, in 2013 railways in Canada carried out 425.1 billion ton-kilometers of travel,[18] trucks accounted for an additional 251.4 billion ton-kilometers. In Germany, there were 113 billion ton-kilometers (310 billion on roads and 59 on waterways).[19] Overall, freight transport in Germany adds up to 5,951 ton-kilometers per person, in Canada it is 10,517. So Canada does transport goods farther per person, nearly double that of Germany.

Without going into a detailed comparative analysis of greenhouse gas emissions for both countries, just looking at the amounts attributable to the transportation sector, while transportation does impact Canada's overall greenhouse gas emissions, it is clear that transportation doesn't explain a near doubling of total greenhouse gas emissions in Canada over Germany, despite Canada transporting goods farther. So does Canada have greater per capita emissions than Germany because it transports goods farther, or is it something else?

By looking deeper into the numbers, we can see that while transportation does account for a higher amount of emissions per capita in Canada versus Germany, it isn't the entire picture. But where we can learn the most from this article is Goldstein's suggestion about what we use instead of a per capita measure for emissions: "But there's another method of measuring a country's greenhouse gas emissions that is every bit as legitimate as doing it based on population. . . . That's doing it based on the size of the country."[20]

Goldstein goes on to explain that the statistics division of the United Nations did in fact calculate emissions per land area. Not surprisingly, Canada had some of the lowest emissions per area in the world, 59.11 tonnes per square kilometer. China is higher at 681.3 tonnes, 632.91 for the United States, 489.77 for India, 92.40 for Russia, and 213.4 for Indonesia. But densely populated Germany and Japan come in at 3,449.80 and 2,355.42 tonnes per square kilometer, respectively.

It is easy to fall into the trap of thinking that Goldstein stumbled upon a "gotcha" moment. By these numbers, Germany and Japan are some of the worst villains when it comes to emissions. Their per square kilometer emissions are incredibly high. But Germany and Japan have some of the lowest per capita emissions in the world. What is going on here?

The logic in Goldstein's article is flawed, but it isn't immediately obvious why. By looking deeper, we can understand not only the fallacies of Goldstein's argument, but discover an important tool to understand metrics. Every metric, when closely examined, carries with it implicit assumptions about how the world works, where causality lies, and, most important, how best to enact change and improve. In Goldstein's example, the assumption is that emissions intensity by land area is the best way to measure carbon emissions. Reduce our carbon emissions per land area, and we improve the situation. But is this correct?

There are two ways to test whether a metric makes sense. The first is to analyze the ways the metric can be improved, and critically examine whether those methods are reasonable, achievable, or in fact counterproductive. The second is to find examples of where the measurement improves, but the actual outcome is poor. First let's look at the ways we can improve Goldstein's emissions per land area.

There are three basic ways we can improve a countries emissions per land area. First we can simply decrease the average emissions for each person. If we decrease the amount each person emits, and the land area stays the same, the metric improves. No issues here. Second we can reduce the number of people in the country. Fewer people on the same land area means less emissions per area. Last we can increase the land area of the country. More land means less emissions per area.

Looking at these strategies, does anything seem counterproductive, unachievable, or absurd? The first is pretty standard: Reducing emissions per person is something that would work for almost any measure of carbon emissions. The second is a bit less clear. By reducing the number of people in a country, we reduce its emissions per area. That is true, but is that what was intended by using the metric? Was Goldstein simply suggesting that some countries simply reduce their population? Perhaps he was, but it definitely wasn't clear in his article. Finally, increasing the land area of the country seems like a dubious method to reduce emissions. There are only two ways this could possibly happen: Either the country creates more land (it isn't unheard of, the Netherlands is a country that is mostly composed of reclaimed land from the sea), or it takes sparsely populated land from another country. In either of these cases, no actual improvements to reducing emissions are achieved. Taking land from another country just shifts the emissions from one country to another, and creating new land doesn't decrease total emissions, which is what is needed to mitigate the effects of climate change.

So looking at an argument such as Goldstein's, when we really dive into the metric, what we find is that Goldstein isn't really arguing that we should lower our emissions per land area, because that is a zero-sum game (we can't add any more land). He is simply (but perhaps unintentionally) arguing the world should have fewer people. When Goldstein argues that, for example, Europeans should emit as much carbon per square kilometer as Canadians, he is either saying that Europe should get larger (which, save for massive geo-engineering projects, is impossible), or that there should be fewer Europeans. Yet, by the same argument, there should also be fewer Canadians. And if the strategy to reduce emissions requires reducing population, wouldn't reducing the population of Canada be more effective than Germany or Japan? Canada does emit more carbon per capita than either (although, Canadians are very nice people).

Now let's look at the second strategy, imagining examples where the metric improves, but the outcome is worse. For this case, let's look at an extreme, if implausible, scenario. We could imagine a single person occupying half of the world and emitting just slightly less carbon as everyone else on Earth combined. This person would have a lower carbon intensity per area as the other eight billion people on the planet but would be responsible for nearly eight billion times as much emissions per capita as the rest of humanity. By Goldstein's metric, they are doing better for the climate than the other eight billion people. Is that reasonable?

The point of this exercises is not to evaluate if this extreme case is probable or even plausible, but to use it as a thought exercise to understand if moving in one way or the other makes sense. If fewer people living on the same area of land but creating more emissions per person is preferable to more people living on less land but creating lower emissions per person, then we should also be able to say that one person occupying half the land in the world, but who has slightly lower total emissions than the entire rest of the world, who occupy the other half, is also a good thing. That is obviously wrong.

It is completely ludicrous to imagine someone living on half of the land on Earth and emitting half of the carbon in the world. But it is not implausible that some people use more land than others with greater carbon emissions, as Canada does. Nor is it implausible to imagine where more people live on slightly less land with lower carbon emissions per person, but higher emissions per area, as does Japan and Germany. The extremes of the scale let us better understand small movements along it.

When we theorize the ways a metric can be improved, but the outcome worsened, we gain a better understanding of what really lies behind a metric. With any metric, if you can think of ways to improve the metric without actually improving the goal behind the metric, the metric is likely flawed. If the only plausible methods of improving the metric are either unachievable, absurd, counterproductive, or strategies that would be adopted anyway with alternative metrics, the metric you are using is likely designed poorly.

However, there are times when improving a metric, even one that uses the right denominator, can still lead to counterproductive efforts. This happens when the measurement focuses narrowly on one aspect of a complex system and ignores the rest. That is the subject of the next chapter.

CHAPTER 5

THE FOREST AND THE TREES

Simplifying Complex Systems

I am sitting on a coffee shop patio in Calgary's Beltline district on a sunny May afternoon. It is 2012. I am meeting with a "mobile mortgage specialist," someone who is employed by my bank to sell mortgages. We are meeting near my work, which I guess is part of the convenience the mobile mortgage specialist offers. In preparation for the meeting I was asked to bring my last two years of tax assessments, a pay stub, and some other information relating to my income.

As we sit drinking our coffee, we discuss the particulars of what type of mortgage I can qualify for and the associated details: the down payment, the fixed interest rate the loan will be at for the first five years, and the insurance I will need from Canada Mortgage and Housing Corporation. We discuss my financial status: income, expenses, debts. We also discuss other costs I can expect: condominium fees, utility bills, property taxes, which all impact what I can afford.

To the banks and mortgage lenders, the relevant information needed to determine how much I can afford is purely financial: my income, credit history, current debts, expected condominium fees, utilities and property taxes, and of course my credit rating, a reflection of how well I pay back loans and other forms of credit. These are all entered into a formula that calculates the expected amount of my mortgage, my monthly payments, the interest rate I will have, and other such details. The purchase of my home is going to be the largest investment I have made. My mortgage payments will be the largest expenditure I have each month. I am not unique in this regard.

In 2011, the year before I purchased my condo, the average Canadian family had total expenditures of $73,457 (including taxes and insurance), with total spending on goods and services totaling $55,151. Of this, $15,198 was spent on the household's primary accommodation (rent, mortgage payments, and the like), or 27.6 percent of total spending on goods and services. This is the largest expenditure for most Canadian families. For those living in single-person households, such as myself at the time, expenditures on the primary residence were $10,125 out of an average total of $40,915, or 24.7 percent of expenditures.[1]

The questions I am asked regarding my mortgage are important, and not just for me. Knowing how much house I can afford is of the utmost importance to my bank, who is lending me the money. It is important to Canada Mortgage and Housing Corporation, who insures my mortgage against default. And it is important to the government and Canadians in general, because as many learned in 2008, nothing brings down an economy like a housing crash (although Canada came out of the 2008 crash much better than our neighbors to the south, partly due to the role of Canada Mortgage and Housing Company, but this book isn't going to get into that). With so much riding on my decision to buy a house it is peculiar what my mortgage broker doesn't ask me: "Where do you want to live?"

This may seem like an odd question to some. Where I choose to live shouldn't be of much concern to my mortgage lender. For where I choose to live is my choice, my personal preference of neighborhood amenities, commuting distance, proximity to schools, or being in a "good" neighborhood. The bank should only be concerned with whether I can afford it.

Yet it becomes important when we look at the second-largest household expenditure: transportation. In 2011 the average Canadian household spent an astonishing $11,229 on transportation, 20.4 percent of all expenditures. This is more than after-tax personal spending on health-care, education, and food combined (granted, in Canada most education and healthcare is paid by the government using income and other taxes). Suffice it to say, transportation is a considerable expenditure for most households.

The choice of where I live is important because the location of my residence is the largest determinant of how much I am going to spend on transportation. For me, the choice between a condominium in Calgary's Beltline—the trendy, urban neighborhood adjacent to downtown—and a far-flung suburb like Mahogany or Rocky Ridge is not just a difference in lifestyle, it is a matter of thousands of dollars a year in transportation costs. By living in Beltline, not only could I walk to work, but I could get groceries, go out for dinner, buy household goods at the drugstore, get my hair cut, go to the bank, shop for clothes, and visit friends, all without a car. And in Calgary, a city of just over one million people, where the average downtown parking costs are second in North America only to Manhattan (downtown parking averaged close to $500 per month), not having to drive to work makes even more sense.

The transmission in the ten-year-old sedan I inherited from my parents failed two months previous, and I decided not to buy a new car at the time. Instead I would rely on walking, transit, car2go (which launched in Calgary a few months previous), the occasional car rental on week-ends, and, admittedly, borrowing my parents' vehicle to get around for more than a year. So while the average Canadian single-person household spent $5,345 a year on transportation, I would expect to pay about a fifth of that (my monthly average for car2go, transit passes, and car rentals was about $100).

But to my bank, these transportation considerations are not taken into account. In fact, my mortgage advisor suggests that if I want a more affordable place, I should move further away from downtown. From a pure cost of housing perspective, this makes sense: housing further away from downtown does generally cost less. But as those housing prices drop, the cost of transportation goes up. The question we should ask is "do the savings on the home make up for the increase in transportation costs?" At least one study in the United States suggests not.

The Center for Transit-Oriented Development and the Center for Neighborhood Technology jointly published a study in 2006 titled "The Affordability Index: A New Tool for Measuring the True Affordability of Housing Choice."[2] What the study did, and what was so different from the typical practice of mortgage lenders, was it included both the cost of housing and the cost of transportation in the calculation of household spending. Granted they used aggregate-level census data and there were limitations to the numbers they had available, nevertheless, the exercise was important, and the findings are interesting.

In Minneapolis/St. Paul for example, the combined costs of housing and transportation for "inner city" neighborhoods were generally between 37 and 43 percent of households' incomes, while in suburban areas it was between 47 and 54 percent (this is holding household income levels constant, so the effect is not just due to incomes varying from one area to another). While the costs of housing were decreasing the farther households moved away from the center of the city, the costs of transportation were increasing. And they were increasing more.

Mortgage lending requirements are an example of what can be referred to as "an incomplete metric." It is a metric that attempts to measure some phenomenon, in this case the cost of living, but only captures a part of the picture, missing out on a lot of what makes up that whole. While I only focused on transportation, there are many other factors that affect the cost of living, such as heating and home maintenance, both of which may be reflected in the price of a home. A less-expensive home may not necessarily mean a lower cost of living.

The problem with this is not just that the measurement is inaccurate, but that it actually leads to behaviors that are contradictory. In the case of mortgages, by neglecting to include transportation costs, banks actually incentivize homeowners to increase their cost of living in order to qualify for a mortgage. The Center for Housing Policy termed this "Drive 'Til You Qualify."[3] Collecting data on housing and transportation costs in the largest twenty-eight metropolitan areas in the United States, the Center for Housing Policy found that as the average commuting distance of households grew, their combined housing and transportation costs did as well, despite the fact that housing costs generally decreased as commuting distance increased.

Mortgage lenders ultimately want you to be able to make payments on your house. Mortgage borrowers defaulting on their loans is not a desirable outcome for banks. At least this should have been the lesson learned from the 2008 crash. Banks are concerned with what you can comfortably afford so that the mortgage payments can keep coming. While a mortgage lender may push you to get a larger mortgage, it doesn't want to push too far in case you default. For the bank, keeping your cost of living at a manageable level is desirable. Inadvertently, by neglecting to consider the cost of transportation on your cost of living, banks are actually increasing your cost of living by encouraging you to live farther away. That is the problem with only counting part of the whole. Mortgage lending is not the only metric that misses the whole picture and results in behaviors that are counter to the original intent of the metric.

||||||||||

Metrics that pit one part of a system against another are common in the business world. One of the areas where this is prominent is in the world of insurance. One insurance executive claimed that he spends nearly half of his time adjudicating disputes between sales and underwriting. The reason is that the sales staff are evaluated on the sales volume they achieve, while the underwriters are measured on the quality of the risk of the insurance policies they issue. In order to meet sales targets, the sales staff have to sell insurance to riskier and riskier clients, which deteriorates the risk quality of the clients who the underwriters have to take on.[4] Insurance companies, wanting to increase their profits, pit one division against each other, increasing sales volume, but also increasing risk, undermining their profitability.

Another example comes from the world of call centers. For many call centers, employees are measured on how quick they complete calls, called "average handling time." The rationale behind the metric is that employees can increase their productivity by reducing the time they spend on the phone with customers, eliminating useless small talk, and focusing on the issue at hand. The problem is that, because they are incentivized to reduce call time, employees start taking extreme measures to get their average handling time down: They hang up on customers. The resulting impact on customer satisfaction could be catastrophic, with customers choosing to spend their money elsewhere due to poor experiences with customer service. The problem with average handling time is that it measures only one part of the function of the call center—resolving the issue quickly. By neglecting other important aspects of the job, such as improving customer satisfaction, call centers are pitting one part of the business against another.

In the world of business, companies are tasked with the goal of generating profit for the owners or shareholders of the company. Sounds simple enough. When companies begin to reach a certain size, understanding and managing the entire organization becomes cumbersome, so their components have to break into manageable departments and functions: product development, marketing, supply-chain management, retail and sales, customer service, human resources, production, and so forth. As understanding how each department relates to the others and to the ultimate goal of generating profit are sometimes maddeningly complex, often businesses attempt to manage each department as a separate entity, giving it its own performance metrics and often, budget.

Sales is responsible for selling the product and so is measured on how many sales are made. Marketing is responsible for reaching the target market with advertisements and messaging, so they are measured on the number of impressions, leads, engagements, customers, and things like spending per customer. Production is responsible for reducing costs and maintaining quality. Supply chain is responsible for getting the product to market in a timely manner and ensuring the right amount of product is on shelves and little goes to waste. Simply optimize each department, and your business will succeed. Right?

What many in business fail to recognize is that these individual performance goals may actually work against each other and may ultimately undermine profitability. Take the insurance example. Salespeople were incentivized to generate sales volume, but they were not responsible for ensuring a good risk portfolio, so they constantly undermined the underwriters' goals. Human resources may be given goals to reduce hiring time and the cost of new hires, but this may result in poor quality candidates being selected, eroding productivity and quality of work. Interorganizational conflict is pervasive in every type of business. Often the greatest competitor a business will face is itself.

One example of an organization that understood the interplay between the various components of its business, and how one part of the system affected another, is Zara. Zara is a clothing business that does one thing better than almost any other clothing retailer: They get new styles from the fashion show onto the rack at the store quickly. Their market is heavily influenced by the latest trends in fashion, and making sure products are on racks in time is paramount. Zara produces nearly 450 million items a year.[5] While many of its competitors had moved production to places like Bangladesh, Taiwan, Vietnam, or China in order to reduce production costs, Zara went in the opposite direction: It moved a lot of its production to Europe. Most of what Zara sells is produced in Spain, because the company realized that low manufacturing costs in Southeast Asia also implied a longer time to market. Given its focus on capturing the latest fashion trends, Zara realized that longer shipping and production times meant that much of the clothes produced outside of Europe would sit unpurchased on shelves at the end of the season. By moving its production to Spain, Zara was able to offset the increased production costs with lower waste.[6] While unsold stock makes up for 17 to 20 percent total merchandise in the industry average, Zara has less than 10 percent of its stock made up of unsold items.[7] By recognizing that maximizing the whole is not just a matter or maximizing the parts, Zara was able to gain a competitive advantage.

Understanding the interplay between different components of a system, and that optimizing each component doesn't necessarily lead to optimization of the system, is an important concept for organizations to grasp. Failing to do so results in suboptimization and counterproductive measures. That failure, unfortunately, is something many of us are guilty of. One area where we are guilty of it concerns our understanding of the impact of the food we eat and where it comes from.

Where does your food come from? Is it from a local farm, or is it shipped from far away? Do you try to eat local? If so, why? Is it because you want to support local farmers? Is it because local food is healthier? Or is it because the cost of transporting food such long distances is so wasteful? The notion of eating local has been around since, well, forever. Hunter-gatherers never ate food that came from much farther away than a person could walk in a day. With the agricultural revolution that began some ten thousand years ago and the surplus food production that resulted, people began trading, storing, and transporting food over longer and longer distances. Most food, however, was still traded and consumed very close to where it was grown. Yet even early on in our history, luxury foods, such as spices or salt, were traded over long distances. It wasn't until modern transportation systems came about (such as long-distance shipping and rail networks) that much of the food we eat, and not just spices and luxuries, came from a long distance away.

The modern trend of eating local food has its roots in a 1994 article by Angela Paxton titled "The Food Miles Report: The Dangers of Long-Distance Food Transport."[8] The article was one of the first looks into the implications of how food travels to get to our plates. The report highlighted aspects of our modern food system that were, and still are, surprising to many. While many concerns about our modern food system are discussed in the report, the focus, as indicated by the title of the report, is on the implications of the distance our food travels to get to our plates. The 2011 reprint of the article sums up the thrust of the article nicely: "Citizens don't want the same food pointlessly crisscrossing the globe, wasting precious energy, causing pollution, trading unfairly, and leaching jobs from the countryside."

Whether they are apples that are transported fourteen thousand miles from New Zealand or green beans transported four thousand miles from Kenya, both to be consumed in the United Kingdom, the distances that food travel are astonishing.[9] The impact of long-distance transport of food is not just the amount of energy the food requires to be transported. Long-distance food transport requires preservation and packaging of food, both of which reduce the health value of food, while also requiring more resources.

The concept of "Food Miles" was popularized by Alisa Smith and J. B. MacKinnon in their 2005 book *The 100-Mile Diet: A Year of Local Eating*. The book was an instant success. The locavore movement was soon under way. Grocery stores began stocking their shelves with more local produce. Local farmers' markets made a comeback. City dwellers skipped the big-box grocery store and drove out to rural markets so they could eat local, do better for the environment, and support the local economy. Restaurants started advertising where their food came from, featuring the farms and the people behind the food you were eating. Knowing the pork you were eating came from Sullivan Farms, only thirty miles away, brought a sense of comfort. Not only was your choice better for the environment, you felt you were helping out the Sullivans. Eating local felt good.

No doubt there was a lot more to our food culture than simply the distance it traveled. Soil erosion; fair labor practices; over-reliance on fertilizers; environmental degradation due to pesticides, herbicides, and insecticides; and health effects are just some of the implications of the food we choose to eat. But for the local food movement, faced with a food system so complex, the negative effects too convoluted to fully understand, using food miles as a measure for the sustainability became the best way to ensure we were eating right. But is it?

Let's look at one example. Compare the two countries of origin of the flowers that the British buy for their loved ones on Valentine's Day: the Netherlands and Kenya. The Netherlands would seem obvious as the more sustainable choice. Transporting flowers from the Netherlands to the United Kingdom requires an incredibly short trip across the English Channel by boat. The trip from Kenya is neither short nor energy efficient. The flowers are flown in by plane. Yet, if you were to undertake a thorough calculation of the total amount of carbon dioxide emitted for each batch of 12,000 flowers grown and sent to the United Kingdom (we will discuss how these calculations are done later), you would find that while the Dutch flowers emit 35,000 kilograms of carbon dioxide (just under 3 kilograms per flower), the Kenyan variety only emits 6,000 kilograms of carbon dioxide (0.5 kilograms per flower).[10] Why the huge discrepancy?

The problem is that food miles, as the name implies, measures only one aspect of the food-production system: transport. All the steps before transport, including raw materials for production (fertilizer, seed, water, pesticides); energy in the form of gasoline or electricity; and production and packing (labor, energy, machinery) are not included in the calculation. Nor are the steps after transportation included, such as consumption (food preparation, other raw materials) and disposal (recycling, waste, transportation).

While it may seem that transporting food halfway across the world would be a heavy energy burden, the transport of food only accounts for a very small portion of the energy that goes into the food system: approximately 4 percent of food-related emissions in the United States. The bulk of the energy consumption and emissions can be traced back to the production stage of the process, accounting for 83 percent of the total.[11] It may seem counterintuitive that transport would account for so little of the food life cycle costs. Clearly, transporting an apple from New Zealand to the United Kingdom would use a staggering amount of energy and emit a lot of carbon dioxide. The trip is incredibly long. Yet the emissions are relatively low. Why is this?

The main reason is that not all modes of transportation are equal. While driving a car is a very carbon-intensive activity, long-distance shipping is not. In fact long-distance ocean shipping is the most energy-efficient mode of transportation in the world. Emissions from oceangoing container ships average between 10 and 15 grams of carbon dioxide per ton-kilometer (6.9 to 10.3 grams per ton-mile), which is lower than rail transport (19 to 41 grams per ton-kilometer or 13.0 to 28.1 grams per ton-mile), trucking (51 to 91grams per ton-kilometer or 34.9 to 62.3 grams per ton-mile), or flying (673 to 867 grams per ton-kilometer or 461.0 to 593.9 grams per ton-mile).[12]

If you were to buy a few bags of tomatoes (let's say 5 kilograms or 11 pounds; quite a lot of tomatoes) and were to drive 1 kilometer (0.62 miles) to the grocery store in a car that gets 100 kilometers per 6 liters of gas (2.55 gallons per mile, which is pretty good fuel efficiency for city driving), the amount of carbon dioxide you emit would be 750 grams (each liter of gasoline burned equates to roughly 2.5 kilograms, or 5.5 pounds, of carbon dioxide produced). A high-efficiency container ship could move a ton of tomatoes 5 kilometers (3 miles) with the same amount of emissions. Let me state that again. A container ship can transport a full ton of tomatoes five times the distance that you transport only 5 kilograms of those tomatoes, while emitting the same amount of carbon. Or it could transport the same 5 kilograms of tomatoes a staggering 1,000 kilometers while emitting that same amount of carbon dioxide.

To put this in perspective, driving your car to the grocery store accounts for 48 percent of all the transport miles associated with food (total miles, not per ton of food, which is important). The reason this is so high, despite the trip distances being so short, is that when you drive your car, you transport only a few bags of groceries at a time. A New Panamax classified container ship can carry 12,000 20-foot containers, each having a volume of 1,172 cubic feet. That is over 14 million cubic feet of storage space. Moving that same volume in personal cars would take hundreds of thousands, if not millions, of trips.

As a percentage of the emissions attributed to the supply chain, 13 percent is attributed to this trip to the supermarket. The long-distance container ships transporting apples from New Zealand, coffee from South America, and spices from India contribute a total 12 percent emissions. And remember: That is just the transport part of the picture; it doesn't include production, processing, packaging, or consumption.

So why do those flowers from Kenya require so much less energy than those from the Netherlands? What is offsetting that huge amount of carbon emitted by flying those flowers from Nairobi to London? While the Dutch rely on greenhouses to grow their flowers, the Kenyans rely on sunshine.

The "Food Miles Report" states that "consumers are not fully informed of the effects of the food they are buying; and that the full cost of production and transportation are not reflected in the shop price." Yet one of the recommendations of the report is to "introduce national labelling schemes showing food miles and/or itemized till receipts to show country/countries of origin of foods" or require products to "carry information to consumers to show the distance fresh food has been transported, and the mode of transportation used."[13] But such a labelling scheme would miss the point.

Even the "Food Miles Report" notes that "it is usually more energy efficient to grow products in their natural climatic conditions and then ship them to the country of destination, rather than intensive agricultural methods to grow them in appropriate climates"[14] Yet, that is exactly what reliance on food miles as a metric of the sustainability of food does:

It encourages us to eat food that is grown locally and transported only a short distance, even if that food is grown in a very energy-intensive manner.

This isn't to say that food miles are a bad concept, just like mortgages are not a bad concept. But they are a bad concept when they are taken out of context and not considered along with other factors, such as the other 96 percent of the emissions from the food we eat. Eating food that is easily grown locally, using local soils and local sunshine, and adapted to the local environment may make sense. Eating local food from a greenhouse doesn't.

This is not to say that being cognizant of the distance food travels to our plate is a bad thing. Nor that food choices are not important, for they do have impact our environment, our health, our economies, and the livelihoods of millions of people across the globe. However, when we reduce the impact of our food choices down to a simple measurement—how far food travels to get to our plate—we not only miss a huge part of the picture, we sometimes do the exact opposite of what our intention was in the first place. (For the record, if you want to reduce the environmental impact of the food you eat the best thing you can do is to eat less red meat.)

Any metric that measures only a small part of a complex whole has the potential to lead to counterproductive ends. It can cause us to focus on the wrong thing, neglect important actions, and lead us to think we are helping when in fact we are harming. It is only when we look at the whole picture, at all the things that go into, come out of, impact, or otherwise influence the phenomena, do we get an understanding of what is really going on. Only then can we see if what we are doing is useful, if we are making the right choices, or if we are doing things efficiently.

So how do we do this? What was the process that was used to calculate the carbon emissions of Dutch versus Kenyan flowers? To tell that story, we have to go back to 1978 to see why the Coca-Cola Company decided to introduce the first plastic soft drink bottle to the world.

||||||||||

In 1969 Harry E. Teasley was a manager at Coca-Cola, working in the packaging department. Born in Hartwell, Georgia, Teasley graduated from the Georgia Institute of Technology and had begun working at Coca-Cola shortly after. During his time there, Teasley became increasingly more interested in understanding everything that went into the packaging process. Coincidently, at the same time, Coca-Cola was contemplating whether to start manufacturing its own beverage containers (they purchased them from a third party at the time). Teasley was the right man for the job. Coca-Cola was using glass bottles and steel cans for the popular drink, but were considering starting to use plastic bottles instead. Their greatest risk in making the switch was the environmental backlash they would face by choosing what many thought was an environmental villain: plastic.

Tasked with the job of assessing this environmental impact, Teasley sought outside help. He contacted a group called the Midwest Research Institute (MRI) in Kansas City with the idea. Arsen Darnay, the assistant director of economics and management, agreed to take on the task with Teasley, adding Bill Franklin (a program manager at MRI) and Bob Hunt (transferred from the physics division) to the team. Teasley, Darnay, Franklin, and Hunt then undertook what was the first resource and environmental profile analysis (REPA).

The REPA they conducted on the bottles took into account both inputs (energy, raw materials, water, and energy for transportation) and outputs (atmospheric emissions, transportation effluents, solid wastes, and waterborne wastes) of producing a beverage container.[15] What set the study apart was its comprehensiveness. It didn't just compare how much raw material was going into the products, or just energy, or just water, but as many things as the study authors could reasonably manage. It was legendary in its meticulousness. The results of that particular study were never published and were kept private by Coca-Cola. Teasley would become the president of Coca-Cola foods in 1987 and then became the executive of the Coca-Cola Nestle Refreshments Company in 1991. But similar studies soon followed.

A few years after completing the study, Darnay moved to a position at the Environmental Protection Agency (EPA). With the government increasingly concerned with energy use and environmental impacts, Darnay saw a need to build upon what they had learned doing the study for Coca-Cola. He soon commissioned Hunt and Franklin at MRI to undertake a similar study of nine different beverage containers. This study involved the glass, steel, aluminum, paper, and plastics industries. Over forty materials had to be characterized in detail in terms of energy; raw material; water use; and solid, liquid, and gaseous emissions. Energy and environmental data were developed for fuel, transportation, and electricity operations.[16]

The EPA study came to the conclusion that, when looking at the whole picture, plastic beverage containers were not the villain many thought they were. Coca-Cola came to the same conclusion. Soon after their study was completed, Coca-Cola introduced the first plastic beverage bottle to the world.[17] Recent studies have come to similar conclusions: While plastic bottles may not be as reusable as glass bottles, glass bottles require a lot of energy to produce, offsetting their improved reusability.[18] What the team's study did differently was that it sought to get a comprehensive picture of the impact of a single bottle of Coca-Cola. It wasn't just focused on how the containers were disposed of, or how much energy went into making them. It focused on how much energy went into making the things that made the bottle. It looked at how the bottles were disposed of. It accounted for the extraction, transportation, and manufacture of all the raw-material components in the bottles. Nothing was left out.

After that first REPA conducted by Teasley, Darnay, Franklin, and Hunt, many more soon followed. Over the next several decades the process would be refined, the methodology codified, and standards introduced. And the REPA would transform into what it is known today as the Life Cycle Assessment (LCA). An LCA is a robust and rigorous evaluation of everything (or at least as much as the scope of the study can reasonably handle) that goes into a product or process. Take a coffee cup, for example. A common choice we are faced with is between a disposable cup or a ceramic mug we can wash and reuse.

A life-cycle assessment of these two options would examine what went into each cup: all the energy, all the water, all the material—everything. For the disposable coffee cup, the evaluation would look at the energy it took to produce the raw materials in the cup itself, including both the paper cup and the plastic lid, as well as the packaging for the cup. All of these would be broken down into the marginal impact of each cup, in other words, how much energy it takes to make a single cup.

But that is not where it stops. We can't forget the problem of "per." Comparing a reusable mug to a disposable cup needs to take into account that each is used differently. Obviously a ceramic mug takes a lot more energy and materials to make than a single-use cup, but it is used many more times. So we have to ask the question: How many times on average is the mug used before it is broken, lost, or thrown away? Then we also have to ask how much energy and water it takes to wash the mug after each use and account for that in the calculation. And we can go even further, looking at how much energy and space it takes to dispose of each mug; how much landfill space each mug takes up; and, more important, how much of that landfill space each mug takes up per use. What a life-cycle assessment does is assess all the energy, material, waste, emissions, and so on that a product uses over its entire life cycle, from the figurative cradle to the grave. (For the record, it takes about fifty uses for a ceramic mug to be more environmentally friendly than a paper cup, and it needs to be washed in the dishwasher, which uses less water than washing by hand. Washing a cup by hand offsets the benefits of its reusability).[19]

You are not alone if this sounds daunting. Undertaking a life-cycle assessment is an incredibly rigorous process. There is an International

Organization for Standards process for conducting life-cycle assessments. There are entire academic journals dedicated to the study, process, and best practices for life-cycle assessments. There are university professors whose title is Chair of Life Cycle Assessment. There are entire research institutes and divisions within companies that are dedicated to the field.

Life-cycle assessments are incredibly powerful tools that we can use to understand the full costs of various alternatives. When used properly they can shed light on the complete picture and expose choices that seem good at first, but upon closer inspection turn out to be not so hot. Let's look at a counterintuitive example: why compact fluorescent lights are not necessarily environmentally friendly.

||||||||||

I went to graduate school at something called the Faculty of Environmental Design at the University of Calgary. It was founded by what could only be described as a group of hippies in an otherwise decidedly unhippie city. The school was so deeply rooted in the hippie environmental movement of the 1960s and 1970s that in the early years of the school, the new year would start with the faculty and new students going for a camping trip into the Rocky Mountains for several days with no electricity, running water, or contact with the world outside. This was the epitome of the "back to nature" movement, and the school reflected it.

Michael Gestwick did not fit in with the Faculty of Environmental Design. I had met him on my first day of orientation, and we found a common bond based on our mutual incompatibility of being analytical minds in an overly conceptual faculty. Gestwick already had a master's degree in mechanical engineering before starting his second master's in the program. He was incredibly analytical, thorough, and detailed. He didn't fit well into the world of abstract concepts, design "inspirations," or projects that more closely represented avant-garde works of art than rigorous analysis. Gestwick was an engineer in a world of architects.

Being analytical, Gestwick couldn't accept ideas without incredible scrutiny. Like me, he wasn't satisfied to know just the general concept of something; he had to know the intimate details before he was satisfied. He was the kind of person who wouldn't just challenge ideas, he would do so with incredible rigor and analysis. One of the ideas Gestwick challenged had to do with the types of lights we use in our buildings.

Gestwick wanted to better understand a widely held belief that compact fluorescent lightbulbs (CFLs) were better for the environment than their counterparts, incandescent lights. At this time CFLs were gaining in popularity, and incandescent lights had become an environmental boogeyman. Countries throughout the world were enacting legislation to phase out the use of incandescent lights and encourage replacing them with CFLs. Gestwick wanted to know if this was misguided.

What everyone knew was that CFLs were more efficient at producing light than incandescent lights. A CFL converts between 7 to 10 percent of the electricity it consumes into light, while an incandescent light struggles to reach 3 percent. The problem with incandescent lights is that much of the electricity they consume is converted into heat and lost. At first glance, it seems obvious that the lightbulb that is more efficient at producing light will be better for the environment. What Gestwick wanted to investigate was whether this energy was truly lost and what it meant for carbon emissions.

When incandescent lights "lose" efficiency to heat, that heat doesn't just disappear into the void. In fact some of the time, that heat actually helps heat your home. When you turn on your lights, the waste heat produced goes into your house, which raises the temperature of your house. The rise in temperature is picked up by your thermostat and signals that your home heating system, whether a furnace, radiator, or other system, needs to work just a little less. So while a CFL is more efficient at producing light, it comes with a loss of producing heat. The question is whether that gain in light production is enough to offset the loss of heat production. But more important, the question is: What is the emissions impact of that tradeoff?

That's where the second part of the evaluation comes in: The sources of energy for electricity and home heating vary depending on where you live. Some energy sources, especially renewables, have very low emissions per unit of energy produced, such as wind, hydro, or solar. Some fossil fuels have incredibly high emissions, such as oil or coal. Other fossil fuels are in between, such as natural gas. Even if it is more efficient at producing light, if a CFL shifts your energy burden from renewables to fossil fuels, replacing your lights with more "energy efficient" alternatives may not actually be better for the environment.

The two ends of the spectrum in terms of the energy mix for electricity generation and home heating in Canada are Alberta and Quebec. In Alberta most of the electricity was, and still is, produced by burning coal, which is the worst emitter of carbon per unit of energy produced. However, home heating in Alberta is almost exclusively done by burning natural gas, a much less carbon-intensive fuel source. (Natural gas, although a fossil fuel, has much lower emissions per unit of energy produced than coal or oil.) In Quebec, by contrast, electricity is almost all produced by hydroelectric plants (96 percent of its electricity is hydro), while home heating is still done, surprisingly, with heating oil. So while Alberta has environmentally unfriendly electricity generation and less unfriendly home heating, Quebec has the opposite: environmentally friendly electricity generation and environmentally destructive home heating.

What Michael found out was that in places like Alberta, switching to CFLs was a no-brainer. Not only are you increasing the efficiency of the light you produce, but you are shifting the lost heat energy from your lightbulbs from coal to natural gas, a much preferable option. However, in Quebec, the opposite is true. By replacing your lights with CFLs, you are causing your home heating system to work harder, and that means you are shifting your energy burden from hydroelectric power to heating oil. Even though CFLs are more efficient, using them creates more carbon emissions. It takes a mind like Gestwick's to go into such detail to figure this out. If you don't have a mind like his, don't be discouraged. Luckily, for some things, understanding the big picture is not a complex process and doesn't require a rigorous and exhaustive study. In fact, sometimes it is quite simple.

||||||||||

I was not the best player on my senior high school basketball team. Not by a long shot. I didn't score the most points or, in fact, many points at all. I would miss embarrassingly close shots from six feet away. I was a notoriously bad free-throw shooter; opposing fans would chant "air ball, air ball, air ball" when I lined up at the free throw line. I didn't have the most blocked shots, assists, steals, or rebounds. I fouled out only a couple of times during the season but was close almost every game. I didn't get a lot of court time. Anyone looking at my stats would not pick me out as a valuable asset to the team. But halfway through the season, that changed.

Suddenly I got more court time. I was put in the game more during important moments. The other players and the coach began to view me much differently as a player. I hadn't gotten any better. My skills were pretty much the same as they had been at the start of the season. I still missed six-foot shots. What happened was that our coach started measuring something different. The measurement was something called plus/minus.

For those unfamiliar with this sports metric, this is how it works: Every time we went on the court, a student volunteer would record the score in the game. Then every time we got off the court, he would record the score again. The score was 12–8, I went on. The score was 14–12, I went off. The score was 16–16, I went on. The score was 24–18, I went off. After each game the difference in score for each shift would be tallied. If you got on and the team was up 6 points but only up 2 points when you got off, your score for that shift would be -4. If you were down 4 points when you got on but up 6 when you got off, your score would be +10. Each game you would get a summed total. Then those totals were averaged over several games. When my brother David played, our team scored, on average, 14 points more than the other team each game. When I was on, we would score 12 more points per game. No other player on our team had a plus/minus more than 6.

According to the plus/minus only, my brother and I were the "best" two players on the team; we were twice as valuable as anyone else. Neither of us scored very many goals or got many assists or steals. Yet when we played, our team scored more and the other teams scored less. Instead of looking at the obvious—points scored, assists, steals, free throws, blocks, or rebounds—our coach used something to help him understand the hidden part of basketball.

In basketball, as with most team sports, there is only one ball, puck, or disk on the court, yet there are many players. Even when they are on offense, the majority of the team does not have the ball. What few players, fewer fans, and, unfortunately, not many coaches understand is that what separates a good team from a great team in any sport is what players without the ball are doing. Any good coach understands that it is never a player who scores in basketball, it is a team. While ultimately only one player puts the ball in the net, the team is who helps him or her put it there. Other players set screens to help others get open, position themselves to make room for a drive, or get ready to box out and get a rebound. It was those things that I was good at.

I rarely scored on my high school team, but I did a lot to help my team score. Our point guard would make a move to drive to the net. At the right time, I would move across the key, creating a space for him to drive into, drawing my defender's attention away. I would set picks for the other center on our team, opening him up for a pass down low. I would rarely block shots on defense, but I was good at preventing high-scoring centers from either getting the ball in the first place, or if they did get a pass, it was in a position where it was hard for them to score.

Sometimes, if a really big player was guarding me, I would move out to the three-point line so he couldn't help defend the key. One of the best things you can do on offense in basketball when you don't have the ball is get your defender to be in the wrong place. I rarely scored. Yet I made it a lot easier for my team to do so. And that is why I was the second-best player on my team. "Court sense" is something that is difficult to coach and more difficult to measure. Few understand what it is and how to recognize it. But when they do, it is hard to miss.

That is what plus/minus does in basketball. It accounts for all of the hidden parts of the game without directly measuring them. Points scored, steals, field goal percentage, blocked shots, assists, and free throw percentage don't capture those hidden parts of the game. No metric in basketball, or any team sport, measures things such as "moving across the court to give another player a better chance at a drive" or the ability to get into another player's head and throw his or her game off. But both of those things can help a team win a game.

Sometimes it is useful to use a metric that ignores all the little things that contribute to an outcome, and just focuses on the outcome, because all those little things can confuse us. The player who scores the most points isn't necessarily the one you want on the team. A player may hit several three-pointers in a game but give up a lot of points on defense. The employee who works the longest isn't necessarily the most productive or useful. The clinic that can attend to the most patients isn't the one that necessarily treats them the best.

Metrics such as plus/minus work well when there are multiple factors (in this case players) influencing an outcome (winning the game) and when it is easy to know when a factor is involved or not and when the outcome is simple. When a player is on the bench, he or she obviously is not directly contributing to the game (although his or her morale may be indirectly contributing to the effectiveness of other players), so testing his or her effect on the score is easy. The outcome of a game is to score more points than the other team. It isn't to have more passes.

These metrics ask the simple question: When we do x, does y improve? When Helen is on the court, do we score more? Why focus on all the other things we can measure, like shots, blocks, rebounds, steals or assists? We should measure what really matters. All the rest is noise. The life-cycle assessment and plus/minus are two very different ways to measure the full picture. A life-cycle assessment is an evaluation of all the inputs that go into something. Every watt of energy, every liter of water, every gram of material goes into the calculation. With the life-cycle assessment, the process is additive; there is always something more to account for. The point is to find everything that could possibly (and more important, reasonably) be counted as contributing to production and to figure out how much of it is attributed to each item. With the life-cycle assessment you will never account for everything that can be attributed to a product or process, because you have to stop at some point.

Not so with plus/minus. Plus/minus is reductive; the objective is to reduce everything to a single criterion. It ignores how many passes, assists, shots, fouls, steals, or rebounds a player gets and only counts what matters—the points a team scores. The point isn't to figure out all the things that can help score more points, but rather to eliminate the noise created by such evaluations. Shots, steals, and assists only confuse the matter, because they can distract from the downsides a player has. With plus/minus it is assumed that there are too many hidden, misunderstood, or undervalued contributions a player makes that help a team win a game, so we don't bother with them. Instead we just focus on what matters: Are we going to score more points?

With the mortgage scenario, we use a very simple additive approach. We add housing costs and transportation costs to get the full costs of a particular choice of where to live. We can add more to this, such as energy costs or building maintenance if we want, or we can even add the costs of furniture (living closer may mean living in a smaller place, which may mean buying one less couch), but other costs, such as groceries or entertainment, may not be reasonable to include (I don't imagine where you live drastically affects what you eat, but you never know).

Both processes are useful in the right situation. Life-cycle assessments teach us to ask the question, "What else?" The idea is to keep looking for what contributes to what we are trying to measure. Plus/minus teaches us the opposite: It tells us to not be distracted by all the noise created by the data around us and to focus on what our objective is. Life-cycle assessments try to measure the forest by analyzing all the trees; plus/minus simply looks at the forest.

Many phenomena in this world are complex. There is a lot more to the cost of living than just the cost of the house. The distance food travels to our plate is not the only part of the food system that matters. Businesses are more than just the sum of their divisions. Team sports are more than steals, assists, and shots. We can't reduce complex phenomena to a single measure. Often, measuring one thing blinds us to everything else that is going on.

When trying to evaluate something, don't stop at a single metric, unless the outcome you want is very simple. Ask yourself if what you are measuring really captures the entirety of what matters. Ask if improving one measure may result in making another worse. See if there is anything missing. Don't confuse the forest for the trees. But don't miss the trees for the forest.

CHAPTER 6
APPLES AND ORANGES

Ignoring Differing Qualities

O n May 9, 1940, German forces crossed into Luxembourg from positions in Germany with virtually no resistance. That night, Germany Army Group B advanced into Belgium and the Netherlands. Paratroopers dropped into Rotterdam the next morning. German aircraft were able to destroy half of the Dutch and Belgian air forces in the first day of hostilities. Belgian defenses, while fighting fiercely, had collapsed sooner than anticipated by the British and French. Four days later the Dutch army surrendered. Only a month and a half later, France itself would surrender to Germany.

What would later be called the Battle of France was one of the most stunning military victories in history. In a very short time, Germany had managed to destroy or capture most of the French army; drive the British back across the Channel; force the surrender of the Belgians, Dutch, and French; and effectively secure the western front of the war for years. What is even more stunning than the incredible success of the German Blitzkrieg in the Battle of France is how they fought it: They were outnumbered.[1]

Metrics can provide insight, clarity, and valuable information in our decision making. But they can also obscure, confuse, and deceive. The concept this chapter will discuss is what happens when things that range greatly in quality are incorrectly lumped together under a single measure. When different things are treated the same, it can confuse and obscure the truth. When valuable information is hidden within a metric, it can lead to measures that are counterproductive, ineffective, or even nefarious.

A comparison of the respective sizes of the Allied and German forces before the Battle of France—in terms of men, tanks, and airplanes—would betray the actual fighting ability of the two sides. Despite having a slightly smaller force, German strategy, equipment, training, and pure luck proved to be far more effective than that of France and Britain. The numbers betrayed the result of the conflict.

Many measurements do not boil down to a simple "Which is bigger?" Raw size does not equal value, nor does having more of something equate to being better. Yet this is often how metrics are interpreted. Bigger is seen as always better, more is always more. But that is not always the case. Sometimes less is more, larger is worse. This may be due to inefficiencies in some cases or the law of diminishing returns in others. However, in this chapter we will examine cases where the metric does not truly reflect what is really important, because variable quality is obscured in the metric. Sometimes bigger is not better, because there is more to the measure than what is in plain sight. Sometimes there is something hidden in the measure. Sometimes one is not like the other. Sometimes things that appear the same are different. Sometimes apples are oranges.

||||||||||

In 2018 cancer killed over 600,000 Americans.[2] That is a scary statement. Over 1.7 million more were estimated to be diagnosed with the disease in that year.[3] Cancer is expected to kill one out of every four Americans today. But it wasn't always this way. In 1970 cancer was only responsible for 16 percent of deaths in the United States. In 1958 it was 15 percent; in 1900 it was 4 percent.[4]

What is behind this drastic increase in cancer diagnoses? Is it the chemicals we put in our bodies? It is our lifestyle? Perhaps it is the increased use of technology, such as cell phones, microwaves, computers, and radios. In fact, it is none of these things. The number one cause will surprise you.

While there are multiple causes that contribute to the rise in the percentage of deaths due to cancer over the last several decades, the greatest factor is something few of us would have guessed: heart disease. And the reason why heart disease is responsible for the rise in cancer is even more peculiar. It isn't because more people are getting heart disease. It is because fewer are.[5]

Heart disease is in fact the leading killer of Americans. In 2015 heart disease killed more people than cancer did, with just over 600,000 deaths.[6] But for the last few decades, the incidence and mortality rates from heart disease have drastically decreased. From 2001 to 2011, deaths from heart disease fell almost 39 percent. In 1970 heart disease was responsible for 40 percent of all deaths. In 2002 it was 28 percent.[7] In 2011, 596,339 Americans died from heart disease, which works out to 191 deaths per 100,000 Americans. In 2001 it was 700,142, or 248 deaths per 100,000 Americans (notice how using the per capita rate is important here). The reduction in heart disease is one of the greatest triumphs in public health in the last several decades. Added to this are substantial decreases in mortality from communicable diseases—tuberculosis, diarrhea, enteritis, typhoid, diphtheria, and measles, to name just a few.

Unfortunately everyone has to die somehow. Since fewer people are dying of heart disease and numerous communicable diseases, and as heart disease and many communicable diseases made up the bulk of the causes of death, people who would have died of heart disease or communicable disease earlier in life are now living longer. And many of them are living long enough to end up getting cancer. Simply put, it is not that more people are dying of cancer, it's just that fewer are dying of other things. By default it seems as though cancer is getting worse when you just measure the impact of the disease by the percentage of deaths, or total deaths, for which it is responsible. People have to die of something, and the older a person gets, the more likely that killer will be cancer. So in a very strange way, increases in cancer rates are a good thing. As Dan Gardner points out, if average life expectancy rose to one hundred years, cancer rates would go through the roof. With few other things causing death, almost everyone will get cancer at some point. And this would be great.

The odd case of celebrating increased cancer rates raises an important question: Why is this so backward? How can an increase in a death rate be positive? The reason is because not all deaths are the same. Dying at eight-five after a long life and dying at the age of eight are two very different things. Dying at night in your sleep safe and comfortable in your own home is very different from being randomly attacked and murdered. While we can all agree that death is a tragic thing, we can also agree that some deaths are more desirable and some more tragic than others. This affects how we think about disease.

Imagine two diseases that kill a similar number of people each year. Which one would you focus more effort on eradicating? It is a hard decision to make without more information. Now imagine that the average age of a person who dies from the first disease is seventy and the second disease takes people at an average age of eleven. Now which one would you focus your efforts on eradicating? The answer is simple.

A straightforward evaluation based on the number of deaths per million people would tell us that there is no difference between the two. We all know that isn't right. Yet much of our understanding of diseases and other causes of death boils down to the raw number of people who die from it each year. When public health is discussed in public discourse, the focus tends to be on the "number one cause of death" or the top three, or ten, or whatever. Until the 1990s, even within the public health field, most evaluations on disease focused on these factors: mortality, incidence, and prevalence. But those measurements are misleading. They ignore the nature of those deaths and their impact on their victims. How should we measure the impact of a disease if not by the number of deaths and cases of people living with a disease?

It wasn't until the early 1990s that the concept of only counting deaths, incidence rates, or prevalence rates started to be seriously challenged. While the problem of developing health indices was discussed as far back as the 1960s,[8] it wasn't until the early 1990s that the idea of incorporating the years of life lost to a disease, as well as the number of years lived with the disability of a disease, came into widespread use. This is when the concept of the disability adjusted life year, or DALY (DALY rhymes with tally or rally), was developed and first used in the *World Development Report 1993: Investing in Health*.[9]

DALYs measure health impacts by using time. In the most basic form, it is calculated by subtracting the age at which a disease kills a person from the average life expectancy. A disease that takes a child at five, who would have lived to seventy-five, will be given a years of life lost measure of seventy. A disease that kills someone at sixty-five with the same life expectancy only accounts for ten years of life lost.[10] Add up all those years for each life lost, and you get the first aspect of the DALY, the life years lost, or the LY part of DALY.

The DALY also accounts for something else that simply measuring the loss of life in years does not; it includes the impact of living with a disease or condition. The impacts of a disease are not just from death, and conditions that severely debilitate, but not kill, the people living with them should also be accounted for. Diseases such as diabetes or Alzheimer's typically do not kill people, but they take a terrible toll on the people who suffer from them. Living a healthy, unimpeded life until sixty-five and dying of a heart attack is preferable to suffering from blindness for forty years and dying at the same age of sixty-five. The DALY factors in this impact of suffering from a condition. This is the "disability" in the Disability Adjusted Life Year. Each condition is given a "disability" factor, a number between 0 and 1 that reflects the burden of living with that condition, 0 being fully healthy and 1 being death. For example, the suffering of a person who lives with a condition with a factor of 0.5 for ten years would be equivalent to someone who lives perfectly healthy and passes away five years early. The concept underlying DALYs is that health indicators should include any loss of health status that warrants the devotion of resources to averting it, not just those that cross a threshold for severity of duration. In essence, we shouldn't just count those things that cause death or severe disability, but we should include anything that warrants at least some attention from a public health perspective. Scraped knees don't count, but lower back pain does, for instance.

Another concept, and one that challenges health indices that use the "cost of a disease" as a measure of its impact, is that weightings are completely independent of the affected individual's wealth, status, or education. The impact of a disease for someone living on welfare should be counted the same as for a person who is a Fortune 500 CEO.[11] If we measure the impact of a disease by the amount of wages it prevents people from earning, we skew the measure toward wealthy people.

The way the disability factors are determined are also subject to variation and debate. Some methods survey patients to determine their preference for one health state over another, the evaluations aggregated and compared to determine relative weightings.[12] Others, called health status indices, use aggregate metrics composed of measurements of various physical, mental, and social functions. However, the Global Burden of Disease study chooses to use a measure of disability, or the loss of particular functions due to a disease or condition. For example, losing a finger results in loss of fine motor function. The study then weighs these disabilities into six classes that range from limited ability to perform activities such as recreation or education (a weight of 0.096) to requiring assistance with daily activities such as eating, hygiene, or toilet use (a weight of 0.920). (The weights were determined using various survey techniques.) These measurements also incorporate the duration of the disability.[13] Having knee surgery is a painful experience and rehab is long and difficult, but there is a limit to the discomfort; it does not last forever, at least not at the same intensity as immediately postsurgery. Losing your eyesight, however, is often permanent. The measure takes this into account. DALYs give us the ability to compare not just the number of deaths caused by a disease, but the relative burden of living with it. Conditions on the lower end of the spectrum include things like moderate hearing loss (0.040), iron deficiency (severe iron deficiency is weighted as 0.090), and hepatitis B (0.075). Some of the higher disability ratings come from diseases and conditions you would expect. Living with AIDS without ART (antiretroviral therapy) has a disability factor of 0.505. Tetanus is 0.638. Most meningitis falls around 0.615. One of the highest disability factors is not attributed to what most would think of as a conventional disease; it's actually a psychological condition: depression. Although the impact on individual health from depression ranges greatly, a severe depressive episode is weighted as high as 0.760. This is more severe than blindness (0.600), spina bifida (0.593), Alzheimer's disease and dementia (around 0.666), or even a spinal cord injury (0.725).[14]

Organizations such as the Institute for Health Metrics and Evaluation, the World Health Organization, and others in public health use DALYs to calculate the overall burden of a disease—the total impact of the discomfort, suffering, and death that a disease places on a population.

Using DALYs helps rectify the shortcomings of measuring just raw causes of death. The discrepancy between the number of deaths from a particular disease and its overall burden on health and suffering is most pronounced when considering diseases that primarily affect the young. Take for example malaria, a disease spread by mosquitoes. In 2015 malaria was responsible for an estimated 730,500 deaths worldwide, or about 1.3 percent of all deaths, which may not seem terribly significant. But malaria is a disease that disproportionately affects the young. Globally it is the number one cause of DALY loss for children ages one to four. It drops to the sixth most burdensome cause for those ages five to nine, and beyond that it doesn't even come in the top ten. Yet, malaria is responsible for 2.3 percent of all DALYs lost globally, nearly twice what it would be expected to be if we just looked at the number of deaths. (The total DALYs for 2015 was 2,464,895,400, and 55,769600 of those years were attributable to malaria. To reiterate, this means that 2.5 billion years of life were "lost" in 2015, either to premature death [loss of life years before reaching average life expectancy] or to disability [the "loss" of healthy life years attributable to the disability of living with a disease or other condition].) Because malaria mostly affects young children, its effect on global health is twice as much as its proportion of deaths would indicate. Using DALYs, instead of raw deaths, provides us a better picture of which diseases, conditions, and causes of death have the greatest burden on the population.

In 2015, communicable diseases (such as HIV, malaria) accounted for 30.1 percent of all DALYs, whereas noncommunicable diseases (such as heart disease, strokes, cancer) accounted for 59.7 percent of the same. Injuries made up the rest of the burden.[15] Since 1990 the burden of communicable diseases has dropped dramatically, and the burden of noncommunicable diseases has risen. In 1990 lower respiratory tract infections, neonatal preterm birth complications, and diarrheal diseases were the three top causes of DALYs. They dropped to third, fifth, and sixth overall by 2015, while ischemic heart disease (heart attacks), cerebrovascular disease (stroke), and low back and neck pain took the first, second, and fourth spots.[16] When looking at just causes of death (not accounting for the disability of living with a condition), the trends are similar: Lower respiratory infections, neonatal preterm birth complications, and diarrheal diseases were the top three in 1990, but dropped to third, fourth and fifth in 2015.

For many noncommunicable diseases—most cancers and heart diseases, Alzheimer's, disease, cirrhosis, diabetes, and kidney disease—total DALYs have increased, but adjusting for the age of those affected, the overall burden has often dropped. What this means is that while more people are affected by these conditions, they are affected later in life. This helps explain why we are seeing greater rates of diseases such as cancer: Fewer people are affected by communicable diseases. What is interesting is that in many higher-income countries, some of the leading causes of death and disability combined are not diseases, but rather nonlethal conditions. In the United States, the second leading cause of death and disability combined is lower back and neck pain. Diabetes is third, depression is fifth, drug use is seventh.[17] It is a clear demonstration that death is not the only thing that matters when evaluating public health.

DALYs help us comprehensively understand the burden of illnesses and other conditions on the general health of the population. By adding nuance to the discussion beyond simple numbers of deaths, DALYs help us better focus our resources on those conditions and illnesses that do not take as many lives, but take them very early, or that do not kill people but create tremendous hardship for those affected. By adding more nuance to the metric, we can better allocate resources aimed at improving people's lives. But DALYs, while telling us the relative burdens of various diseases and conditions, do not tell us much about whether the population's health is getting better or worse, at least not directly. Just as if we were to look at just the causes of death, and their relative increases or decreases, it wouldn't tell us much about whether the human race is better off than before, because we wouldn't know if people were living longer or healthier. (This can be indirectly done by measuring deaths per unit of population [for example 100,000 people]. But to do this accurately, one would have to consider things such as the relative age of the population.) For every cause of death that is in decline, others are on the rise, simply because people have to die of something at some time. But what if we were to ask a different question, one that was the inverse of DALYs? DALYs calculate the total loss of life and disability caused by a disease. What if instead we calculated the total number of years people live without suffering or disability? That is what the HALE does.

Where DALYs calculate the total loss of life due to death and disability, HALE (Healthy Adjusted Life Expectancy) calculates the opposite: the number of healthy years one can expect to live. HALE is simply an adjustment to the typical life expectancy (the average lifespan of a population) that accounts for years of life lost to disability (for example, living your last ten years of life with debilitating pain would adjust the life expectancy down).

HALEs give us a clear picture of the overall health of a population, one that is often obscured by causes of death, or difficult to decipher with DALYs. While news reports, Facebook clickbait, and phony health websites try to scare you with statistics of rising rates of certain conditions, the fact is that overall global health is improving. The picture that HALEs provides of global health is a positive one. Globally, life expectancy, for both males and females, has risen every single year from 1980 to 2015 without exception. Male life expectancy has increased from 59.6 years in 1980 to 69.0 years in 2015, females from 63.7 to 74.8.

What DALYs, HALEs, and the Global Burden of Disease teach us is that often metrics fail to differentiate between units of measure that vary widely in quality. Death at the age of five is much worse than death at eighty-five. Living through a major depressive episode is worse than living with mild iron deficiency. Without accounting for these differences, we are prone to overweigh less important conditions and neglect more important others. Put more simply, we must remember to measure quality as well as quantity. Just because there is more of something does not mean it is better.

||||||||||

When we measure things purely by their quantity and do not take into account their differing qualities, we open ourselves up to multiple behaviors that are counterproductive, inefficient, or suboptimal.

First, ignoring the quality of a measure results in inflation of low-quality, but easily countable metrics. Take the example from chapter 2, about the paleontologists in China paying peasants for fragments of dinosaur bones. What the paleontologists failed to account for is that different sizes of fossil fragments had different values. An entirely intact skeleton would be more valuable than, say, a tiny fragment of a thigh bone. But, by failing to account for this by paying for bone fragments regardless of their size, the paleontologists inadvertently incentivized the peasants to maximize the number of fragments they found. The peasants soon discovered a brilliant way to achieve a higher yield of bone fragments—by smashing the bones into multiple pieces!

Metric inflation happens everywhere. In human resources, when departments are measured on the number of applicants hired without any regard to their quality, companies will soon find their ranks filled with poor-quality employees. In IT, if programmers are given incentives based on the number of lines of code they write, they will produce vast amounts of code, very little of it of any use at all. This same phenomenon occurred in the example of the cardiac surgeons in New York and Pennsylvania. The surgeons were measured on their success rate in surgeries, but there was no accounting for the varying degrees of difficulty in the surgeries performed. So doctors responded by refusing to do surgeries on more complex patients, as it would hurt their evaluations. There was no incentive to take on a complicated surgery, as it was more likely to result in a failure and therefore a poorer evaluation.

Organizations that create incentives for undertaking tasks that vary in quality, but only count their quantity, will soon find that workers will be averse to taking on challenging and complex tasks, preferring to "up their stats" by undertaking simpler and easier to complete tasks. This is called "cream skimming." Those being evaluated manipulate the measure by only counting the good stuff, the "cream," and avoiding, neglecting, or discounting the rest.

In private education in the United States, for example, schools are rated on the performance of their students on standardized tests, as we investigated in chapter 2 (and we should be skeptical of evaluating schools solely on test results). In certain parts of the country, voucher systems exist that allow students to choose which schools to attend. The vouchers allow the state funding for education for the student to go to the school that accepts them (often private schools). The problem with this is that the students who use vouchers are typically wealthier students, who typically perform better than lower-income students due to their ability to pay for tutors and by having a more stable family life or parents who can help them with their studies. When private schools point to the fact that their test scores are better than the comparable public schools, is it because they are better at teaching students, or is it because they have better-performing students to start with?

This same phenomenon is evident in postsecondary education. Many top schools will claim that the performance of their students after graduation, in terms of salary, is much higher than their competitors. "Come to our college," they'll exclaim, "our students do better in the workplace after graduation than students from other colleges." However, due to high tuition costs, admission requirements, and other factors, the students attending their schools are more likely to be from wealthy families. We have to ask the question: Are the increased salaries of those alumni really due to the better education they received at the institution, or is it because the student body is simply from wealthier families and is more likely to obtain high-paying jobs whether they attend the college or not?

Stacy Dale and Alan B. Krueger wanted to find this out. Does the school a student attends really affect their success in the labor market, or is their success simply due to other factors, such as their ambition, intelligence, or social connections? Are Ivy League schools really worth what they charge?

Many studies tried to figure this out by controlling for factors like high school grades, standardized test scores, or parental background.[18] What Dale and Krueger did to find out if Ivy League education actually mattered was truly ingenious. They pored through data to find students who were accepted into schools like Harvard, Yale, or Dartmouth, but for some reason decided to go elsewhere. Since they had been accepted into those schools, they must have had the résumés and grades to do so. But, despite being accepted, they decided to attend college elsewhere, maybe due to family reasons, the price of tuition, or dislike of the campus. Then

Dale and Krueger compared the earnings of those students to the earnings of comparable students who did attend those prestigious schools. What they found was surprising: Attending an Ivy League school had no influence on how much money someone made later in life. (The researchers did find that attending an Ivy League school did improve earnings for Black and Latino students, and attributed this to the idea that the social networks that Black and Latino students connect into in Ivy League schools would not have been available to them if they had not attended.) So are Ivy League schools better at providing career opportunities for their students? Not really. Rather they simply just admit more students who would have those same career opportunities anyway.

Cream skimming is akin to you and I having a contest to see who is a better coach. On my team, I get the national all-star team from that year, and your team consists of your immediate group of friends. Is it really fair to evaluate us on the same level? That's effectively what cream skimming does: It selects the best players, patients, projects, what have you and then evaluates against the average. This is why Ivy League schools look so good—they choose the best (and wealthiest) students and then claim they are the best at educating them, when in fact those students would do well anyway, as Dale and Krueger demonstrated.

So how do you respond to the lack of accounting for quality in your measures? How do you prevent cream skimming or the misunderstandings that come from counting varying degrees of quality as the same? One tactic that organizations may take in trying to manage quality is to set a minimum standard that any project, task, or piece of data must reach before being "counted." The idea behind minimum standards is that it will prevent suboptimal results or processes from being counted. But minimum standards likewise suffer from perverse effects.

The first effect is that once the standard is reached, people will see no reason for exceeding it. Once you set the bar, there is no point in going above it. One example of this is standards for home construction and incentives to meet a minimum standard of energy efficiency. Programs that set home efficiency at a score of 80 out of 100, for example, will find that home builders will build homes just efficient enough to meet the standard, but no more. You will find a lot of homes built at an 81 or an 83, but very few built at 95 or 97.

The second perverse reaction to standards occurs when the project doesn't have a good chance of meeting the standard. In these scenarios what often happens is that people simply give up trying to improve the situation. If something only counts if it meets the standard, and that standard can't be met, why even bother trying to improve it? Perversely, minimum standards can actually decrease average performance.

Imagine the following hypothetical scenario:

A team of thirty-two staff members is tasked with completing sixteen projects. Two staff members are assigned to each project. However, the team can reassign one staff member to another project in order to improve its quality. At least one staff member must be left working on each project. If only one staff member is assigned to a project, it will achieve the lower result shown below. If it is assigned three employees, it will achieve the higher result shown below. Teams can alternatively choose not to prioritize projects and leave two staff members on the project. Projects with two staff members achieve the average score. The projects, and their possible outcomes, are provided below.

- *One project can achieve a score between 40 and 55 (average 47.5).*
- *One project can achieve a score between 55 and 70 (average 62.5).*
- *Eight projects can achieve a score between 70 and 75 (average 72.5).*
- *Four projects can achieve a score between 75 and 82.5 (average 78.75).*
- *Two projects can achieve a score between 82.5 and 90 (average 86.25).*

Management can incentivize the team in three ways. In scenario A, the team is given no incentives. The team distributes staff equally, with two staff members on each project. Each project achieves its average score.

In scenario B, in order to improve the team's performance, management sets a minimum standard for each project. Management selects a score of 75. For each project that meets that standard, the team receives a monetary reward. Accordingly, the team decides to assign extra staff members to the eight projects that can improve their score from 72.5 to 75, reassigning them from all other projects. The team will increase the number of projects meeting the standard from six to fourteen.

In scenario C, management does not implement a minimum standard. Instead it incentivizes the team to achieve as high an average score as possible. The team is incentivized to focus their efforts on where it will have the most impact. The team therefore puts an additional staff member on every project other than those scoring between 70 and 75. The average scores of the teams, based on the strategies they adopt, are as follows:

Scenario A: 73.13
Scenario B: 72.5
Scenario C: 74.06

In this hypothetical example, creating minimum standards actually works against the overall performance of the projects. Teams that are given incentives to meet a minimum target allocate resources only where they can help the projects overcome a threshold. But in this scenario, getting a project over a threshold means resources are allocated from other projects, and those projects would gain more benefit from additional staff. Look at the averages. Not only does the scenario where the team tries to meet minimum standards (scenario B) underperform the scenario where the team is encouraged to improve the average (scenario C), it also underperforms the scenario where the team just goes about its business as usual.

By incentivizing a threshold, management inadvertently induced staff to lower the overall quality of work. The team put its effort into projects where their efforts had the lowest marginal impact. This scenario, while hypothetical, has real-world implications.

Take, for example, measuring on-time deliveries in supply-chain management. Imagine a company decides to measure the percentage of deliveries that are on time but doesn't account for the average number of days late. If the team meets a certain percentage of on-time deliveries, it will be given a bonus. But like the previous scenario, the company may discover that the percentage of on-time deliveries may decrease, but the average number of days late may increase. Why? Because once a delivery is going to be late, why care if it is ten days late or one hundred days late? Likewise, if a delivery would be early, why care if it is ten days early or five days. All that matters is making it on time. If the measure is blind to how late a delivery is, and only cares if it is late, it will incentivize late deliveries to be really, really late and early ones to not be very early.

When setting a standard, it is important to consider not only how many measurements meet that standard, but also how many exceed it or fall short, and by how much. If organizations fail to do this, they will soon find many more of their processes exactly meet the standard, but they'll also find that those that exceed the standard do not exceed it by very much, and those that do not meet it at all fall far, far short of it.

||||||||||

With any metric, we have to ask if there is a difference among the things being measured. Death from cancer is different from dying from heart disease. Living with AIDS or a major depressive episode are different from living with insomnia. Many measurements we use lump together quite dissimilar things in the interest of simplifying a phenomenon. This often makes sense. When we create models to understand our world, we have to make simplifications, otherwise the model would be just as complex as the phenomena it is describing, defeating the purpose of the model. Therefore, most metrics have to lump together things that have slight differences in order to help a measurement make sense.

However, sometimes this simplification goes too far. Significant differences can be glossed over, their importance lost. The death of a person in their nineties who lived a healthy life being counted as the same as a death of a six-year-old is a good example. A similar error occurs often when maps are used to convey many types of data. Maps are best used to convey information related to area. If we want to know the area of a forest or desert or how much sunshine different areas receive on a landscape, showing it visually on a map is a good idea.

What maps are terrible at is representing data about population. The number of people living in a given land area varies drastically between different regions. Take two extremes: the metropolitan area of Tokyo and the country of Canada. The Tokyo metropolitan area has a slightly greater population than the entirety of Canada, with over thirty-seven million people living in the metropolitan area. Canada has just over thirty-six million people. The greater Tokyo metropolitan region covers only 13,572 square kilometers (5,240 square miles), while Canada covers 9,984,670 square kilometers (3,855,103 square miles), making it the second-largest nation on Earth. Canada is approximately 735 times the size of Tokyo. These two areas are vastly different in size yet contain similarly sized populations. Representing them on a map drastically distorts this fact, showing Tokyo as merely a blip compared to the massive expanse that is Canada. Yet, as ridiculous as this example is, maps are commonly used to convey data about populations.

No other example of how maps misrepresent data is as widespread and abused as electoral maps in the United States. There are two common ways electoral maps are shown in the United States: a national-level map showing state-by-state results, or state-level maps showing county-by-county results. Both of these examples reveal some serious distortions. One of the best examples of these distortions was the 2016 federal election.

At the national level, there is great disparity in terms of both the population and area of the states. California is the largest in population, with over thirty-three million people living there. It is followed by Texas (just over twenty million), New York (eighteen million), and Florida (fifteen million). Wyoming is the smallest state in terms of population, with just under half a million people, followed closely by Washington, DC (which isn't technically a state, but for the purposes of population comparisons, we will treat it as such here), Alaska, and North Dakota.

Similar disparities are found in land area: Alaska is the largest state with over 570,000 square miles of land, while Washington, DC, is much smaller with only 61.4 square miles (both figures exclude bodies of water). Alaska is not alone in being a big state with few people. Montana has over 145,000 square miles of land, but less than a million people. On the other end of the spectrum, the state of New Jersey is home to nearly eight and a half million people in only 7,417 square miles.

What this means is that maps that show electoral results grossly misrepresent the truth. The population of Connecticut is underrepresented by a factor of three when compared to California. At the extreme end, voters in Washington, DC, which is the smallest jurisdiction in the union, are visually represented eighty-five hundred times less than the largest state, Alaska.

Presidential elections in the United States are not a simple popular vote. The electoral college system assigns different electoral college votes to each state, which, other than a few states, award all their votes to the winner of the state. Without going into the complexities, inequities, distortions, and absurdities of the electoral college itself, when looking at how the data are represented on a map, the college displays incredible distortions. Looking at how many electoral college votes are represented for each 10,000 square miles in a state, there is a huge discrepancy. Alaska has 0.05 electoral college votes for each 10,000 square miles. Montana has 0.2. Maryland has 10.2. Hawaii has 6.22. Washington, DC, has 489. The area represented by each electoral college vote for Washington, DC, is nearly ten thousand times smaller on the map than it is for Alaska.

Looking at a national-level electoral results map of the United States does little to indicate the results of the election. More than anything it simply shows that some states are larger than others.

This disparity is even more profound at the county level. The largest county in population in the United States is Los Angeles County in California, with a population of just over 10 million people. The smallest (as of 2015) is Yakutat City and Borough in Alaska, with a population of just 613 people. The smallest county, in area, is City of Falls Church in Virginia, with only 5.2 square kilometers (2 square miles), while the largest is the North Slope Borough in Alaska, at 229,720 square kilometers (88,695 square miles). The population of these two counties is just over 13,500 and 9,500, respectively. A map showing the preferred presidential candidate by county would make North Slope Borough around forty-four thousand times more prominent than the City of Falls Church. In fact, the county of City of Falls Church would never register on any map showing voting patterns by county, simply because it is too small.

But it is not just the fact that counties differ in population that causes problems of perception. The political divide in the United States is shifting toward an urban/rural divide, rather than a divide between states. As urban areas have large amounts of people in small areas, they are poorly represented on maps, as the amount of map space dedicated to each voter is smaller in urban counties than rural ones. Even if every single county in the United States had the same population, the maps would still overrepresent rural areas due to how much area that population takes up.

This is especially evident in the 2016 presidential election results from the state of Illinois. Hillary Clinton won the state in the election, with just over 55 percent of the vote. Yet, at first glance, the election results map for Illinois would make anyone think the state is heavily Republican. The election results map is almost entirely red with only a few spots of blue. Clinton only won 12 of the 102 counties in the state; the total area of those counties only makes up 14 percent of the area of the state. If we were to look at land area only, the state looks strongly Republican. But that isn't the case.

The issue is that a handful of counties—Chicago's Cook County and those immediately surrounding it—account for 65 percent of the population of Illinois. So, while Donald Trump had won nearly every county outside of Cook County and the surrounding counties, by winning Cook County, Clinton had essentially won Illinois.

One way to address this distortion is to change the way we use maps to represent data about population. Instead of portraying large areas (such as a state) as a single data point, maps can use dots to represent, say, one thousand people, to represent the data. Dot maps, however, run into problems when especially large urban areas contain such a large concentration of people that the dots end up running into each other and the comparative size of a population is difficult to determine.

Another way is to use what is called a cartogram. A cartogram is a map generated by a computer algorithm that weighs the area of region based on population (or whatever phenomena you are measuring) and was developed by Mark Newman from the University of Michigan. In a cartogram, places like Washington, DC, and Connecticut appear larger than normal, while Wyoming, Alaska, or North Dakota appear smaller. The problem is that cartograms can look distorted and lose the ability to identify the spatial location of areas. So while the problem of properly representing population is solved, the maps can become so distorted as to become unrecognizable.

All of this is probably obvious and boring. Electoral statistics usually are. But the fact is most of us cannot help but look at an electoral map of the United States and draw conclusions based on the area of the states. We look at the map and think: "Gee, that is a lot of blue, the Democrats must be winning" or vice versa. It is hard to avoid. The same goes for data on birth rates, crime, income, age, sports affiliation, and frankly any information regarding population. Sparsely populated areas with unusually high birth rates, crime rates, high incomes, or tendencies to cheer for the Spartans can seriously distort our perceptions of what is really happening. Simply put: Do not use maps to convey information about population.

The same thing occurs when we come across any metric where variable things are lumped together as a single measure. Just as we cannot help but draw conclusions from electoral maps, the same goes for when we evaluate professors based on the number of papers they publish, when those papers could be forgettable articles or groundbreaking works. Einstein only published three articles in his lifetime, but those three articles revolutionized physics as we know it. Or when we evaluate a policy on the number of businesses it impacts, when some of those businesses employ tens of thousands of people and others have less than a dozen. The same goes for statistics on job creation, when the jobs could be high-paying professional jobs or low-wage menial labor.

The apples and oranges fallacy is often abused when someone boasts a large number of something, but fails to recognize the incredible variation within those numbers. This takes many forms: Twitter followers, calories consumed, hours worked, tasks completed, products sold, jobs created, website visits. In all these cases, there is great variety in what is being measured. Not all Twitter followers are the same. Some may be bots. Eating three hundred calories of fruit and lentils is different from eating three hundred calories of butter. A job that does not pay enough for someone to make ends meet is different than one that provides a living wage. You get the point.

All manner of metrics conceal the true value of what they are measuring by choosing the wrong unit of analysis. These shortcomings can be addressed in several ways. The metrics can be weighted based on what the actual objective is, such as how years of life lost weigh the number of years lost prior to life expectancy, or how cartograms weigh areas by population. But most important, simply recognizing these errors can help us identify the problem before we make the mistake.

CHAPTER 7

NOT EVERYTHING THAT CAN BE COUNTED COUNTS

The Lamppost Problem

This job is so easy. Just keep the hounds off. A parker. A 250. Someone walking down the street. So what? I did a 250. What's the big deal? He doesn't want to give you his information? Who cares? It's still a 250.

—Sergeant Raymond Stukes of the 81st Precinct in New York's Bedford-Stuyvesant during a roll call, instructing officers how to meet stop-and-frisk quotas

A police officer is walking down the street at night. Turning onto another street, he sees a man fumbling about underneath a lamppost. As he approaches the man, he sees that the man is intoxicated. As he gets closer, it becomes clear the man is in fact quite intoxicated, and it appears he is searching for something.

"May I help you?" the officer asks as he approaches.

"Oh, hey there. Yeah, for sure. I lost my keys," replies the man.

Being a good policeman, the officer offers to help and begins searching for the man's keys. He looks under the nearby bench, along the curb, all through the grass. A few minutes pass, and it becomes clear to the officer the keys are nowhere to be found underneath the lamppost.

"Are you sure you lost your keys right here?" he asks the man.

"No," says the man. "I lost them back in the woods there."

Quite irritated, the officer replies, "If you lost your keys in the woods, then why are you searching under the lamppost?"

"Oh," replies the man, "because this is where the light is."

||||||||||

On October 31, 2009, Adrian Schoolcraft was feeling ill at work. He asked his supervisor for permission to leave early, got the OK, and went home. Arriving at home, he changed into shorts and a T-shirt, took some night-time cold medicine, and got into bed. Several hours later, a group of men entered his apartment, pulling him from his bed and overwhelming him. The incident would result in Schoolcraft being admitted to the hospital for six days.

What is unusual about this story is that Schoolcraft was a police officer with the 81st Precinct of the New York Police Department in Bedford-Stuyvesant. What's even more peculiar about this story is that the men who entered his apartment that evening were also police officers. One of them was his precinct commander, another was the deputy district captain.

||||||||||

Nineteen years earlier, on Sunday, September 2, 1990, Brian Watkins, a twenty-year-old from Utah waited on the platform for the D train with his parents, brother, and sister-in-law. The family was on their way to dinner at a restaurant in Central Park. While waiting on the subway platform, a group of young men surrounded Watkins and his family. They attacked his mother and father, slashing his father's pants and assaulting his mother. When Brian and his brother tried to intervene to stop the attack, one of the men in the group drew a knife and stabbed Brian in the chest. He died on the platform.

Brian's murder would spark outrage in New York and across the nation. The story ran not only in every local paper, it was covered in newspapers across the country. Stories ran in the *LA Times*, the *New York Times*, the *Chicago Tribune*, and many other dailies throughout the nation. *People Weekly* ran a cover story on the event, called "Death of An Out-of-Towner." The headline in the *Chicago Tribune* was, "For New York, the End Is Here," describing the event as "another signature event in the downfall of a once wonderful city." *Time* magazine's cover story fifteen days later was titled "Rotting of the Big Apple."

It is an understatement to say that in the late 1980s and early 1990s the New York City subway was a dangerous place. In the year Brian Watkins was murdered, twenty-five other victims would lose their lives on the New York City subway system. And it wasn't just murders that plagued the subway. The year 1990 was the peak of a crime wave in New York. As many as 17,497 felonies took place on the New York City subway: robberies, rapes, assaults, and thefts, in addition to the twenty-six murders that year.[1] Crime was increasing unchecked. Subway robberies alone rose 21 percent in 1988, 26 percent in 1989, and another 25 percent in just the first two months of 1990.[2] There were over two thousand murders in the city that year.[3]

In addition to the felonies, minor infractions were also out of control. Fare invasion was endemic. In 1990 the number of people jumping turnstiles and finding other ways to get around paying a fare reached its peak with over fifty-seven million fare evasions occurring during the year, costing the city nearly sixty-five million dollars in lost revenue. Those who weren't skipping paying the fare were often faced by gangs of thugs who would take over the fare gates, charging riders a fare themselves. On top of the robberies, fare evaders, and illegal fare collectors, homelessness on the subway was at endemic levels. There were an estimated five thousand homeless people living in the subway. Over eighty of them died in the subway system in 1989 alone.[4]

New Yorkers were afraid to take the subway. In 1992, 97 percent of passengers reported taking some sort of defensive action when riding the subway, such as actively avoiding certain people, areas of the stations, certain subway cars, or subway exits notorious for being dangerous places. In that year 40 percent of New Yorkers felt that reducing crime was the top priority for improving the subway system. Only 9 percent of New Yorkers felt that the subway was safe after eight o'clock at night.[5] The situation was untenable. Someone had to do something. That someone was William Bratton.

Bratton began his police career in Boston in 1970, rising through the ranks of sergeant and lieutenant. Then in 1980 he became the youngest ever executive superintendent of the Boston Police Department, the second-highest post in the department. He may very well have continued his rise through the Boston Police Department had he not made the mistake of telling a journalist that he had intentions of becoming the police commissioner, which didn't sit well with the current one. He went on to become the chief of police for the Massachusetts Bay Transportation Authority and the Superintendent of the Boston Metropolitan District Commission. Bratton was an ambitious and talented policeman. And in 1990, he became the chief of the New York City Transit Police.

Bratton's task was no small one. By 1992 the New York City Transit Police would have forty-one hundred officers, making it one of the largest police forces in the United States. It had more officers than the Boston Police Department.[6] Nearly three million passengers rode the subway every day in New York City. Bratton was faced with endemic levels of crime on the nation's largest public transportation system. Where would he start? To understand Bratton's strategy for making the subway safe for New Yorkers, we have to learn about George Kelling.

George Kelling was a former probation officer and childcare counselor who became a criminologist after obtaining a PhD in social welfare in 1973 from the University of Wisconisn-Madison. Kelling and another criminologist, James Q. Wilson, got the attention of police, public safety advocates, politicians, and William Bratton when they published an article titled "Broken Windows" in the *Atlantic* in 1982.[7]

The Broken Windows analogy actually had come from another researcher, a psychologist named Philip Zimbardo from Stanford. Zimbardo had conducted an unusual experiment in 1969 on social disorder and the state of the physical environment. Zimbardo obtained two cars, removed their license plates, put their hoods up, and parked them on the street. One of the cars was parked in the Bronx, the other in Palo Alto, California. The car in the Bronx was vandalized within ten minutes of being left by Zimbardo, as a family of four removed the radiator and battery, followed by others who smashed windows and tore off parts; neighborhood kids eventually used the car as a makeshift playground. The car in Palo Alto sat for a week untouched. Until, that is, Zimbardo took a sledgehammer to the car, after which others from the neighborhood joined in the destruction. Within a few hours, the car had been flipped over and destroyed. In both cases, most of the vandals were "well dressed, apparently clean-cut whites."[8]

The analogy that Kelling and Wilson drew from Zimbardo's experiment is that if you let a broken window go unfixed, you invite other forms of vandalism, destruction, and antisocial behavior. A smashed window leads to children disrespecting rules, adults ceasing to scold them, buildings becoming abandoned, weeds growing, groups of teenagers congregating and harassing passersby, fights ensuing, people drinking in public, and soon citizens being attacked and robbed. And it all starts with a broken window.

The term that Kelling and Wilson used to describe the deterioration of the environment of the street was *disorder*. According to Kelling and Wilson, disorder—the broken windows, abandoned lots, graffiti on buildings, loitering groups of teenagers—leads to serious crime. When people see an environment like the one described, they feel that since no one cares about the general state of the environment, they probably won't care about more serious crimes, like robbery.

And it is not just that criminals become emboldened, regular citizens react to disorder as well. They start taking defensive measures. They avoid going out at night, they avoid disputes with anyone they view as suspicious, they stop attempting to regulate order in their neighborhood, and they stop calling the police, because they don't trust they will do anything.

And so, an environment that neglects to care about the small things soon has to deal with the bigger ones. Kelling's Broken Windows theory was simple at its core: Reduce disorder, and you reduce crime. To Bratton, the New York City subway was a perfect embodiment of disorder.[9] Disorder in the subway was an entire ecosystem. Gangs robbing riders, graffiti on cars, homeless sleeping in the tunnels, riders jumping turnstiles and evading fares—all of them were outcomes of an environment of endemic disorder. Fare evasions were not just minor infractions and misdemeanors to Bratton. By wantonly flaunting the law, fare evaders were reinforcing an environment that bred and nurtured disorder. By jumping turnstiles, fare evaders were not just robbing the transit system of revenue, they were tacitly giving permission for others to flaunt the law as well. To combat crime on the subway, Bratton knew he had to take on the entire environment. So he got to work.

Around the same time that Bratton was appointed as the New York Transit Police commissioner, a transit police lieutenant named Jack Maple began developing the initial structure of a crime analysis system that would eventually be spread around the world. Maple believed that to be more effective, transit police should be more proactive, that they should anticipate where crime was going to occur and deploy resources to those areas before crimes were committed. Maple started mapping out the crime that was occurring in the subway, noting the number and types of crime occurring in each subway station, to determine if there was a pattern to the crime in the subway. Maple didn't have powerful computers to analyze the data, or even any analysis tools at all. He began by marking the data on maps he printed out and put on his apartment wall. The crimes were recorded with crayons. He called his maps "The Charts of the Future."[10] It didn't take long for William Bratton to recognize the utility of what Maple had developed. By mapping and analyzing crime trends, the transit police could deploy officers preemptively and more effectively.

Using Maple's crime hot spot maps, Bratton implemented a targeted attack on repeat offenders, especially youth gangs. Rather than be satisfied with nabbing one member of a group involved in an attack, Bratton instructed his detectives to go after all of them, even if it meant bringing witnesses into schools to identify suspects. Bratton would also cut the time it took to act on warrants from thirty days to twenty-four hours.[11] Bratton also conducted widespread fare evasion sweeps. The strategy involved putting more plainclothes officers to work in the subway. Uniformed officers had little to no impact on reducing fare evasion, as offenders would just not risk jumping a turnstile with the police in sight. Not only did these sweeps catch fare evaders, they also deterred other crimes, as the offenders could be searched for weapons and checked for warrants. One in seven people caught for fare evasion ended up being wanted on a warrant for another crime. Apart from fare evaders and robbery gangs, Bratton also cracked down on things such as panhandling, illicit merchants, smoking, drinking, and even things such as lying down in the stations. Homelessness was tackled not only with enforcement, but by also offering round-the-clock transportation to shelters.

The tactics worked. Felonies dropped every month from October 1990 to October 1995. Felonies dropped 64 percent, robberies dropped 74 percent. Fare evasion was cut in half by 1994, and two-thirds by 1995, saving over forty million dollars in previously foregone revenues. Homelessness dropped 80 percent.[12] But Bratton's work wasn't done.

In 1994 Bratton's success in the New York City subway attracted the attention of the newly elected Republican mayor, Rudy Giuliani, a

US attorney who ran on an anticrime campaign, beating the incumbent, David Dinkins.[13]

As one of his first orders of business, Giuliani appointed Bratton as the commissioner of the New York Police Department (NYPD). Immediately after being appointed commissioner, Bratton did two things: He set a goal of a 10 percent reduction in felony crimes for that year, and he appointed Jack Maple, the man who had tracked subway crime on maps in his apartment, as his deputy.

By the time Bratton and Maple took over the NYPD, their system of tracking and mapping crime data had become more sophisticated. The crayon markings on maps hanging on Maple's apartment wall had evolved into a rigorous system using computers and spreadsheets.[14] By 1995 the crime data collection and reporting system got itself a name: CompStat (either short for Computer Statistics, or Comparative Statistics, no one seems to know which). That system would define NYPD strategy and tactics for the next several decades and would spread to dozens of other cities in the United States and the world.

Prior to his arrival to the NYPD, and the implementation of CompStat, Bratton found an organization centered around the avoidance of risk and failure, with precinct commanders constrained by regulation and procedures. Little strategic direction was provided; precincts were micromanaged. Bratton did away with that. Under CompStat precinct commanders were given a lot more room to organize their own operations without interference from headquarters. Instead, central command would provide strategic direction and hold precincts to account for their success. Officers would be encouraged to make arrests and "assertively" enforce quality-of-life laws. CompStat on one hand gave precinct commanders a lot more independence to run their precincts the way they desired, but on the other hand made them intensely accountable for the statistics coming out of headquarters. Each precinct commander was held accountable for the crime rates in his or her precinct.[15] As Bratton put it, "We began to run the NYPD as a private, profit-oriented business. Profit was crime reduction, and the competition was the criminals."[16]

The CompStat system involved four key pillars: accurate and timely information, effective tactics for specific problems, rapid deployment to problem areas, and relentless follow-up to ensure the problem was solved.[17] The implementation of CompStat revolved around semiweekly meetings where the top executives would meet in rotation with precinct and detective squad commanders. In these sessions crime trends, identified through thorough geospatial analysis, would be reviewed, tactics planned, and resources allocated. Commanders would have to report back at least once every six weeks, creating an environment of immediate accountability.[18] This system allowed the NYPD to identify tactics that worked in one precinct and rapidly adopt them to others.

Behind the CompStat meetings was an intensive data collection and reporting system. Crime data were entered into the system, geographically tagged and reported every week. But the system had to prioritize what crimes mattered most, and to do that it turned to what is called the Uniform Crime Reports.

The Uniform Crime Reports (UCR) were developed in the 1920s by the International Association of Chiefs of Police and the Social Research Council. Initially the organization determined that seven crimes would be used to compare crime rates between cities: murder, forcible rape, burglary, aggravated assault, larceny, and motor vehicle theft (arson was added in 1979).[19] These crimes would become known as "index crimes" (and later as "index 1 crimes" after 1985, when a second, less serious category was established). The first UCR was published in 1930, with crime data from four hundred cities covering forty-three states. From then on, the UCR would become the predominant method by which cities reported crime.

The UCR not only reported on the number of crimes committed (or more correctly, reported), it also published data on the number of arrests, or what were called clearance rates, or the rate at which crimes were solved. This data helped the public, media, politicians, and the police themselves understand the problem of crime, and how effective police departments were. With a standardized system, the public had a way of comparing the crime rate not only year to year, but between cities. Was New York more dangerous than Boston? Was LA safer than Atlanta? Was crime increasing or decreasing in Detroit? The UCR gave an answer to these questions.

CompStat relied heavily on the UCR. It provided not only a standardized system of crime reporting that the NYPD could use to compare itself to other cities, it provided precinct commanders with a list of serious crimes they could focus on. CompStat originally began with a focus on major crimes, the UCR index crimes, but it quickly moved onto "Quality-of-Life Enforcement," where minor infractions such as pot smoking, graffiti, and vandalism were tracked and reported on.[20] CompStat had become the systemization of Broken Windows policing. Along with implementing CompStat, Bratton also continued to increase the size of the New York police force. It didn't hurt that just prior to Giuliani being elected, the previous mayor, David Dinkins, and his police commissioner, Ray Kelly, had lobbied President Clinton for funding to drastically expand the police force.[21] The number of officers increased dramatically from around twenty-seven thousand in 1993 to forty-one thousand in 2001. Foot patrols, which were expanded under the previous commissioner, Ray Kelly, were pulled back. For Giuliani and Bratton, foot patrols were too soft and didn't accomplish the results Bratton was looking for.[22]

Through his tenure as the chief of the New York Transit Police and later as the commissioner of police, William Bratton had initiated an incredible drop in crime. In just three years crime in New York would drop 40 percent. Homicides dropped 50 percent, and they dropped in every single one of New York's seventy-five precincts. Assault and robbery dropped in nearly every precinct as well. As for the crime reduction target he set out in 1994, Bratton exceeded it, achieving a 12 percent drop in crime. And he did so again in 1995, with a 16 percent decline.[23] That decline continued after Bratton's tenure, with drops in crime continuing throughout the 1990s and into the twenty-first century.

The CompStat system itself spread to Washington, DC, Austin, San Francisco, Dallas, Detroit, Vancouver, Minneapolis, and even London and Australia over the following years. William Bratton even took the system to LA, where he served as police commissioner from 2002 to 2012. By 2004, just ten years after it began in New York, CompStat spread to over a third of all police departments in the United States that had more than one hundred officers.[24] The Broken Windows policing strategy of combating crime and disorder, and the CompStat system that implemented it, proved to be one of the most effective crime-fighting undertakings in modern history.

Or did it?

|||||||||||

Adrian Schoolcraft was a shy, soft-spoken, at times cerebral, and generally antisocial kid. He didn't drink or smoke, and he didn't make friends easily. Growing up in suburban Texas as a child to parents who were only twenty and nineteen years old when they had him, Adrian wasn't anything of a social butterfly. His father was an ex-military police officer, his mother worked at a bank. He didn't play many sports, spent a lot of time to himself, never really had a girlfriend, and preferred to spend his time reading or playing video games.

After graduating high school, Adrian spent four years in the US Navy as a medic. After being honorably discharged, he tried attending college, but dropped out after spending only one semester at the University of Texas in Austin. He worked at Walmart and Motorola for some time, but he was laid off of the latter job after two years. After that he moved to Jonestown, New York, to live with his parents. Then September 11 happened.

Unlike many stories of inspired Americans joining the military or the police force in response to the events of September 11, Adrian didn't feel compelled out of a sense of duty to serve his nation. Rather, his mother convinced him to try and apply as a police officer, given that the NYPD was recruiting in the area. Adrian took the admissions test, scoring near the top of the class. That is how Adrian Schoolcraft, one of the most famous whistle-blowers in its history, came to join the NYPD—somewhat reluctantly, after being persuaded by his mother.

When Adrian Schoolcraft began his academy training with the NYPD in 2002, CompStat had been in effect for several years. Just before Adrian joined the force, Michael Bloomberg had become mayor of the city and had appointed Raymond Kelly as his police commissioner, the first person to be appointed to the job two separate times. CompStat had been making and breaking careers in the NYPD since Commissioner Bratton had implemented it eight years earlier. The two intervening commissioners, Howard Safir and Bernard Kerik, hadn't changed the system, CompStat still dominated the NYPD. Commanders were promoted or reassigned based on their precinct crime rates. If you got the right numbers, you got promoted.

Ray Kelly didn't just continue the CompStat system, he expanded it. Not only were precinct commanders responsible for the crime rates in their precincts, they were also held accountable for activity reports of the number of arrests, summonses, and other enforcement actions that officers undertook in their areas. Under Kelly, even minor enforcement actions, such as stop-and-frisks or community visits, were tracked. And under Mayor Bloomberg, who was obsessed with productivity, the system thrived.

After completing the police academy, Schoolcraft spent his first eight months as a patrol officer on a program called "Impact," a training program for new recruits, after which he was assigned to the 81st Precinct in Bedford-Stuyvesent in Brooklyn in July 2003. Bed-Stuy, as it is more commonly known, was not a precinct that many police officers wanted to be assigned to. Bed-Stuy was essentially a dumping ground for police officers who didn't have any connections that could get them a better placement, officers who had trouble with headquarters, and those who ran afoul of their bosses. It was the same precinct that Frank Serpico, the famous whistle-blower from the 1970s, was assigned to. Bed-Stuy had been the epicenter of black activism and politics in New York for decades. Spike Lee's *Do the Right Thing* took place in Bed-Stuy. Jay-Z, Lil' Kim, The Notorious B.I.G., Mos Def, and Ol' Dirty Bastard all called Bed-Stuy home. One sergeant described Bed-Stuy as, "You're not in midtown Manhattan, where everyone is walking around smiling and being happy. You're in Bedford-Stuy, where everyone probably has a warrant."

For six years Schoolcraft stayed in the 81st Precinct. He would make seventy-one arrests, seventeen of which were for felonies, forty-two for misdemeanors, and twelve for violations. He would earn two lesser medals for "excellent police duty" and "meritorious police duty." For the first several years of Schoolcraft's career, things were pretty hum-drum. He was a decent police officer, receiving good evaluations and not making much of a ripple in his precinct. He did complain a bit, disliking being put on forced overtime, and he felt that the practice, which was common in the NYPD at the time, was unsafe and led to accidents and injuries due to overworked and sleep-deprived cops.

But nothing ever came of it. In October 2006, that would begin to change.

In that month, Steven Mauriello joined the 81st Precinct as an executive officer. A year later, he would become the precinct commander. Mauriello was a numbers man if anything. His approach to policing favored productivity and numbers; it was an approach that fit well with the CompStat system. His tactics as precinct commander were clear: Get your numbers up or face consequences. Officers who didn't meet the performance standards set out for them were threatened with relocation. Those tactics were fully supported by the Brooklyn North Borough

Command, under the direction of Michael Marino, which began holding its own CompStat meetings and tracking not just index crimes, but statistics as minor as the number of tickets each officer wrote or the number of sick days he or she took.

From late 2007 on, the pressure in the 81st to get productivity numbers up increased. Sergeants started putting pressure on Schoolcraft to get his numbers up or face consequences. Schoolcraft felt that this pressure to meet enforcement quotas clashed with his idea of policing. For Schoolcraft, policing wasn't about meeting quotas, it was about being a partner with the community. "You pull someone over for a seat-belt violation, they have their ID, all their papers, you don't need to give them a ticket . . . Just warn and admonish. You don't need to hammer the regular people." Yet Schoolcraft started noticing others around him changing their behavior. He saw that lieutenants or sergeants from the precinct would look over an officer's shoulder when he or she filled out reports, second-guessing the way the incident was classified. In some cases, Schoolcraft witnessed other officers filling out fake reports for stop-and-frisks, known as "ghost 250s" (stop-and-frisks were coded as a 250 in the NYPD), with made-up names of people.

He started making notes in his memo book about the behavior he saw his fellow officers undertake, but, more important, he noted the behavior of his superiors. Schoolcraft wouldn't play along. He refused to make fake reports, or to increase his enforcement numbers simply to hit a target. In December 2008 Schoolcraft's individual poor performance on these activities, such as arrests and summonses, resulted in him being given the worst evaluation he had ever received as a New York police officer—a score of 2.5 out of 5. He decided to appeal it. The day after he notified his command he would appeal his evaluation, a note was posted on his locker: "If you don't like your job, maybe you should get another job." He had another meeting on February 20 with a lieutenant who reiterated the message: Get your numbers up. Another one followed on February 22, this time with Precinct Commander Mauriello, a captain, two lieutenants, and three sergeants. Again, Schoolcraft was asked to get his numbers up, again Schoolcraft resisted.

"I've taken action on anything I've observed, whether a summons, an arrest or a warn and admonish." Schoolcraft didn't want to play the game. Schoolcraft did what few on the force would do: talk back to his bosses. He hired a lawyer. He appealed his poor evaluations. In another incident, he accused his superiors of falsifying documents. He wrote notes of the conversations he had with his superiors and other patrol officers in his memo book. On March 13 one of his sergeants confiscated Schoolcraft's memo book, discovering that Schoolcraft was recording critical notes about his superiors. By then command knew Schoolcraft was document- ing their actions. Schoolcraft wasn't making any friends.

Throughout 2009 Schoolcraft had attempted to alert the higher- ups of these attitudes and the misconduct he felt was occurring in his precinct—to an NYPD district surgeon and a department psychologist in April of that year and to a psychologist in July. They did not take his complaints seriously. Instead, after his meeting with the psychologist, they put him on desk duty due to anxiety. In August, Schoolcraft sent a letter to Charles Campsis, the head of Internal Affairs, saying he had witnessed two precinct supervisors tampering with civilian complaint files. Adrian's father even contacted David Durk, who had helped Frank Serpico expose corruption in the NYPD in the 1970s, for help.

Another meeting took place on October 7, this time with the Qual- ity Assurance Division (QAD), which audits crime statistics. Schoolcraft was told the QAD took the complaint very seriously. But nothing came of it. Instead he was told in mid-October that he was on "forced monitor- ing." And then came the night of October 31.

At the start of his shift on October 31, still on desk duty, School- craft's memo book was confiscated by Lieutenant Timothy Caughey. This was the memo book that contained Schoolcraft's notes about quota pressure, a lack of training, the threats he received from his bosses, notes about the downgrading of crime, questionable orders he was given, and more. Caughey took the memo book into a room with a copy machine and locked himself in the room for three hours. When he came out, he had copies of the book, one of which he placed on Precinct Commander Mauriello's desk. Schoolcraft became incredibly nervous. Sensing something was up and feeling threatened by the way Caughey was looking at him, Schoolcraft decided to leave. He went to his supervisor, Rasheena Huffman, intending to ask to leave early, saying he had stomach pains. She was on the phone, so he left a note and quickly headed home. Upon arriving at his apartment, Schoolcraft took some nighttime cold medicine and got into bed.

Shortly after he had left the precinct office, the captain on duty sent a lieutenant to Schoolcraft's home to see if he was there. The lieutenant would be joined by several other police officers over the next several hours. Within a few hours, a deputy chief, two deputy inspectors, a captain, and several lieutenants and sergeants from four different units would arrive outside Schoolcraft's apartment. All in all, about a dozen NYPD policemen were involved. Included in that group was Mauriello and the deputy chief of the Brooklyn North borough command, Michael Marino. All of this for one AWOL police officer.

After numerous attempts to contact Schoolcraft on his phone, or by knocking on his door, the police eventually entered his apartment by obtaining a key from his landlord. Upon entering his apartment, the other policemen instructed, pleaded with, and forcibly told Schoolcraft to return to the precinct, but he continually refused. Some officers insisted he was having mental issues and was an emotionally disturbed person. Schoolcraft insisted he just wasn't feeling well, and if he was to go back to the precinct, it would be against his will.

After much more back-and-forth, Marino eventually lost his patience, yelling at the other offices, "Alright, just take him, I can't fucking stand this anymore." Four policemen grabbed Schoolcraft from his bed, slammed him to the floor, pulled his hands behind his back, put a boot on his face, and handcuffed him. The officers put him in an ambulance and took him to Jamaica Hospital in Queens. He was admitted to the psychiatric ward as patient 130381874. For the first nine hours of his visit, he was handcuffed to a gurney and not allowed to use the phone, get water, eat, or use the bathroom. During his hospital stay he was continually monitored by police officers and was never given a reason for his admittance to the psychiatric ward. He spent six days at the hospital and was billed $7,195 for his stay. After being released from the hospital, Schoolcraft and his father Larry tried contacting everyone they could about the incident. Oversight agencies, lawyers, policemen Larry knew, the FBI, federal prosecutors, district attorneys in Brooklyn and Queens, the Patrolmen's Benevolent Association, the police union, police union lawyers. Anybody they could think of, they tried to contact about the incident and what his fellow police officers had done to Adrian. No one listened. Even Internal Affairs, who had pledged a thorough investigation of the incident, didn't have anything to show for it. Instead of being taken seriously, Schoolcraft was suspended without pay.

Shortly after, Adrian and his father moved back to Jonestown in upstate New York. Even there, NYPD officers would continually visit the apartment and ask Adrian to return to work. He refused. They set up surveillance on him. Over the next several months, Adrian and his father tried contacting district attorneys to no avail, and they even filed a notice of claim about the incident to the court, alleging that the NYPD and Jamaica Hospital had violated his civil rights, slandered him, libeled him, subjected him to cruel and unusual punishment, damaged his character, and revealed his confidential medical information. They even convinced a reporter from the *New York Daily News* to write a front page story on the incident, but it barely made a splash.

Then, in March 2010, the Schoolcrafts got in contact with Graham Rayman of the *Village Voice*, a local newspaper in New York. Adrian sent Rayman a rather cryptic e-mail that contained a recording he had made of one sergeant telling officers in his precinct to refer robbery complaints to the detective squad. It didn't seem like much, but Rayman was intrigued, so he agreed to meet with the Schoolcrafts at their rented apartment in Jonestown on March 16. After a few minutes of talking, and taking some photos of Adrian, Rayman asked if Adrian had any more recordings. Adrian responded, "Oh, about one thousand hours or so."[25]

||||||||||

The Schoolcraft tapes hit the New York media like a tidal wave. Here was a police officer, not just with a few anecdotes, or some unsubstantiated claims of wrongdoing in the force, but nearly a thousand hours of recordings detailing police misconduct in the precinct. Schoolcraft had been taping nearly every roll call, patrol conversation, meeting, or other discussion he had been having for more than a year. And he had the tape of the events from Halloween night.

Rayman published the findings from those tapes in a series in the *Village Voice* starting on May 4; it examined the content of the tapes and followed the fallout. Similar stories would soon run in nearly every media outlet in the city as the scandal unfolded. Rayman would eventually write a book on the events, and his "NYPD Tapes" series would win the New York Press Club's top prize, the Gold Keyboard Award.

The content of the tapes was damning: An entire ecosystem of corruption was taking place in the 81st Precinct. Officers were pressured to manipulate statistics in two ways. They were told to maintain high levels of "activity," such as stop-and-frisks (known as 250s) and arrests, but also to find ways to reduce the amount and severity of crimes reported. Patrol officers were given quotas for stop-and-frisks and arrests and expected to meet them. At numerous roll-call meetings, commanders reiterated that officers were to get their numbers up, no matter what it took. Officers were told to write up minor offenses, such as littering or blocking the sidewalk (known as C summonses), with little regard to their usefulness. One sergeant on Schoolcraft's tapes, referring to stop-and-frisks, said, "Anybody walking around, shake them up, stop them, 250 them, no matter what the explanation is, if they're walking, it doesn't matter."[26]

On the other hand, reported crimes were downgraded in order to not show up on index crime reports or to be dismissed altogether. Officers would make it difficult for victims to report crime through a variety of means. Burglaries would have to be reported to the detective squad directly, adding another hurdle in the process. Other victims would be called back and harassed or otherwise pressured to downgrade the crime they reported.[27] One victim, who had been beaten and robbed, had his crime downgraded to "lost property," because the victim didn't get a good look at the suspects. Another man reported being berated by Mauriello for trying to report a stolen car. An elderly man said that the police wouldn't take a report of him being burglarized, stating there was no evidence. Victims of crimes who couldn't come into the precinct office to report them—because they had to get to work, had kids to take care of, or didn't want to be seen getting into a squad car—wouldn't have their complaints filed.

The scandal would rock the NYPD throughout 2010 and for several years to come.

Shortly after the *Village Voice* started their series on the Schoolcraft tapes, local elected officials, clergy, and community groups demanded Mauriello be removed in a May 26th letter written to Police Commissioner Kelly. The letter stated that "not only did officers treat our community as if it were the subject of a military occupation, but they were also dismissive of criminal complaints made by residents."[28] By October, officers from the 81st Precinct were faced with charges: commander Mauriello, for failing to record a grand larceny and impeding the police department's investigation; four others for failing to report a robbery complaint. Others were charged with filing false arrest paperwork. Mauriello would eventually be transferred to the Bronx.

The NYPD would quickly claim that the incidents in the 81st Precinct were isolated and not indicative of a widespread problem. But the cracks were already forming for the NYPD. Other whistle-blowers started coming forward. In May 2010, shortly after the first NYPD tapes article came out, a retired forty-three-year-old detective first grade named Harold Hernandez contacted Graham Rayman. Hernandez was a respected detective in the NYPD, receiving nineteen excellent police duty awards, four meritorious duty awards, and three commendations. The story he would reveal to Rayman was shocking.

On November 3, 2002, a woman heard noises outside her apartment. She went to her door, looked through the peephole and witnessed a man forcibly pushing a woman into the apartment across the hall. She immediately called 911, and two officers rapidly responded to the call. They kicked the door of the apartment across the hall open, found a woman tied to a chair, and, upon searching the apartment, located the perpetrator hiding in a closet. The man, Daryl Thomas, was taken into custody, and Detective Hernandez was sent in to interrogate him. It didn't take much interrogating for Hernandez to get Thomas to reveal that he had previously committed similar attacks, seven or eight of them. Thomas had been stalking women in upper Manhattan. He would accost women at the door of their buildings, threaten them with a knife, and try to force them into their building. If the women resisted, he would flee.

Hernandez convinced Thomas to confirm the dates, times, and locations of the other incidents. He went to the records to see if the crimes had been reported. They had. What shocked Hernandez was that the crimes Daryl Thomas had committed had all been misclassified. Each previous case had been reported to the police, and, in every case, the police reporting the crime had found a way to classify Thomas's attack so it wouldn't be a felony. The attacks had been classified as criminal trespassing or criminal possession of a weapon. "They used every nonfelony you could think of," Hernandez said.

When a pattern of serious crime occurs, such as Thomas's attacks, it is identified by police and a response is triggered. Increased patrols may be put into an area, plainclothes officers may be deployed, detectives can be assigned, or the sex crimes unit alerted. But all of these resources require the problem to first be identified. In the case of Daryl Thomas, because of the pressure for police to report low crime rates, Thomas was never flagged as a serious threat to public safety. Hernandez never heard of Thomas before that night. He should have. A predator was allowed to continue attacking women.

Another whistle-blower came forward in August. Adhyl Polanco, who was born in the Dominican Republic but grew up in Washington Heights, joined the NYPD in 2000 after deciding not to follow his father's footsteps into a life of crime. Polanco worked in the 41st Precinct in the Bronx, in an area called Hunts Point. According to Polanco, in the 41st Precinct, quotas for arrests, summonses, and stop-and-frisks were happening as well. Officers were pressured to conduct stop-and-frisks, mostly on young African American and Latino men, usually high school students, in an environment that was "all about activity and numbers." Polanco also witnessed illegal searches, illegal stops, and even phony charges put on people in order to meet quotas. Polanco himself was told to downgrade crimes or neglect to report stolen property. In one example, Polanco responded to a "shots fired" call, but was later told to report it as "a sharp object" going through a window, since the precinct didn't want to report an attempted murder.[29]

These small enforcement actions and offenses weren't small to the people of the community though. A minor summons could land people in jail. A summons required the person to present themselves at court, but they often couldn't do so. The next time they were stopped, they had a warrant and could go to jail. The practices put a strain on the relationship with the community, which came to see the police as untrustworthy and more likely to harass them then protect them.[30] In other precincts, the story was the same.

The accusations that Schoolcraft and other whistle-blowers brought forth were corroborated by others. Earlier in 2010 a survey of nearly one thousand retired NYPD captains conducted by criminologists John A.

Eterno and Eli Silverman found that the problem was widespread. Many of the captains who responded to Eterno and Silverman's survey claimed to have known about the practice of downgrading crime in the NYPD. Some of its findings were shocking:

- Sixty percent of captains had little confidence in the accuracy of crime statistics.
- Ninety percent felt crime went down less than the NYPD claimed.
- Most believed it only dropped by half as much as claimed.
- Stop-and-frisk pressure grew during the Bloomberg and Kelly era.
- Thirty-eight percent felt pressure to downgrade crime, close to 90 percent knew of three or more incidents of downgrading crime.[31]

The report revealed even more practices that officers would undertake to get crime statistics down and enforcement statistics up. One such practice involved officers checking eBay in order to find prices for items reported stolen in order to lower their reported value and therefore downgrade the crime from a grand larceny to a misdemeanor.[32]

Other survey respondents claimed that precinct commanders would go to crime scenes to persuade victims to not file complaints or to change their accounts to lower crime classification. Before Adrian Schoolcraft and his tapes, cracks were already starting to form in the authenticity of crime reporting in New York. The first case of fraud was uncovered just one year after CompStat was initiated: The *New York Daily News* obtained a memo from the Bronx's 50th Precinct in which the commander had instructed his officers how to downgrade felonies to misdemeanors. A few years later, in 1998, then-Commissioner Safir had to disclose that subway crime had been underreported by nearly 20 percent for years. Other cases of downgrading crime made headlines. In 2002 a rape in the Bronx was revealed to have been categorized as a lower level crime. In 2003 in the 10th Precinct in Manhattan, over 203 felonies were reported to have been downgraded to misdemeanors. And in 2003, again in the Bronx's 50th Precinct, officers were found to have refused to take multiple robbery complaints of several restaurant delivery people. Commissioner Kelly had successfully avoided any serious fallout from these previous incidents, insisting these were just a few bad apples in an otherwise rigorous and trustworthy system.[33] But none of these scandals really shook the NYPD the way the Schoolcraft tapes did.

Police Commissioner Ray Kelly had to react. The problem was more than just a few isolated incidents in a couple of precincts. In January 2011 Kelly appointed a panel of three former federal prosecutors to investigate the crime reporting and recording practices throughout the entire department. They were given three to six months to complete their report. It would take nearly two and half years for the report to come out in July 2013, titled the "Crime Reporting Review."

The "Crime Reporting Review," while commending the NYPD for helping the decline in crime for the last twenty years, was also critical of how crime reporting was manipulated in the department. The report noted that "a close review of the NYPD's statistics and analysis demonstrates that the misclassification of reports may have an appreciable effort on certain reported crime rates." It also stated that "patterns of misclassifying support the anecdotal evidence, including that certain types of incidents, may be downgraded as a matter of practice in some precincts." Most important, it noted that "the focus of the NYPD and the general public on the year-over-year declines in crime as reported by the NYPD, if over-emphasized, serve to undermine the integrity of that statistic and undermine CompStat as an effective law-enforcement tool."[34]

Not only that, the report found that the risks of suppression (not recording crimes at all) may have been more substantial than the risk of downgrading crimes. With downgrading, such as the type Detective Hernandez found with the upper Manhattan predator case, at least there was a paper trail that could be audited and victims could be contacted to corroborate reports. When no report is filed in the first place, following the trail is a bit more difficult. The only way to audit these cases was to go back to 911 call data (called SPRINT audits) and check to see if the calls were properly followed up. But these audits are limited; they miss all the other ways citizens report crime, such as through beepers, cell phones, voice mails, and face-to-face reporting.

For decades, the NYPD was covering up false crime reporting. Crime decreases were not as great as they had been reported. On top of that, police officers were given quotas for arrests and minor infractions. It was Goodhart's Law all over again. At the center of all of it was William Bratton's golden child: CompStat.

What the report concluded is that the particular implementation of CompStat itself was a cause of the problem. The desire for officials to see continued crime reduction led to manipulation. As time went on, and crime rates continued to decline, it became harder and harder for police commanders to show better numbers. There is only so much the crime rate can go down. As the Patrolmen's Benevolent Association secretary, Robert Zink, said in 2004, "When you finally get a real handle on crime, you eventually hit a wall where you can't push it down any more. Comp-Stat does not recognize that wall, so the commanders have to get creative to keep their numbers going down."[35]

The same was stated by whistle-blowers. As Adhyl Polanco, the whistle-blower from the 41st precinct claimed, "The reason was CompStat. They know what they are going to be asked for in CompStat, and they have to have a lower number—but not too low."[36] Eterno and Silverman's survey came to similar conclusions. The enormous pressure from Comp-Stat to downgrade crime was felt throughout the force. That pressure was leading to ethically questionable actions by police officers throughout the NYPD. Low crime rates benefited everyone. Precinct commanders got raises and promotions. Patrol officers got days off and other perks. The police commissioner got commendation for achieving such incredible reductions in crime. The mayor could tout the low crime numbers as a selling point for the city: New York was a safe place to do business, to live, and to work. Low crime meant more tourists, more economic development, more revenue. And there were many ways that the rank and file of the NYPD found to keep crime rates low.

Zink explained the multiple ways police found to achieve lower reported crime rates:

> *Don't file reports, misclassify crimes from felonies to misdemeanors, under-value the property lost to crime, and report a series of crimes as a single event. A particularly insidious way to fudge the numbers is to make it difficult for people to report crimes—in other words, make the victims feel like criminals so they walk away just to spare themselves further pain and suffering.*

The scandal in New York wasn't anything new. Other cities had already experienced their share of crime suppression scandals. In 2001 in Philadelphia, a newspaper investigation found that over seventeen hundred cases of rape were classified in a way so that the police didn't have to report them. In 2003 in New Orleans, five police officers were fired for downgrading crimes. In Atlanta a 2004 investigation found that twenty-two thousand 911 calls had vanished from the records in 2002.

In some cities CompStat was to blame. In 2009 the Florida Department of Law Enforcement found that the pressures of CompStat in Miami led to underreporting of crime. In Dallas police were caught classifying people who had been beaten with lead pipes as a case of simple assault rather than felony assault. In Baltimore police were caught downgrading the value of stolen property in order to classify the robberies as misdemeanors rather than felonies.[37] The heavy-handed practices of the NYPD coming out of CompStat also led to a massive increase in the number of lawsuits and complaints filed against the police force. The focus on enforcement quotas was also a major instigator of a major controversy in New York: stop-and-frisks. A stop-and-frisk is where a police officer stops a person on the street and searches him or her under reasonable suspicion. The practice was legalized with a 1986 Supreme Court decision that established that the police could, without a warrant, stop and search a person on the street so they could intervene in what they could reasonably suspect to be criminal activity. That court decision, called *Terry v Ohio*, would establish the legal basis for stop-and-frisks and would also give the practice their name: Terry stops.[38] The important thing about the Supreme Court decision was that it required the police to have reasonable suspicion that a crime was occurring or about to occur. That was seldom the case in the 81st Precinct, and it was seldom the case in the entire city of New York.

Under Commissioner Kelly, the use of stop-and-frisk had skyrocketed.[39] In 2011, the year that Commissioner Kelly launched the "Crime Reporting Review," the New York Police Department conducted over 686,000 stop-and-frisks. The controversy around stop-and-frisks was not just the fact that the police were overdoing them, it was who they were doing them to. Stop-and-frisks were disproportionately conducted on the city's African American population.

While African Americans only made up 23 percent of the residents of New York City, they were involved in 52 percent of stop-and-frisks over a twelve-year period. Whites, while making up 33 percent of the population, only accounted for 10 percent of stop-and-frisks. What is even more upsetting is that in those stop-and-frisks, contraband and weapons were only found in 1.8 percent and 1.0 percent of stops of African Americans, but in 2.3 percent and 1.4 percent of whites. African Americans were being stopped more often, despite being less likely to be carrying weapons or contraband than whites.[40]

Stop-and-frisks would be challenged over and over again in the courts. In January 2012 alone, forty lawsuits were filed against the NYPD for stop-and-frisk complaints.[41] A lawsuit filed by the Center for Constitutional Rights against the City of New York, *Floyd et al. v. City of New York*, in New York's Southern District would be instrumental in deciding the legality of the practice. Ultimately the practice was deemed unconstitutional. According to the attorneys involved in the case, Schoolcraft's tapes were the smoking gun, showing clear evidence that the NYPD was using quotas for the practice, with little regard to the reasonable suspicion they were supposed to exercise. In the decision on the case, the judge found that the NYPD had not only violated the Constitution, but it had perverted the goal of using stop-and-frisk against "the right people, the right time, the right location" into a tool of discrimination against poor people of color.[42] The Bloomberg administration filed to appeal the decision to the federal courts.

Stop-and-frisk had become the focal point of community protest against police tactics. Regular citizens became anxious and afraid of the police while just going about their regular lives. These events taken together—the downgrading and suppression of crime reporting; the enforcement quotas, including aggressive stop-and-frisk tactics; the whistle-blower scandals blasted across the headlines of major newspapers throughout the city—led to a deterioration of trust in the NYPD.

But one could argue, the drop in crime that CompStat instigated was worth it. Sure, some people were harassed, others falsely arrested, and some serious crimes went unreported. But it was worth it, because New York was a safer place after CompStat than it was before. CompStat had instigated one of the greatest drops in crime the United States had ever seen. Or did it?

The problem is that crime just didn't drop in New York starting in 1990, it dropped everywhere. David Greenberg, a professor of sociology from New York University, pointed out that crime decreased in places like Los Angeles and San Diego, which didn't implement the CompStat system. CompStat wasn't implemented until 1994, and it just continued the already existing trend.[43] New York City's crime drop, while substantial, wasn't an outlier. It is true it dropped by a greater degree than in most other cities, but not by much. Criminologists to this day debate the ultimate causes of the drop in New York's crime rate, and the drop in crime across the United States. But one thing is clear: CompStat wasn't the sole cause.

Going back to Schoolcraft, the QAD did in fact investigate Schoolcraft's allegations, as well as the incident of October 31. During the course of the investigation, forty-five other officers were interviewed, and hundreds of documents were reviewed. Their report came out in March 2012, nearly two and a half years after the incident. The report substantiated eleven of the thirteen allegations Schoolcraft made, including the downgrading of crime complaints; instances of reports being delayed, rewritten, or never filed; and instances of victims being ignored or pressured. The investigation also found a range of other crimes in the precinct that were altered, rejected, misclassified, went missing, or simply were never entered. The report concluded: "When viewed in their totality, a disturbing pattern is prevalent and gives credence to the allegation that crimes are being improperly reported in order to avoid index crime classification. This is indicative of a concerted effort to deliberately underreport crime in the 81st Precinct."[44]

As for Schoolcraft's lawsuit against the NYPD, it finally came to an end in 2015. He was awarded six hundred thousand dollars in compensation, plus back pay, for the incident. Schoolcraft was vindicated, but he never returned to the NYPD.

Adrian Schoolcraft became the whistle-blower who cracked open the perverse system that was CompStat. He could do so not because he was a popular, respected, and well-liked police officer on the force. He wasn't. Schoolcraft was a shy, introverted man who would probably fit better in a software development company than on the nation's largest police force. But Schoolcraft was, for all intents and purposes, someone with nothing to lose. In the words of his father, "Adrian was different. He had no friends on the job, no history in the city, he didn't want to become a detective, he didn't want to work overtime, he didn't have the house, the mortgage, the wife and kids, so they didn't have the management tools they use to pressure most other people."[45]

||||||||||

To understand where things went wrong, why officers were so focused on "downgrading crime" or upping their enforcement numbers, we have to go back to George Kelling, the man who developed the Broken Windows theory. In 1992, just as Bratton was implementing his subway strategy, Kelling wrote another article, this time for the *City Journal*. In that article Kelling was critical of the reliance on statistics.

Kelling pointed out that New York City, despite its fairly high crime rate in 1992, actually had lower crime that most other large cities in the United States. Eight other cities had higher homicide rates, twenty-one had higher incidents of rape, seventeen had higher burglary rates, eight had higher rates of auto theft. Some cities were actually much worse than New York. In Washington, DC, the murder rate was 2.8 times higher than it was in New York City. Cleveland's reported incidents of rape were 3.5 times higher than New York's. New York, according to the statistics, was actually a much safer city than many others in the country.

Yet, as Kelling pointed out, when a New York politician held a focus group and asked participants what they thought of the statement "New York City is tough on crime," they were met with incredulous laughter. To Kelling this reaction was the result of police strategies, tactics, and methodologies that were overly driven by statistical and bureaucratic measures of performance. Those statistics didn't reflect what citizens actually care about. Those measures were primarily driven by the UCRs. There were several things that Kelling noted about the UCRs. First, the formal measures of the UCRs have little to do with community needs.

The UCRs only report on index crimes, the "major" crimes, but for most people, it isn't murder or auto theft that they are concerned with. Even with crime rates rising for decades, individual cases of serious crimes are rare. Added to this is that over 40 percent of serious crimes do not involve strangers, but take place between family members, friends, rival gang members, or other acquaintances. Random crime of a serious nature is not as common as many people think. What people do care about is the general environment of disorder, which often involves less-serious crimes. These are the literal Broken Windows Kelling referred to in his original article in 1982.

Second, recorded crime is actually a poor measure of actual crime taking place. A low level of reported crime may indicate a low level of crime, but perversely, it can also indicate that citizens don't bother to report crimes, either because they don't trust the police or they don't think the police will do anything about it. In this manner, crime rates can actually be quite deceiving. Was the higher reported rate of rape in Cleveland indicative of more cases of rape, or was it that victims in Cleveland were more trusting of the police and more willing to report their victimization, trusting the police would do something about it?

Third, using arrests as a metric of enforcement is problematic. Often it is simply an incentive for police to either make arrests for harmless actions or for the police to allow situations to get out of hand so that arrests are required. Kelling uses a theoretical example of an officer witnessing a dispute between a Black citizen and a Korean shop owner. The dispute escalates into violence, and the officer steps in and makes two arrests. But is this a success? Sure, the officer can chalk up two arrests to their stats, but what are the consequences for race relations and conflict within the community? Had the officer stepped in earlier, de-escalated the situation, and calmed tensions, wouldn't that have been a better result, despite the officer not being able to "count" any enforcement action? Marquez Claxton, a retired detective and the director of the Black Law Enforcement Alliance in 2013, put it succinctly:

> *The difficultly is that you can't quantify prevention. There is no number which says I stopped seven burglaries today. People have made careers out of summonses and arrests, but that's not even the main component of police work. In today's police department, the officers are ostracized unless they have their numbers. You're punishing officers who say their job is not to be the hammer.*"[46]

Fourth, the UCRs don't differentiate between the various intents of crime. Not every burglary is the same. Not every murder has the same effect on people's perceptions of safety. Kelling noted that a simple case of vandalism can take on an entirely different perception of threat depending on what it depicts: Some graffiti on the side of a dumpster may be entirely harmless, but a swastika painted on the front door of a Jewish home is a very serious crime.

For Kelling the focus on stats betrayed what real police work was supposed to do: create an environment of order and safety. Stats didn't say anything about whether people felt safe to go out at night or trusted the police to investigate complaints. For Kelling there were three examples of police work that exemplified actions that would actually lead to increased safety and better relationships between the police and the population they served: two operations in New York in the 1970s—Operation Crossroads in Times Square and the Bryant Park situation and the Newark foot patrol initiative in the 1980s.

In the 1970s Times Square was a pretty dangerous place. Drug dealing occurred in the open in the square, tourists were harassed by panhandlers, and the area had a general feeling of danger. Previous police action in the area involved "sweeps," where officers would be deployed to the area and loiterers would be arrested, much like Bratton's fare evasion sweeps of the early 1990s. But in Times Square, shortly after the sweeps, the loiterers were back on the street again. It was a merry-go-round of police enforcement that went nowhere. Eventually the police tried something different. It was called "Operation Crossroads."[47]

First, the police decided to actually get a handle on assessing the environment so they could understand the results of their actions. They hired trained civilian professionals to count instances of "disorder": drug dealing, drug use, non-food vendors, loitering, open-air gambling, and so on, to get an understanding of the baseline situation. Then the police adopted a tactic that was rather different from the previous sweeps: They would deploy a lot of officers to the area but took very little action. Loiterers were not arrested, and sometimes neither were drug dealers. Instead, police were instructed to use as little enforcement as possible. They would order, counsel, educate, and cajole loiterers and drug dealers to "move along." People would only be arrested as a last resort. The tactics worked. The counts of "disorderly behavior," done by impartial civilians, showed that the area was made safer. And few people had to be arrested.

The same situation occurred in Bryant Park, the plaza outside of the main branch of the New York Public Library. The park was infamous for drug dealing, which was so bad it even caused the Parks commissioner to threaten to close the branch. The same tactics were used; civilian counts of disorder, as well as counts of "positive activities" like people reading, eating, or conversing in the park, were undertaken to establish a baseline condition to evaluate the success of the program. The police again implemented a low-enforcement tactic in the park. They arrested very few drug dealers, instead resorting to simply asking the dealers to move along.

Again the strategy worked: Positive activities in the park increased by 79 percent; the number of drug dealers, buyers, and users decreased by 85 percent; and loitering and drug-related uses declined from 67 percent to 49 percent of activities. That may not have been as much as the police were hoping for, but the drug dealing that did happen was done more discretely, which made other people in the park feel safer. The experiment proved that the police didn't need to arrest anyone to deter drug dealers; simply having an officer in the park was enough to prevent a lot of dealing.[48]

When Kelling wrote his Broken Windows article in 1982, he referenced a foot patrol initiative in Newark. The initiative went against everything that the police believed at the time. It took officers out of their cars, making their response time slower. For the police officers themselves, foot patrol was hard work—they were outside a lot and exposed to the weather, and foot patrols made it difficult for them to make good arrests.

Yet the morale of the officers improved, and the citizens felt safer with officers patrolling on foot.[49]

This spoke to Kelling's criticism of police work at the time that police departments were too focused on responding to crimes that had already occurred, relying on the rapid response of patrol cars to arrive at crime scenes quickly rather than what Kelling felt was a better use of their time—foot patrol. Kelling had personally tagged along during the foot patrol initiative in Newark and it opened his eyes to what good police work could do. Kelling was particularly critical of the pitfalls of police patrols using vehicles. As Kelling explained in a 1992 article, "Police need to change their own minds about their mission, and give up the view that police work consists of racing around in patrol cars, apprehending criminals after the fact, and feeding them into a 'criminal justice system.'"[50]

What was important about Operation Crossroads, the Bryant Park experiment, and the Newark foot patrol initiative was that while they all involved a lot of resources and was purposely highly visible, they were also low-enforcement operations. In Times Square and Bryant Park, very few arrests were made. Officers were instructed to use various ways to deter disorderly behavior. Only as a last resort would an officer undertake an arrest. In Newark, crime rates didn't significantly decrease (at least not UCR index crimes). But what did improve in all situations was that citizens felt that the police were maintaining order. The police cared. They were trusted.

Compare this to the actions of many officers in the 81st Precinct. Citizens were harassed in order to keep enforcement numbers up and reported crime rates down. Somewhere, things went wrong. The idea of working with communities to identify areas of concern, develop strategies together, and create a feeling of safety was usurped by almighty statistics.

Kelling's ideas, while not perfect by any means, were nevertheless perverted into a system that cared more about numbers than it did about the purpose of what a police force is supposed to do.

Following the NYPD tapes scandal initiated by Adrian Schoolcraft, the resulting "Crime Reporting Review," and the *Floyd et al.* court case, things did change at the NYPD. Bill de Blasio, the New York City public advocate from 2010 to 2013, won the mayoral election in 2013 in a landslide. He had made opposition to the stop-and-frisk policy a centerpiece of his campaign, and upon his victory, de Blasio made major changes to the NYPD. De-escalation training was implemented for officers, the use of police body cameras was implemented, and the stop-and-frisk appeal to the federal courts was promptly dropped. On top of that Ray Kelly was removed as the police commissioner, and at the start of 2014, William Bratton was brought back to lead the NYPD for a second time, serving until September 2016.

In 2015 Bratton and George Kelling wrote another article for the *City Journal*, defending the Broken Windows strategy, but also offering some reflection on what had gone wrong in the twenty years since it was first implemented in 1994. Bratton and Kelling recognized that stop-and-frisk had been abused. The stops had been, according to Bratton and Kelling, an "ad hoc" measure of productivity. Stop-and-frisks decreased substantially starting in 2014, going from the high of 686,000 in 2011 down to 45,000 in 2014. Unsurprisingly, the lower rates had no discernible impact on crime.

Bratton created a system that valued stats above all else. If precinct commanders couldn't get their UCR numbers down, they were humiliated in front of their peers at CompStat meetings, denied promotions, or reassigned. But we cannot blame Bratton for the overreliance on statistics or the UCRs. Bratton was just responding to a political climate that demands action. And almost always, that action requires numbers to go up or down.

This is the same pattern we have seen before. Someone develops a new way of tackling a problem or comes up with a new concept: combating crime by tackling disorder, giving doctors more control over their practices, investing in fundamental scientific research, aligning interests of CEOs with shareholders.

These are all good ideas. But then they get quantified. Physicians are measured by their ability to bill for each service they provide. Researchers are measured by how many articles they publish. CEOs are compensated based on the quarterly earnings of their company or are given short-term stock options. Broken Windows policing transforms into quotas for misdemeanors, summonses, arrests, and minor infractions, pitting police officers against the public they are intended to protect.

Broken Windows policing and the strategies that William Bratton employed in New York to reduce crime are not fundamentally flawed at their core. Credit should be given to Bratton and Kelling for their role in reducing crime in New York. And while the tactics may not be as effective as Bratton, Kelling or other proponents of Broken Windows and CompStat claim, nor as nefarious as the detractors assert, it isn't the theory behind the tactics that are flawed, it is the way they are implemented. As Eterno and Silverman, the criminologists who conducted the survey of retired NYPD captains state "CompStat was originally a positive development but morphed into a numbers game."[51]

CompStat can be an incredibly useful system to help identify trends and geographic patterns in crime and respond to those trends with the deployment of resources. But when precinct commanders' promotions, bonuses, and salaries are put on the line, the tool becomes a perverse weapon. When this happens, CompStat is transformed from a tool used to identify and evaluate crime to a metric that can be manipulated. Precinct commanders begin to juke the stats by putting pressure on their subordinates to misclassify crime. Citizens are pressured to change reports or withdraw them altogether. Whistle-blowers like Schoolcraft are intimidated and harassed by colleagues. Regular citizens, with no criminal inclinations, are harassed, arrested, and abused by the police in a drive to up the stats and generate revenue. Lives are destroyed, and sometimes they are tragically lost. And in the process, the police lose something that can't be measured in the same way UCRs or stop-and-frisk quotas can: the trust of the public.

As David Sklansky wrote, "Shiny video screens, interactive maps, and 'mathematical prophesy' have allures that are not shared by, say, a poorly attended community meeting in a church basement."[52] Building trust with community requires thousands upon thousands of actions every day by police. It is those meetings in church basements, the discrete conversations residents have with patrol officers informing them of criminal activity in the neighborhood. It's the conversations in living rooms with the parents of at-risk youth. It's the officers who let drivers not wearing seat belts off with just a warning. These are the things that really matter. And none of those things can be measured in the same way a quota for misdemeanor enforcements can. Sometimes the role of the police is to not take action. Not conducting a stop-and-frisk can be more important than doing so. Not writing up a C summons, even if it means not getting your numbers up, can be more important in building trust with a resident. The obsession with metrics in the police forces in the United States, and increasingly in other countries, has perverted the goals and functions of the police. The costs to people's livelihoods, to their quality of life, to their constitutional rights, and to their trust in those sworn to protect them are high. But sometimes the cost of our obsession with metrics is much, much higher.

||||||||||

It was something new to all of us. It was an entirely different type of military operation than we'd ever been in on . . . there wasn't any front line, it was no place, it was everyplace. It was in your kitchen, it was in your backyard.
—General P. D. Harkins, Military Assistance Command, Vietnam Commander, 1962–1964

Every quantitative measure we have shows that we are winning the war.
—Robert McNamara, Secretary of Defense, 1962

His is not an army that sends coffins north; it is by the traffic in homebound American coffins that Giap measures his success.
> —P. J. McGarvey, author of *Visions of Victory*,
> referring Vo Nguyen Giap, Commander in Chief
> of the People's Army of Vietnam

We will fight to find victory. Everything depends on the Americans. If they want to make war for 20 years, then we shall make war for 20 years.
> —Ho Chi Minh

In the process of data collection, the data had become an end unto itself.
> —Gregory Daddis, Department of History, United
> States Military Academy

||||||||||

The war in Vietnam didn't begin in the way most wars do. The Vietnam War did not so much start, rather it just happened.

In 1954, the United States found itself in a problematic situation. With the 1954 Geneva convention the French and Vietnamese had agreed to a cease-fire, ending ten years of armed conflict between the two. Vietnam was split in half, with the communist Viet Minh government, led by Ho Chi Minh, ruling in the north, and the previously French-supported government, led by Ngo Dinh Diem, ruling in the south. The separation of the two halves of the country was not initially expected to last, with elections planned to unite the two parts of the country shortly after the cease fire. Elections took place in the south portion of the country in October 1955, with Ngo Dinh Diem, now an American-supported politician, claiming 98.2 percent of the votes, and 133 percent in Saigon!

The United States found itself in a strange situation. It was supporting a government that was showing blatant signs of corruption, in a country that had not only been fighting against the French for ten years, but also against the Japanese occupation during World War II before that. The Americans were only initially acting in an advisory position to Diem's government, under something called the Military Assistance Advisory Group.

During Diem's rule, communists in the south organized themselves into a political and armed resistance, called the National Liberation Front. Diem called them the Vietcong, a term the United States would adopt. Over the next several years, the Vietcong resistance grew, with political organization and propaganda focused especially in rural villages. Slowly the armed conflict between the Vietcong and the government under Diem grew. By 1961 the number of violent clashes between the Vietcong and government forces had grown to nearly two a day. The South Vietnamese government forces seemed incapable of containing the resistance. The situation was becoming grave, and the United States feared the Vietcong would eventually overthrow Diem's government and establish a communist state in the South. That was an outcome that they did not want to see happen.

In February 1962, the United States set up the Military Advisory Committee, Vietnam (MACV), which would become the official command of the operations in Vietnam. MACV would be responsible for American military policy, operations, and assistance for the duration of the war. Outwardly MACV was confident and clear in its direction in the war. This was a war that could be won easily and quickly. General Paul D. Harkins, the first commander of MACV, a sixty-year-old World War II veteran, was confident that "we have taken the military, psychological, economic and political initiative from the enemy."[53]

Inside military command, however, the picture was different. The Americans were not sure exactly what their objectives were, how to achieve them, or even how to understand if they were achieving them. Edward Lansdale, the defense secretary's deputy assistant for special operations said that "the truest thing that could be said about the situation in Vietnam today is that the accomplishments do not match the efforts being made."

Right from the beginning of American involvement in Vietnam, MACV faced problems establishing a system of measurement for the war.

The country was geographically diverse, the understanding of the exact nature of the threat was unclear and continually shifting, and the military command didn't have a clear purpose or direction. Harkins was quoted as saying, "It was something new to all of us. It was an entirely different type of military operation than we'd ever been in on . . . there wasn't any front line, it was no place, it was everyplace. It was in your kitchen, it was in your backyard."[54] The problem with the war in Vietnam was that it wasn't a conventional war.

There was no front line. There was no enemy territory, at least not in the same way there was in World War II or the early stages of the Korean War. In a conventional war, either you are moving forward, killing enemy troops, or you are holding ground against attack or retreating.[55]

Success is easily measured. But in Vietnam, it was hard to tell where the lines were. The enemy seemed to be everywhere, and nowhere. For many officers, Vietnam was filled with uncertainty. Political allegiances, population security, and ideological strength—important factors in counterinsurgencies—defied measurement. How do you measure a war where you can't count the territory you conquer, don't know who or where your enemy is, and you don't know if a village is under enemy control or not?

Early in the conflict, military officers attempted to get a handle on how the war was going, and how to measure success. Between 1960 and 1962, Lieutenant General Lionel C McGaar had directed his officers to provide rudimentary measurements for the number of violent incidents, weapons seized, or people killed in conflict. Lansdale, the deputy assistant to the defense secretary, had suggested that measuring villagers' attitudes toward Vietnamese troops or the effect of Vietcong propaganda on the population would be useful in gaining an understanding of the situation on the ground. Lansdale felt that earning the friendship of the Vietnamese people was instrumental and suggested measuring such things as the willingness of villagers to care for the wounded civilians, the degree to which they shared rice with the hungry, or their propensity to repair destroyed structures.[56] But all this changed in 1962.

If anything could be said about Robert McNamara, it is that he was a numbers man. He studied economics, math, and philosophy at UC Berkeley, graduating in 1937. From there he went to work for Pricewaterhouse. Then he went to teach accounting at Harvard, where he was the highest paid, yet youngest associate professor in the department. He then entered the Air Force in 1943, serving as a captain in the Office of Statistical Control, where he analyzed the efficiency of bombing operations in the war against Japan. At the OSC McNamara and the others brought a statistical approach to the war. They measured everything they possibly could. They measured the number of tons of bombs that could be dropped per gallon of fuel for various bomber types. They created an inventory of all the spare parts available at every base so that new supplies didn't have to be ordered. Their efforts saved the US military 3.6 billion dollars in 1943 alone.[57]

After the war, McNamara and a group of ten other former officers and the commanders from the Office of Statistical Control grouped together to form a consultancy. The group was quickly hired by Ford Motor Company. Ford, reeling from the death of its founder, Henry Ford, was in the hands of his grandson, Henry Ford II. The company was disorganized, ruled by men loyal to Ford's grandfather, who had no real direction or even defined responsibilities. Like the Air Force before the Office of Statistical Control, Ford barely kept any records or data on what they did, other than a cash statement provided to the bank. Bringing in the team McNamara belonged to could reverse all that.

Employees of the company started calling the group "The Quiz Kids," because they wouldn't stop asking "Why?" The group took the name as inspiration for what they would call themselves: the Whiz Kids. The Whiz Kids' work for Ford was nothing short of amazing. The group would reform the chaotic, money-losing organization in a matter of years, improving the safety of the vehicles and refocusing the company on producing small and simple vehicles rather than the large models popular at the time. McNamara himself moved up through the ranks of the company and became the first nonfamily member to be president of the company.

The Whiz Kids believed in one unifying philosophy: All decisions could be based on numbers. And in 1962, one of them, Robert McNamara, became secretary of defense for the United States.[58]

In contrast to the unease that senior officers felt toward the conflict, and their struggles with dealing with a complex, nebulous and shifting situation, McNamara felt Vietnam was a perfect environment for statistical analysis. For McNamara and his team, a reliance on statistics was a "reasoned approach to highly complicated problems of choice in a context of much uncertainty." These complex problems were perfect targets for statistical analysis—the hard numbers would cut through the fog of uncertainty. For McNamara, nothing couldn't be solved by math. The situation that McNamara found in Vietnam after his appointment as secretary of defense was one of an "absence of the essential management tools needed to make sound decisions on the really crucial issues of national security."[59] Quickly after his appointment, McNamara created the civilian Office of Systems Analysis (OSA), which would be responsible for analyzing the numerous statistics that would be collected throughout the war theater. With the structure in place to collect, analyze, and act on data coming out of the war theater, McNamara then turned Vietnam into the largest data collection and analysis effort in the history of war.

By late 1963 MACV, under instructions from McNamara, instituted Directive Number 88, an officially sanctioned criteria for evaluating progress in the war. It measured nearly everything possible: the rate of Vietcong defections, the ratio of enemy to friendlies killed in action, the percentage of Vietcong crops destroyed, the number of civil guard units trained, the average number of days spent in offensive operations, Hamlet pacification measures, enemy incident rates, tactical air sorties, weapons losses, security of bases and roads, population control, and area control. Dozens upon dozens of different metrics were directed to be collected and reported by military commanders all the way down the chain of command.[60] And so the data flowed in. Hundreds of thousands of troops, provincial advisors, military advisors, US civilian officials, US intelligence officers, Vietnamese military units, government agencies, and civilian development teams collected and fed millions upon millions of points of data up the chain of command to MACV in Saigon and the OSA in the Pentagon. On top of the quantitative measures, thousands of detailed narrative assessments were produced by military and civilian officers. The amount of data was so immense, National Security Council staff member Chester L. Cooper described it as, "Numbers flowed into Saigon and from there into Washington like the Mekong River during the flood season."[61]

Analysts in Saigon and Washington tabulated millions of reports and compiled their own. Data were entered into a staggering number of catalogs and computer databases: The Hamlet Evaluation System, the Terrorist Incident Reporting System, the Territorial Forces Effectiveness System, the Pacification Attitude Analysis System, the Situation Reports Army File, the Revolutionary Redevelopment Cadre System, the Assistance in Kind System, the Refugee System, the Village and Hamlet Radio System, the People's Self-Defense Force System, the VCI Neutralization System, the Southeast Asia Province File, Project Corona Harvest, the System for Evaluating the Effectiveness of South Vietnamese Subsystems, and the Air Summary Data Base.[62] The list goes on and on. The government had to publish a pamphlet called the "Introduction to the Pacification Data Bank" just to help analysts navigate the sheer volume of reports and databases being produced. At the height of the analysis effort, there were fourteen thousand pounds of reports produced daily.[63]

This emphasis on numbers bred interest in more numbers. The number of indicators kept increasing. By April 1964, over one hundred indicators were to be measured by military and civilian personnel in the war effort. There was so much data that there were teams created just to review the amount and quality of data coming in. In late 1963 and early 1964, MACV had an entire team devote six months of full-time analysis of reviewing and evaluating nearly five hundred reports to understand the nature and quality of data coming in.[64] Data had become an end in and of itself. MACV struggled with understanding how progress was being made in the unconventional conflict in Vietnam. The sheer volume of data did not provide much help. Throughout the war the military command struggled to find a consensus on how to defeat the insurgency, let alone know if they were doing so. The leadership couldn't agree on where the main threat lay, so field commanders were never given clear direction on what to prioritize: securing villages from Vietcong intrusion, searching and destroying Vietcong units, or clearing areas of Vietcong influence.

Analysts in Saigon and Washington were under intense pressure not only to obtain, collate, and understand absurd amounts of data, but to show progress.

The other problem with data in Vietnam was that most of the data were military in nature; political and social measures of the war, the kind Lansdale had advocated for prior to McNamara's arrival on the scene, were largely ignored. Casualties, military activities, and operations were used to larger degrees than other measures of success. For example, the security of an area was measured in terms of the number of incidents occurring, but this provided little insight into whether a village was "secure" or not. Fewer incidents could indicate that a village was in fact under Vietcong control. There seemed to be no rhyme or reason to any of the data. There were over one hundred indicators of progress in the war, but no one prioritized which ones mattered most, or how they were to be interpreted. One report from 1968 counted the number of cakes of soap issued to Vietnamese villagers.[65] Data that made sense in one area, such as body counts of enemy dead in the central highlands, where the United States was fighting North Vietnamese army, didn't work in evaluating whether a village in the Mekong Delta was freeing itself from insurgent influence.[66] The nature of the war itself escaped measurement. Officers were instructed to put relentless pressure on guerrillas. But if Vietcong activity had ceased in an area, was it because they had been defeated, or was it because they had just decided to disperse and lay low until a better opportunity to attack presented itself? Was a village that wasn't experiencing any attacks doing so because the Vietcong was in control of the area? Officers were instructed to assess the effectiveness of the Vietcong, how it related to the local population, and the effectiveness of its communications and intelligence networks. But they were never told how to evaluate these things.

On top of the sheer volume of data flowing into Saigon, there was no system to validate much of it. Troops in the field were tasked with reporting data that often did not exist, in formats that made little sense.[67]

The lack of clarity in how to measure what was being asked of them often resulted in data being reported erroneously, if not completely fabricated. Thomas Thayer, the head of the OSA, admitted that most of the data he was dealing with were of poor quality. Almost no measure that was collected during the war—the number of insurgents, the number of attacks by Vietcong, the capability of the South Vietnamese military, estimates of civilian casualties, hamlet security, political attitudes of the local population, the number of refugees—achieved any degree of accuracy or reliability.[68] Often officers simply reported what their commanders wanted to hear. Embellishment was an even bigger problem for data coming from South Vietnamese government forces, who were notoriously corrupt and ineffective.

The sheer volume of data and reports in Vietnam, the questionable accuracy of the reporting, and the lack of a clear direction in determining what really mattered left the command in a quagmire. Despite the hundreds upon hundreds of reports on various aspects of the conflict, the war seemed to be going nowhere. But for McNamara, the data were what would win the war. After 1965, exactly what data that were thought to win the war would change dramatically, and with dire consequences.

In 1965 the United States faced a deteriorating situation in Vietnam. Despite rosy pictures often presented in the data, many in command felt that if things did not turn around, the United States would face an imminent communist victory in South Vietnam. This situation had led to the replacement of General Harkins with William Westmoreland as the head of MACV. And in June 1964, Westmoreland intended to change the course of the war.[69]

In August 1965 MACV issued a three-phase concept for operations in Vietnam. First, by the end of 1965, the plan was to reverse the losing trend of American and South Vietnamese forces by focusing on the security of logistical and military bases, strengthening the Republic of Vietnam armed forces, and increasing operations against Vietcong bases. Second, by 1966 the Americans and South Vietnamese would go back on the offensive, attacking more bases and expanding their Pacific operations. And third, after twelve to eighteen months, MACV predicted, the Vietcong and North Vietnamese would be defeated and their remaining forces destroyed.[70]

General Westmoreland brought more discipline to measurement in the conflict. He advised that the one hundred–plus indicators used in the war effort be reduced to a few basic yardsticks: population control, area control, communications control, resources control, as well as a comparative analysis of Vietcong and Republic of Vietnam armed forces. But one measure would come to dominate the strategy in Vietnam for the remainder of the war: body counts. Westmoreland's overall strategy was simple: kill more of the enemy.

The strategy was attrition. If the United States simply killed more Vietcong and North Vietnamese soldiers, they would win the war.

According to Westmoreland, if the United States continued to cause massive losses on the part of the Vietcong and the North Vietnamese army, they would hit a "crossover point" at which the enemy could not sustain the casualties inflicted upon them.[71]

This strategy wasn't entirely unfounded. The way the military command saw the war was that their role was to prevent the unification of Vietnam by force. They were not seeking to overthrow the communists in the north, just prevent their expansion into the south. Their goal wasn't to overthrow Ho Chi Minh. In that sense, the American command didn't feel the communists were fighting for the survival of their state or their own survival. The war wasn't a "death struggle." If the United States simply convinced the communists the fight wasn't worth it, they would eventually relent. Westmoreland believed there was a point at which the communists would be "convinced that military victory was impossible and then would not be willing to endure further punishment." Ironically, for Westmoreland, the crossover point was reached in the spring of 1967, one year before the infamous Tet offensive.[72]

There were many ways this strategy could work according to the military command. First, by depleting North Vietnamese and Vietcong forces, the Americans would deny them the ability to win the war. With no hope of beating the American and South Vietnamese forces, the North Vietnamese would simply give up in discouragement, as had the communist insurgencies in Greece in 1946 to 1949, the Philippines in 1945 to 1954, and in Malaya in 1948 to 1960 had done. Second, the losses could convince the communist leadership to negotiate to save face. If they couldn't win the war, perhaps the communists would agree to a negotiated settlement, as had occurred in Korea. Finally, the continual losses of men and equipment could also lead to discouragement among the allies of the Vietnamese, namely the Soviets and the Chinese, and they would eventually cut aid, seeing the conflict as fruitless. Once support was withdrawn, the Vietnamese communists would have no choice but to sue for peace.[73]

This attrition strategy wasn't new to the United States. In fact the United States had adopted an attrition strategy just over fifteen years earlier in Korea.

For the first eight months of the Korean War, Americans and their UN and South Korean allies fought against the North Korean forces over territory, and the battle lines constantly shifted. But starting in the spring of 1951, President Truman made the decision not to try and occupy North Korea; the American strategy had shifted to one of attrition. In December 1950, General Matthew B. Ridgway became the eighth Army commander and a significant influence in the military strategy in Korea. For Ridgway, the American strategy in Korea had to shift from annihilation to attrition. His goal was "not the seizure of territory but the maximum destruction of hostile persons and material at the minimum cost to our forces." For Ridgway, Korea would become a "meatgrinder, to chew up Chinese manpower at a rate that even the Chinese could not afford" and the job of the US military was "to kill Chinese . . . to deal out maximum damage at minimum cost."[74]

Ridgway followed through on his actions. His operations were even named to fit the tactic, such as Operation Killer and Operation Ripper. When given the opportunity to seize strategic areas, such as the capital, Seoul, Ridgway objected, instead choosing to focus on simply killing as many of the enemy as possible. Even after the army regained control of Seoul and the Chinese and North Koreans had been ejected from South Korea, Ridgway considered it only a "qualified success."[75]

In Korea, with attrition becoming the dominant strategy in the war, body counts became the metric for which the military would evaluate its progress. Officers and soldiers received medals and promotions based on their body counts. The reliance on the body counts wasn't necessarily due to a lack of geographic movement either, as the United States was advancing and pushing the enemy out of South Korea. Instead it was a tactic to impose as high a cost on the enemy as possible in order to bring them to the bargaining table.[76]

And so, as in Korea, a strategy of attrition was adopted in Vietnam.

An attrition strategy shifted the focus of the war. In a war of attrition, the focus is not on attacking strategic objectives, gaining territory, or even evaluating an enemy's political influence or strategy. As compared to a geographic war, the goal isn't to seize and hold territory. Rather it is to kill the enemy. A war of attrition requires an army to crack its enemy's morale, instilling attitudes of defeatism in its forces, and possibly shifting its leadership to more moderate positions. To do this, it has to inflict unrelenting punishment on its enemy.[77]

Military command was confident in the strategy and the ability to wear down the morale of the communists. According to Westmoreland, when the enemy "loses one man, it's equivalent to our loss of more than ten."[78] McNamara agreed. As he later said, "We tried to use body counts as a measurement to help us figure out what we should be doing in Vietnam to win the war while putting our troops at least risk."[79] McNamara shared Westmoreland's analysis; near the end of 1965 he estimated the chance of success at 50/50 for the war to be won by 1967.[80]

This strategy also provided an easy solution to the confusion and chaos of data in Vietnam. Rather than relying on hundreds of metrics to figure out how success was being measured, an attrition strategy was easily measured through just one: body counts, or how many enemies were killed. Body counts provided a simple, straightforward way to measure progress. Simply kill more Vietnamese and kill them more than they kill you. According to Douglas Kinnard, a brigadier general during the war who would later conduct surveys of his fellow generals after the war and become famous for his dissent against the war, "Some substitute had to be devised to measure progress in a guerrilla war,"[81] and that measure had become body counts. This strategy changed the focus (or lack of focus) of soldiers on the ground from a plethora of confusing metrics to two: body counts and kill ratios.

McNamara and Westmoreland mandated that body counts be tallied, both by American forces and the South Vietnamese army. Adapting to using body counts came fairly easily to the rank and file. Search-and-destroy missions were already part of the modus operandi for the army, so officers and soldiers didn't have to learn anything new. They just had to put more focus on counting the dead.

The emphasis on body counts made their way down through the ranks, being used to evaluate success at all levels of military command. Officers and units were given promotions, medals, and even time off for achieving high body counts and kill ratios. Few other metrics allowed officers to stand out among their peers (nobody was evaluated on the number of cakes of soap they delivered), and so body counts became the yardstick by which officers and units were evaluated. But like many metrics discussed in this book, body counts became distorted in ways that neither Westmoreland nor McNamara anticipated. They weren't immune to Goodhart's Law.

In many military units body counts became informally, but implicitly, tied to promotion and became the primary gauge of performance. One division commander, Julian J Ewell, was infamous for the pressure he put on his unit to report high body counts. He gave them quotas and threatened to replace his officers if those quotas were not met. Another division, the 25th infantry, held a "Best of the Pack" contest that awarded points for the highest body counts. The 503rd infantry division did the same, compiling a performance indicator chart that rewarded points to soldiers for body counts and captured prisoners.[82] Many others followed suit.

The pressure to achieve high body counts meant that military commanders often inflated their reported kills or counted dead civilians as enemy combatants. As Alain C. Enthoven and K. Wayne Smith wrote, "Padded claims kept everyone happy; there were no penalties for overstating enemy losses, but an understatement could lead to sharp questions as to why American casualties were so high with the results achieved."[83] Counts were especially inflated when a confrontation went in the enemy's favor. No commander wanted to admit losing more men than the

Vietcong or the North Vietnamese, so they just upped the enemy body count. Fabricated reporting was widespread. There was no system to prevent double counting of the dead. Some units claimed all the dead as combatants, some units double counted, others just made up the numbers. One commander was reported as instructing his soldiers, "If you come across dead bodies, you count the dead bodies. You re-sweep the area, recount the numbers, double it, call it a day."[84]

Counting bodies was further complicated by the fact that the communist fighters made it a point of emphasis to recover their dead from the battlefield, or at least hide them from the Americans and South Vietnamese. Counting enemy dead was also hard due to difficult terrain. On top of that, counting the dead from airstrikes or artillery strikes was near impossible. The emphasis on reporting kills may even have resulted in the killing of civilians in order to achieve higher counts, or at the very least, counting killed civilians as enemy combatants in order to increase the score. Operation Speedy Express in the Mekong Delta in 1969 was one operation where civilian deaths resulted from the pressure to achieve high body counts.[85]

There were also flaws in the ways in which body counts were classified. In 1966 MACV classified a "killed in action" as being "based on actual body count of males of fighting age and other, male or female, known to have carried arms."[86] This definition did not include probable kills while also counting all males of fighting age in the counts. By not including probable kills, MACV created a conundrum for its soldiers and officers. To get a confirmed kill, an actual body had to be counted. The result, in some instances, was that American soldiers risked their lives in order to physically observe and count a dead body. Strategically, the tactics made little sense. If a Vietnamese soldier was dead or alive, going to search for him didn't change that fact. It only put the lives of soldiers at risk. One general officer after the war recollected, "I shudder to think how many soldiers were killed on body-counting missions. What a waste."[87]

On the other hand, the pressure on achieving high body counts may have led officers to carry out unnecessary missions of questionable strategic importance, let alone being morally sound. There were numerous anecdotes of soldiers being wounded or killed on missions simply designed to increase the body count. Despite that, the emphasis on body counts was unrelenting.

The result was highly problematic and flawed data on body counts. Much anecdotal evidence claims that the official reporting on body counts was highly inaccurate. Thomas Thayer, in the OSA, noted in his reports that the data he was given were of poor quality.[88] Other intelligence staff filed numerous complaints that the military staff was inflating enemy losses, while underestimating enemy strength. Douglas Kinnard, a brigadier general during the war, conducted surveys of his fellow generals after the war. He asked them about the practice of counting the dead. Sixty-one percent agreed that the body counts were inflated. In the same survey, 55 percent of the generals responding felt the body counts were also misleading, as they didn't indicate progress.[89]

Despite the reservations of numerous analysts, lower ranking commanders, and civilian observers, Westmoreland and McNamara placed a shocking amount of faith in the accuracy of the body count statistics. Enthoven and Smith note that based on captured enemy documents, Westmoreland claimed to know the exact body count of casualties, on both sides of the conflict, to within a 1.8 percent accuracy. The OSA, interpreting the same documents, felt the body counts were understated by 30 percent![90] Officially, a few years after American withdrawal and the conclusion of the war, the Department of Defense reported 46,498 American dead, 220,357 South Vietnamese dead, and a toll of 950,785 communists killed in battle.[91] (Some say the losses for the Vietnamese were closer to 500,000 to 600,000). Officially, the ratio of Americans and South Vietnamese killed to communists was over 3.5 to 1. Just counting American casualties, it's over 20 to 1. It's hard to put a lot of faith in these numbers, especially the number of communists killed. The Vietnamese have never reported the numbers of combatants they estimate died in the war.

The reported body counts instilled a false sense of progress in the military command. As the number of kills continued to climb, McNamara and Westmoreland became more and more convinced that the war was going in their favor. From 1965 to 1968, the story told by body counts was one of increasing American effectiveness in the war. During that time, the kill ratio increased from about 2.0 to 6.0. McNamara and Westmoreland saw this as an indication that American troops were becoming more effective as the war progressed and that the Vietnamese fighting ability was declining. But nothing was further from the truth.

Westmoreland's strategy was based on the belief that somehow if some quantitative point of losses was reached, the North Vietnamese would lose the will to fight. It was as if there was some magic number, or magic ratio, that once crossed, the war would be over. The strategy assumed not only that the United States knew how the North Vietnamese were thinking, it also assumed the United States knew more about the North Vietnamese then they knew about themselves.[92]

Yet Westmoreland and McNamara were not complete fools to think the strategy could work. Attrition had worked in both World War I and World War II, where incredible loses had precipitated the surrender, or withdrawal of various sides of the war. And the amount of losses by the Vietnamese were considerable. For the Vietnamese, the war was one of the deadliest in modern history. With a population of nearly sixteen million North Vietnamese and fourteen million South Vietnamese, the total losses would be around 2.5 to 3 percent of the total population of the countries. Since 1816, no other country had lost that many people in war except in World War II, where the Soviet Union and Germany each lost around 4.4 percent of the population, or World War I where Germany lost 2.7 percent of its population, France lost 3.3 percent of its population, and Romania lost 4.7 percent.[93] Despite these staggering losses, the communists' morale never seemed to deteriorate. Defeatist factions never arose in North Vietnam, or among the Vietcong.

The North Vietnamese command, including Ho Chi Minh and Vo Nguyen Giap, had surprisingly little concern with the level of casualties they suffered. The staggering amount of losses never seemed to deter them from their belief in victory. Ho Chi Minh was single-minded in his commitment to victory. For him, it was an existential war, despite American thoughts to the contrary.

What is incredible to understand in retrospect is that despite suffering some of the heaviest losses in military history, the Vietnamese leadership was undeterred. Ho Chi Minh once said, "You can kill ten of my men for every one I kill of yours, but even at those odds, you will lose and I will win."[94] Vo Nguyen Giap took an almost nihilistic perspective on the death of his men: "Every minute, hundreds of thousands of people die on this earth. The life or death of a hundred, a thousand, tens of thousands of human beings, even our companions, means little . . . Westmoreland was wrong to count on his superior firepower to grind us down."[95] Giap was shockingly unphased by losses. These are not the words of men who are looking to save face or fighting a war of convenience. These are men who are willing to fight to the ultimate end. Ho Chi Minh claimed in 1965 that they were prepared to fight for "five, ten, twenty-five years, even longer."[96]

The intense conviction for victory wasn't just a mindset shared by Minh and Giap. That same intensity was ingrained in the rank and file of the communist forces. Konrad Kellen, a World War I psychological warfare officer, was amazed at the resolve of the North Vietnamese and Vietcong soldiers. Conducting extensive interviews with prisoners, Kellen described their resolve as "incredible" and said they had "apparently inexhaustible courage and morale."[97] Their commitment to the war was unshakeable despite being informed repeatedly that the war would be long and fierce.

This resolve was evident in the battles that the Vietnamese fought and how they viewed the war. In most battles, the communists came out on the losing end. What is incredible about the Tet offensive, one of the battles cited as a major turning point in the war, was that the Vietnamese lost. Badly. Estimates of Vietnamese losses during that operation suggest that nearly thirty thousand men lost their lives, with very little American casualties on the other side. In another operation, the Easter Offensive of 1972, near the end of the war, the casualty estimates for the communist forces was between fifty thousand and seventy-five thousand![98]

Oddly, however, Kellen found that the Vietnamese were not particularly committed to Communism. Rather, they were committed to their cause to not lose the war and a deep, personal hatred of the United States, a hatred more intense that the Nazi's felt toward the Russians in World War II. Kinnard described the Vietnamese as "the best enemy we have faced in our history."[99]

What the communists likely understood was that the war was definitely not an existential war for the Americans. They witnessed a gradual loss of American resolve, saw the opposition to the war growing back home on American soil, and decided that they could outlast the Americans. American soldiers were sent far from home, sitting in hot jungles among a population they did not know, speaking a language they did not understand for a global political strategy that they didn't comprehend or didn't care about. The Vietnamese, by contrast, were fighting in their home country, against the latest in a long line of Imperial occupiers.

For the Vietnamese, it was a war of liberation. They fought it as such. Giap's strategy in the war was to inflict as many casualties on the Americans as possible, with almost no regard for minimizing his forces' own losses. In contrast to the Americans, Giap didn't care as much about kill ratios; he was focused on making the Americans suffer. P. J. McGarvey, author of *Visions of Victory*, said of Giap: "His is not an army that sends coffins north; it is by the traffic in homebound American coffins that Giap measures his success."[100] In a way, Westmoreland and McNamara had one thing right about the war: They were fighting a war of attrition. They just didn't know it was them who would lose it.

‖‖‖‖‖‖‖‖‖

If this book were a ranking of the worst failures of metrics, the American experience in Vietnam would be in the top spot. In the beginning of the war, under the command of General Harkins, American strategy suffered from a lack of focus. In this environment metrics were used to mask the lack of a comprehensive approach to the war. As Fred C. Ikle observed, the military was so wrapped up in the day-to-day it had trouble seeing the big picture.[101] Military leaders were overwhelmed with everyday minutiae, with little background or context to understand any of it. Not knowing how to fight the war, the military command tried to make up for their lack of focus by simply overwhelming themselves with data.

Surveys after the war would find that only 29 percent of officers believed that their objectives were clear or understandable. Ninety-one percent felt that if the war was to be fought again, they would choose "defining the objectives" as the key recommendation. Only 2 percent believed that the systems used to measure the war were valid.[102] During the war, no one seemed to have a clear idea of what the end state of the war was supposed to look like.

In the absence of a clear strategy and clear assessment of goals, policy makers will micromanage, and they did so in Vietnam. The sheer volume of data collected and analyzed doesn't speak to a rigorous assessment and clear direction for the war, rather it was a result of a complete lack of direction and the chaos that resulted. The reporting and analysis in Vietnam had the appearance of incredible accuracy and rigor, as reports were presented in heavily quantitative formats, but there were huge gaps not only in the accuracy of the data, but also their usefulness. What value someone would obtain from knowing how many cakes of soap were distributed to Vietnamese villagers is anyone's guess.

The avalanche of data also reinforced the lack of strategy. How does a policy maker make any sense of the direction of progress or decide on a strategy when he or she is faced with thousands of pages of numbers, completely decontextualized from anything at all? In counterinsurgencies, as with any complex situation, choosing what not to count is just as important as choosing what to count. That message wasn't heard in the first phase of Vietnam.

In the second phase of the conflict, when General Westmoreland took over the command and shifted the strategy to a war of attrition, the pendulum had swung entirely in the opposite direction. Now the army had a singular focus, but one that was misguided. Metrics played a role, this time as a tool used to ignore the fundamental flaws of the attrition strategy. Throughout the latter part of the war, McNamara and Westmoreland would point to increasing body counts and kill ratios as evidence of success in the war. The assumptions behind the strategy were never really considered or challenged. Instead the numbers kept coming in, the reports kept being written, and the narrative of the Americans winning the war kept being told.

But throughout the war, almost no attempt was made to really understand the root causes of the insurgency, the intentions, values, and aspirations of the population, or whether the assumptions the United States' strategies were based on were true. There was almost no effort to integrate the qualitative analysis of hundreds of civilian advisors working in Vietnam into the OSA analyses. The advice of people such as Lansdale, who stressed that understanding the political motivations of the population were instrumental to understanding the war, went ignored. Instead the Americans relied on a very centralized, quantitative analysis of the war.

While some, such as Thomas Thayer, had serious reservations about the quality or accuracy of the data being reported, many in the command put almost religious conviction into the numbers. While it is convenient to assess briefings and executive summaries as providing an almost mathematical path to success, in war, as in many other things, that path isn't always clear, and it isn't always quantifiable. Simple and concise assessments of the war should have been treated with considerable caution. As Ben Connable described, in war, overly aggressive drives to reduce uncertainty by collecting more data can be counterproductive, as precise and accurate data are not always available or reasonably collected.[103]

Vietnam was perhaps the most complex war the United States ever fought. They were battling a conventional army, the North Vietnamese, who were supported by powerful allies (the Chinese and the Soviets), and at the same time were fighting a powerful insurgency, consisting of tens, if not hundreds, of thousands of experienced combatants. They were trying to prop up an ally that was horribly corrupt and incredibly inept, while trying to gain the trust of a local population whose country had been fighting foreign occupation for decades. All the while they were dealing with the morale of the troops on the ground and an increasing political resistance at home.

Faced with an incredibly complex political, geographic, cultural, and social condition, the military command chose to turn to the familiar and comfortable world of numbers. And by doing so they failed to understand the deeper motivations behind the war. The emphasis on data in Vietnam wasn't a sophisticated or rigorous approach to understanding the war, it was a way to avoid dealing with the complexities of the situation. McNamara believed that he could bend the world to fit his analysis, refusing to accept that some things defy quantification. He believed that numbers could make sense of any situation.

Like so many managers who overemphasize numbers and neglect everything else in their jobs, McNamara used data to mask the fact he couldn't comprehend the nature of the conflict, the psychology and motivations of the Vietnamese, or the complex political, cultural, and sociological factors influencing the war. Data analysis wasn't a tool to improve understanding, it was a tool to disguise a lack of understanding.

Body counts became a cop-out, a crutch to lean on when faced with the complex realities of the war.

It is easy to start to believe that the numbers are real. If we are collecting the data, that data must be relevant. How can it not be? If we can measure it, how can it not be the truth? Numbers mean that we know something for certain, and if we know something for certain, then it is true. And if things that are true are things we can put numbers to, then they must be the only things that are true. It is easy to fall into the trap that it is the numbers that matter, and nothing else. It is easy to believe that numbers are the only thing that can make sense of the world. Sometimes metrics aren't a way to shine light on an issue. Like the drunk in the lamppost story, metrics are often an excuse to avoid looking in the right places. Sometimes metrics can be an excuse to hide from the truth. Bernard Fall was an Austrian Jew whose family had fled to France during World War II. He became a war correspondent for the French in the first Indochina War and acted as a war correspondent in Vietnam on five different tours during the American involvement there. While critical of the Diem regime, he was supportive of the American involvement, believing it could stop the communists from controlling the country. He died from a bouncing betty land mine in 1967. Before his death, he commented on the use of body counts in the war. For him, body counts were used "simply because the essential political target is too elusive for us, or worse, because we do not understand its importance."[104] He was right.

CHAPTER 8

NOT EVERYTHING THAT COUNTS CAN BE COUNTED

Measuring What Matters

O n June 12, 1996, a crowd of Levi Strauss employees waited in San Francisco for an announcement from their CEO, Bob Haas. Levi's workers in Britain were taken to the cinema to watch the announcement on video. Standing before the crowd Haas announced a new incentive plan for the company. Every employee, all thirty-seven thousand of them, from the executive team down to the person operating the sewing machines, would receive an entire year's salary as a bonus.[1] The employees were thrilled. Other locations held celebratory barbeques and satellite parties. Bob Haas saw the bonus as an incentive plan for innovation at the firm that would encourage employees toward "continued striving for new standards of excellence." The total bonus was estimated to be worth nearly 750 million dollars.[2] There was one catch, however. The employees had to have been working at Levi's at least three years from the date of the announcement, and the company had to reach a goal of $7.6 billion in revenue.[3]

The next year, things went south. Sales, achieving an all-time high at $7.1 billion in 1996, started falling. On November 3, 1997, the company announced it was closing eleven plants and laying off over six thousand workers.[4] Market share among the key demographic of male teenagers dropped by half. In the next two years, Levi's would plan on closing twenty-nine factories in North America and Europe, eliminating over sixteen thousand jobs. Sales in 1998 dropped 13 percent, to less than 6 billion dollars, far below the 7.6 billion dollar goal for the bonuses.[5]

There were a lot of reasons for the drop in sales. Competition from other emerging brands like the Gap, Sears, and J.C. Penny on the low end of the market and Tommy Hilfiger and Calvin Klein on the high end were taking market share from the clothing company. Others blamed the lack of innovation and ability to keep up with trends. The Levi's 501s pant legs were too narrow for kids in the 1990s. They tried to be everything to everyone and lost their competitive advantage at what they did well: selling jeans to make people look cool.[6] The company additionally had high manufacturing costs compared to their competitors, as Levi's continued to make its jeans in the United States.[7]

Apart from the emerging competition from brands like Tommy Hilfiger and high manufacturing costs from plants in the United States, Levi's had another thing working against it: its incentive plan. Initially the plan was almost unbelievable. Employees were overjoyed that they could receive a full year's salary as bonus pay. It was too good to be true. Morale skyrocketed.

Levi's employees were incredibly proud to work at the company. But when the sales numbers for 1997 started coming in, and the first plant closures and layoffs began, the tide turned.

What started out as a morale booster for the company quickly became the opposite. The bonus plan, and its promises of huge bonuses, was quickly viewed as out of reach and entirely unobtainable. Morale was sapped, and employees began to feel hopeless. The bonuses would never be achieved given that revenues were not only not increasing, they were dropping—and fast.

As early as 1997, employees saw the writing on the wall: There was no way they would ever reach the 7.6 billion dollar goal. In 1999, the year of the goal the bonus was based on, revenue fell to 5.1 billion dollars, far short of the 7.6 billion dollar goal.[8] In 2000, 344 million dollars of the planned bonus had to be put back into the company instead of being used to pay staff.[9]

Contrary to what Hollywood movies may tell you, people generally are not motivated by impossible odds. When things look truly desperate, most people don't respond with one final, incredible effort. More often, they give up and resign themselves to the situation they are in. People can be demotivated with metrics because the goals are just out of reach. Organizational psychologists call this expectancy theory.[10] The theory, put in the simplest of terms, says that your motivation is based on how reasonably you can expect to meet your goal. You can find motivation to, for instance, do an extra four laps after you complete your swim. You can push yourself that last bit up the mountain to reach the summit or work an extra fifteen minutes each day in order to get a day off later in the month. But if you were asked to run the Marathon des Sables, a six-day, 156-mile ultramarathon through the Sahara desert, you likely wouldn't find the motivation to do so. We can be motivated for things that are within our reach, but things that are out of what we can reasonably expect to accomplish are simply daunting.

The second part of this theory is called instrumentality. This is the understanding that you have the tools to actually succeed in your goals, and that your efforts will result in the desired outcome. For example, you can easily push yourself to complete a run, but that same effort won't necessarily lead to results if you are trying to complete a maze. The effort doesn't match the result.

In roles where people undertake multifaceted tasks in complex systems that require cooperation with numerous other people, not just within their organization, but outside as well, metrics can in fact be demotivating. In large team environments, an individual's efforts may not result in improved performance of the team, as there are multiple other factors (and people) upon which success depends. When outcomes are beyond someone's ability to influence them, measuring people on those outcomes can be incredibly frustrating.

This is what happened at Levi's. The bonus plan, while motivating at first, soon was seen as unachievable and started having the opposite effect. Employees became discouraged, bitter, and hopeless. How would an employee who works on a factory floor work harder to make up for a sales loss in the billions? Would a sales manager in the United Kingdom really feel that if she ran her store better, it would improve the sales targets of a multinational company? The employees were not motivated to innovate, instead they resigned themselves to a situation they felt beyond their control.

In 1975 Steven Kerr, a professor of management, wrote an article with the straightforward title "On the folly of rewarding A, while hoping for B."[11] In the article Kerr outlined instances where organizations had rewarded one type of behavior, while hoping for another. The article became a classic in management and psychology courses, and still serves as an example of how metrics can be poorly designed. For example, Kerr noted that doctors, not being perfect, will sometimes err in their diagnosis, and they could err in two ways. The first (called a type 1 error) is where a doctor gives a diagnosis, but the patient is actually healthy. The second (called a type 2 error) is where a doctor fails to diagnose a sick patient, telling him he is healthy. Both have downsides. In the first, the doctor can cause needless anxiety and use up limited resources treating a patient who has nothing wrong with her. In the second, the sick patient may continue to suffer or worse, die, because the physician didn't properly diagnose the ailment. But by and large, doctors commit the type 1 errors far more often than type 2 errors, meaning that a lot of people are diagnosed with conditions they do not have. Why? Because the punishments for making a type 2 error are large—not only does the doctor feel immense guilt, but malpractice lawsuits can be career-ending. So doctors err on the side of caution. The incentive (or rather disincentive) drives the behavior.

In sports, Kerr noted that coaches want to instill values of teamwork, a proper attitude, and a cooperative spirit. Yet, players are assessed based on their individual stats—their points, rebounds, and steals—and not on the team's efforts. So players think of themselves first. In business, Kerr noted a practice where one company tracked the number of "times" an employee was absent from work, rather than the number of "days" they were absent, so a ten-day absence was counted the same as a one-day absence. Consequently, employees, once they had gotten close to their maximum number of sick "instances," would simply extend their time off as long as they could, knowing the length of their absence didn't matter.

Kerr's article was a lesson in misplaced rewards. If you reward the wrong thing, you get the wrong thing. So if we just measured the right thing, we would get the right thing, right? Performance metrics are built on that very basic premise: If you measure someone on something and give him or her an incentive to perform based on that metric, then his or her performance will improve. It sounds simple enough. If I pay you based on how quickly you stack a pile of rocks, you will stack rocks as quickly as you can. The belief is that the same goes for selling a product, providing better healthcare, teaching children, or improving productivity. Conventional business practice and management is in large part based on the idea that incentives motivate people. Managers have made careers out of claiming to improve performance simply by choosing the right metrics and creating the right incentives. The refrain by Peter Drucker is popular in every field of business and management: "If you can't measure it, you can't manage it." But what if that isn't the case? What if, instead of motivating behavior, metrics can in fact be demotivating? What if, in fact, by measuring something, you can no longer manage it? What if, by rewarding A, you don't actually get A? This isn't just Goodhart's Law again. This is different. Goodhart's Law deals with how people learn to game a system once a measure becomes a metric. This is a fundamentally different question: Do metrics motivate people?

This issue is at the very heart of performance management and the raison d'être for nearly every metric we use. The assumption is that people respond to incentives. There are numerous examples of instances where employees have responded to financial incentives. One economist showed that at a windshield installation company, when employees were paid based on the number of windshields they installed, rather than paid a set salary, they installed more windshields. In fact the increase in productivity was nearly 50 percent almost immediately.[12] But there are several cases that demonstrate just the opposite.

▌▌▌▌▌▌▌▌▌▌

In 1970 Edward Deci, a psychology professor at the University of Rochester, conducted an unusual experiment.[13] He, with the help of some other psychologists, recruited a group of psychology students for the experiment. (Who else to conduct experiments on other than students? I mean, their participation is free.). Each participant sat down at a table with a researcher and was given a puzzle. The puzzle was called Soma, a game developed and sold by Parker Brothers. Soma contained seven different blocks made up of three or four one-inch-by-one-inch cubes arranged in various shapes. The object of the game was to build different configurations of 3D shapes shown on pieces of paper using the blocks. It is basically 3D Tetris. Each session lasted an hour and the students were given thirteen minutes to complete each puzzle. The students did this session three separate times.

The manipulation in the experiment was that during the second of the three sessions, half of the students were given a small sum (one dollar) for each puzzle they solved under the thirteen-minute time mark, providing them an incentive to do the puzzles better. For the third session, none of the students were paid for each puzzle they correctly solved, being told there was not enough money left to reward the students. Like many well-designed psychology experiments, what Edward Deci was trying to figure out wasn't what the participants thought, or were told, they were being tested on. The participants were told, and therefore believed, they were being tested on how quickly they solved the puzzles. But Deci didn't care how quickly the students were completing the puzzles, he was looking for something else.

Psychologists are incredibly creative at conducting experiments that seem to be about one thing but are really about another. In psychology experiments, nothing is random—every event, environmental condition, or coincidence is carefully planned and orchestrated. In one famous experiment, John Bargh and his colleagues at New York University had students assemble sentences using a set of five words. They were given the words out of order and had to make coherent sentences with them. For the experiment half of the students were provided scrambled sentences containing words we normally associate with the elderly, such as *Florida, forgetful, bald, gray*, or *wrinkle*; the other half were given sentences with no such association. The experiment wasn't about how quickly the students completed the sentences. Rather, after completing the task, the students were asked to walk down a hallway to another room to complete another task. The walk down the hall is what the experiment was about. During their walk, researchers timed how quickly the students got from one room to another. Bargh wanted to see if "priming" students by exposing them to words associated with the elderly, it would affect the pace at which they walked from one room to another. It did. Significantly.[14]

In Deci's experiment, the trick came halfway through the session. After the participant attempted two puzzles, the researcher observing the experiment told the participant that the researcher had to go to another room on a made-up pretext (the researcher said she had to go enter data into a computer in order to obtain the next two puzzles). While the researcher was out of the room (for exactly eight minutes), the participant was left alone at the table. The pieces of the puzzle were left on the table, as well as some configurations to work on and some magazines. What Deci was trying to find out was how much the participants kept playing with the puzzle while the researcher was gone. Deci didn't care how quickly the participants completed the puzzles, he wanted to know what they did when they were left alone, and how interested in the puzzle they were. His team recorded how much time each participant spent playing with the game while the researcher was away as a measure of the participant's inherent motivation for playing the game. The results were interesting.

Unsurprisingly, the participants who were paid for each puzzle they played, spent a lot of time working on the puzzle when the researcher was gone during the second session, probably trying to get some extra practice in to improve their chances of successfully completing the puzzles in order to get rewards. But that wasn't what Deci was measuring either. He wanted to know how much time the participants spent playing the game in the third session, when they were told they were not going to be paid for their performance. What Deci was testing was motivation. More specifically, he was testing whether paying students for the task previously undermined their motivation.

Playing the game when the researcher left the room was that measure of motivation. The longer the person played with the game, the more interested in the challenge they were. They were not doing it for a reward, gain, or any social status; for all they knew they were alone in the room. Their motivation for playing the game was purely intrinsic. What Deci wanted to know was whether providing an external reward, the small sum given for each successful puzzle solved, would change the participants' intrinsic interest in the game.

It was the third session that was the one that really mattered. Now that they knew they weren't being rewarded for doing the puzzle, would the participants who had been paid still be as interested in playing the game? The answer was no. After being told they would no longer be paid for completing puzzles, the participants lost interest in the game. They spent less time in the last session playing with the game when left alone than they did in the first session (when they were not paid and not told they would be paid). Those students who were never paid, on the contrary, spent more time playing the game when left alone than they did at the beginning.

What Deci discovered is that not only are intrinsic motivation and extrinsic motivation different things, but that by introducing one, it undermined the other. Once they were paid to do the puzzle, the participants lost their interest in it. Somehow, when money was introduced into the picture, things changed. The puzzles weren't fun and interesting to do, completing them was now a goal to achieve for a reward, and once that reward was taken away, the motivation to do the puzzles was gone.

A similar experiment was conducted a few years later by two psychology professors from Stanford, Mark R. Lepper and David Greene.[15] The two set up an experiment in the nursery school on the campus of Stanford University. Researchers set up a drawing activity in the nursery school. Prior to starting the experiment, the researchers observed which children liked to play with the drawing activity during playtime. The activity was then removed from the classroom during playtime, but the children who were interested in the activity were given the opportunity to do the drawing activity in another room away from the classroom, where they could do the activity by themselves.

Once there, the researchers would do one of three things: They would tell the children they would get a "good player award" with a gold seal and red ribbon if they did the activity; they would not tell the children they were getting the award beforehand, but would give it to them after the activity; or they would not give the children any reward and just allow them to do the activity by themselves.

Then, two weeks after they had conducted the three different reward scenarios with the children, they put the drawing activity back into the classroom during playtime. What they observed was that the children who were not rewarded during the individual activity went right back to the drawing activity. But the children who were given the rewards for the activity in the individual session showed almost no interest in the activity anymore. What the psychologists had discovered was that by introducing a reward, they had undermined the children's intrinsic motivation to do the activity. Play had become work.

In another experiment, researchers observed what happened in a laundry plant when a reward system for attendance was implemented. At the plant management noticed that a small segment of their employees was arriving late, or not showing up without prior notice more often than others. Their punctuality and attendance were hurting productivity.

Management decided to implement an attendance reward system in order to address the issue. Every employee was eligible. If the employees had perfect attendance in a month (no unexcused absences or late arrivals during the month), they were recognized by the company, and one was randomly selected to win a seventy-five-dollar gift certificate. The program lasted ten months.[16]

It seemed like a good idea. An incentive program couldn't hurt, and it would likely encourage those problem employees to improve their attendance in order to get the prize. The cost of the program wasn't that high, other than administrative time used to implement it; the only cost was the seventy-five dollars per month, a pretty small sum. As predicted, the researchers found that attendance in the plant among those with previously poor attendance, the ones who management felt were having a negative impact on productivity, did in fact increase. They had fewer unexcused absences and were late less. From that perspective, the program worked. The late employees had improved their performance in response to the program's incentives.

But what happened to the other employees was quite surprising. For those employees who were normally good at coming to work on time and not missing work unexpectedly, their behavior changed in an unexpected way. First, researchers found that once one of the previously good attendance employees was late one time in a month, and thus no longer eligible for the reward, they actually increased the amount of times they were late. In fact, once an employee was late just once, they were then 5.5 times more likely to be late for a second time that month compared to the situation when the incentive system didn't exist. What happened was similar to the Soma puzzle and nursery art activity experiments. By creating an external reward for their behavior, the laundry plant managers had undermined the intrinsic motivation for workers to come to work on time and not miss work unannounced. Essentially, the external motivation of the competition and the rewards had completely replaced the previous motivations for people to come to work on time. Now that their intrinsic reasons were undermined, those employees found that once they were ineligible for the reward, they had lost the motivation to come to work on time.

But what was even more interesting with this study, and completely unanticipated by management (but predicted by the psychologists), was that those employees who had great attendance records before the experiment, who were rarely late, actually saw a decline in performance in other parts of their job apart from attendance. In the experiment the researchers were not just measuring tardiness and absenteeism, they also measured employees on their productivity in various tasks in the plant such as sorting laundry, pressing uniforms, and the like. For those employees who were normally on time, the award program actually resulted in their productivity dropping by 9 percent. What was happening?

Part of it was that employees who were intrinsically motivated to do other parts of their job well saw the attendance reward system as a kind of underappreciation of their behavior. How was it fair that their performance in other tasks, such as sorting, ironing, cleaning, and so on, was not rewarded and only attendance was? And if the point of showing up on time was for the purpose of getting an award, why bother with any other reason for being on time? Once you are ineligible for the reward, there is no longer a reason to be punctual. The experiment found that external rewards for behavior not only undermined intrinsic motivation for a specific task, it undermined motivation for a whole host of other activities at work.

This introduces a whole new level of risk that external rewards and metrics can bring. Not only can an external reward undermine the specific behavior being rewarded, it can have knock-off effects that can spread throughout a network of related activities and behaviors. How far can the effects go?

||||||||||

I want you to think about any activity you do outside of work that you enjoy doing but requires effort or skill. Maybe it is doing puzzles, painting, running marathons, climbing mountains, or building furniture. Now I want you to think about how you would respond if I offered you a small amount of money, say ten dollars for each "task" you completed in that activity. For each puzzle you completed, each painting you completed, each marathon you ran, each mountain you climbed, or each chair you built, you would get ten dollars for it. Now ask yourself, would you enjoy the activity as much as you did before?

Logically, the answer is that it shouldn't change your enjoyment much, maybe even increase it slightly. Not only do you get to do your favorite activity, but now you get a little bonus cash for doing it. Sounds like a win-win, right? But we all know that isn't the case. If I were paid ten dollars each time I hiked up a mountain, something about the experience would change. In a way, the activity, and my motivation for doing it, would be tainted. I wouldn't think about the activity as something I do for enjoyment, it would become something I do to get ten dollars. And I can think of a lot of ways to make ten dollars that are a lot easier than hiking up a mountain. Just like the children in the Stanford nursery experiment, or the Soma puzzle experiment, the reward somehow taints my enjoyment of the activity.

These experiments highlight a tension that occurs not only in our leisure activities, but in our work lives as well: the difference between intrinsic and extrinsic motivation. Through these experiments (and many, many others done in between and since these studies were published), psychologists, economists, and others have gained a better understanding of just how our motivation works. Intrinsic motivation is a difficult thing to measure, let alone understand what causes it. But the studies discussed above do show one thing: Intrinsic motivation can be undermined by rewards, by extrinsic motivation. There are two ways someone can be motivated, but the two cannot mix. Only one can exist for any one particular activity. First, with Deci's study, the researchers learned that monetary rewards can undermine the intrinsic motivation for a task. This is called motivation crowding. With Lepper and Greene's study, they saw that the rewards that undermine motivation can also be social. Finally, with the laundry study, external rewards cannot only undermine the motivation for a particular task, it can also undermine the motivation for other aspects of a job unrelated to the task being rewarded. Contrary to the conventional wisdom that creating rewards for accomplishment of goals or the completion of tasks will motivate people, these studies show that there are situations where rewards act in the opposite way: They demotivate people.

Why do people climb mountains? There is no extrinsic reward for doing so (at least for the vast majority of people who climb mountains). People are not paid to do it. While others may be impressed by being able to climb mountains, most mountain climbers do not do it to be recognized by others. Nor is the experience particularly enjoyable in itself. Your legs hurt, and you find yourself short of breath very often (maybe that is just me). Weather can be particularly nasty. So why do people climb mountains? Because it gives them a sense of accomplishment. People are intrinsically motivated for a variety of reasons: being able to exercise creativity, fulfilling a sense of duty, feeling a part of making a change, accomplishing a sense of purpose, achieving intellectual stimulation, succeeding in meeting a challenge, and so on. However, metrics, by their nature, often deal only with extrinsic motivation. While people may use metrics to help themselves achieve intrinsic goals, the metrics are only a means and not an end.

This phenomenon is especially true in the public sector. Public sector workers tend to have a passion and idealism for the work they do:

protecting the environment, helping the poor, fighting crime, caring for the sick, teaching youth, and others.[17] Yet when consultants, government officials, or members of the public look for ways to improve performance in the public sector, they often suggest introducing tools such as accountability, performance rewards, or a heavy reliance on metrics. However, what these recommendations fail to recognize is that much of what public sector employees do requires high levels of intrinsic motivation to succeed, because much of what public sector employees do is not easily measurable.

By introducing such tactics, management runs the risk of undermining employees' motivation, turning their objective at work from their passion into a numbers game.

As Erik Canton notes, most jobs involve both observable and unobservable tasks.[18] Your boss cannot follow you around all the time, and unless your workplace is laden with cameras, most of what you do at work isn't recorded. If you are a worker on an assembly line, your activity is easier to monitor. But in large, complex, multitask environments, it is incredibly hard to measure the contributions an employee makes. This is very much like the principal/agent problem from chapter 4. Employers cannot know everything their employees are doing all the time, yet they want the employees' interests to be aligned with the company's. This creates a conundrum for employers.

Many, mistakenly, try and ensure their employees' efforts match the company's interest by focusing on, and measuring, observable behavior. But unobservable tasks rely on employees to be intrinsically motivated to accomplish them. Since it is difficult for a manager to observe aspects of work such as cooperation, quality control, customer service, loyalty, guarding public trust, delivering public goods, protecting the environment, reducing risks for citizens, and so on, they have to rely on trust to ensure these behaviors are being carried out. Yet, when employers start measuring and rewarding observable behavior, they run the risk of shifting their employees' focus on to what is measured and rewarded and discard their motivations to undertake those things that are not easily observed.

Take for instance teaching or nursing. Neither profession is particularly well paid, and both involve tremendous amounts of stress. If someone chooses to work in one of the busiest emergency rooms in the nation, dealing with multiple traumas, belligerent patients, difficult administrators, and the stresses that come with a fast-paced and high-stakes environment, he or she probably already has all the motivation needed. But tell these workers that you will start tracking them on their performance, and you shift that focus. The attention they give to patients, the positive work environment they build, and the care they give to their work will soon be lost to focus on whatever they are measured on. The greater the incentive or disincentives you place on these observable and measurable aspects of the work, the more they will shift away from the unmeasurable and unobservable aspects of work.

It isn't just the public sector where people are intrinsically motivated in their jobs. Those who work in the private sector are not motivated solely by financial incentives. People in the private sector may take on jobs in order to exercise their creative talents, make a difference in the world, feel a sense of accomplishment by taking on difficult tasks, or simply improve customers' experiences. These people are not motivated to do these things because they are paid to do it. Some professions, such as journalism, are horrendously underpaid but attract some of the brightest minds and motivated people there are. Yet, just like in the public sector, measuring and rewarding purely observable behavior in these organizations can similarly undermine their motivation.

When people motivated by the higher purposes of intrinsic motivation are placed in an environment where their value is reduced to a simplistic performance metric, they resist. They feel that their motivations are betrayed, their contribution is belittled, and their efforts are misplaced. Most important, once financial incentives are introduced that undermine intrinsic motivation, it is nearly impossible to get that motivation back. Removing the incentives doesn't seem to work in bringing things back to normal.[19] Once it is gone, it is gone. As Barry Schwartz says, "When you rely on incentives, you undermine virtues. Then when you discover that you actually need people who want to do the right thing, those people don't exist."[20]

Performance metrics can undermine everything that motivates people. When you incentivize a teacher only to ensure their students score high on the final test, and don't value the other contributions they make in the school, you undermine their purpose for being a teacher. Soon you get teachers who only care about test scores and not about any other reason they became a teacher in the first place. By trying to make the important parts of our lives countable, we can lose what really counts.

▌▌▌▌▌▌▌▌▌▌

In 2002, researchers Dan Ariely, Uri Gneezy, George Loewenstein, and Nina Mazar conducted an interesting experiment in a rural village in India. Some local research assistants from a nearby college were hired and sent out to the village. The research assistants told the villagers that they would pay them to play some games.[21]

The games were fairly simple, with varying degrees of difficulty, so a person could do poorly, decent, or excellent at each game. One game involved observing a sequence of different-colored lights and then trying to remember and repeating them back. Another game involved putting specially cut metal pieces into a wooden frame, which had to be done in a particular way in order for everything to fit; it required some creative thinking. Other games involved things as simple as throwing a ball onto a makeshift dart board, or trying to roll a ball upward by pushing together or pulling apart two rods.

The villagers were randomly assigned different levels of incentives if they did better on each of the games. If they did the games well (like remembering six consecutive lights in the light game), they would get half of the reward; if they did exceptionally well (remembering eight lights, for example), they would get the full reward; and if they did poorly on any one game, they wouldn't get the reward. The rewards varied from four rupees to four hundred rupees for each game. These were considerable rewards. Four hundred rupees was nearly an average month's spending for rural India! Some villagers were playing for fairly low stakes, while others were playing for very high ones. If the high-reward villagers performed excellent at every game, they could receive almost half a year's salary!

What is incredible about the experiment was that the highest-paid group—the group that could have won half a year's salary by excelling at all the games—didn't do any better than the groups that were rewarded less. In fact, the highest-rewarded group did worse than the lower-paid groups. The financial incentives offered in fact led to a decrease in performance. This isn't expectancy theory; all the players have the ability to do well, or not, on all the games. They have the tools to do so, and remembering a sequence of eight lights isn't an unreasonable goal to set. Nor is motivation crowding playing a factor here. The games are entirely independent of everything else in the villagers' life. Their motivation to do well on the game isn't influenced by their motivation in other things. This is truly a completely independent game. If they do well, they get rewards, potentially massive ones. So why are those with the potential to win the greatest rewards doing so poorly?

The researchers suggested that the highest-paid group was simply choking under the pressure. With such high stakes, perhaps the villagers were focusing too much, thus disrupting processes that are better done automatically. (Have you ever tried thinking about swinging a golf club, shooting a basketball, or throwing a ball with intent? It tends not to work out so well.) Or perhaps the villagers were so focused on the thought of receiving half a year's worth of pay that they were distracted from the task at hand. Others have found the same thing. Sometimes incentives, especially large ones, when paired with relatively easy tasks can have a detrimental effect on performance. Sometimes too much motivation can rattle us.

||||||||||

Imagine I asked you if you could help me shovel my sidewalk after a large snowstorm. Would you do it? Well, since you don't know me, you probably wouldn't (if you lived in a climate where it rarely snows, you probably wouldn't want to do it no matter what!). Now imagine if I were to pay you one hundred dollars to shovel my sidewalk. You are probably more likely to do it. If I paid you one thousand dollars to do it, you would be even more likely to do it. If I paid you a million dollars to do it, almost no one would refuse my offer. Clearly, the more I pay you, the greater the likelihood of you shoveling my sidewalk.

Now imagine a good friend or family member asks for your help shoveling his or her walk. Would you do it? If you are a decent person, you would probably help out. Now imagine this person offered you five dollars to shovel the walk. According to the concept in the paragraph above, the more money offered, the more likely you are to shovel the sidewalk. Clearly, five dollars is more than nothing, so the extra money should increase the chances of you wanting to shovel the walk. But that doesn't work in this case. Most of you felt a sudden aversion to shoveling the sidewalk once the money was offered. Why?

This is what behavioral economist Dan Ariely describes as social versus market norms.[22] When I ask you to help shovel my sidewalk as a friend, that is a social norm. You are going to help based on your relationship with me, how close you feel to me, and how much you value our relationship. When I offer you money, that is a market norm. You will only shovel the sidewalk based on your evaluation of whether the money is worth your time and effort. The important thing to note about social and market norms, just like intrinsic and extrinsic motivation, is that they don't mix. Once you introduce money into a social transaction, it ceases to be a social transaction and becomes a market transaction. That is what happened in the example when the friend or relative offered to pay you five dollars to help shovel his or her walk. That five dollars wasn't an additional reason to help shovel the walk in addition to the reasons of loyalty, altruism, and friendship, it was an entirely different proposition altogether.

Ariely points out several other examples of how social norms and market norms conflict. In one example, lawyers were given the opportunity to provide legal aid to poor elderly people. At first they were offered thirty dollars to help the seniors, a scenario which most lawyers balked at and refused to take on. Then they were offered to provide the aid, but this time for free. Nearly all of them agreed.[23] When organizations replace one aspect of a social transaction with market transaction, they may soon find that all their social transactions have been replaced by market transactions. When an employee asks to leave early to pick up a sick child from school, and the manager tells them they will have to make up the time another day, the manager sends a signal to the employee that the employee's relationship with the company is purely transactional. You work certain hours and we pay you for those hours. But by doing so, the manager has undermined all the social transactions that the employee provides to the company. Once that employee has been told to make up the time for taking a sick child home, he will unlikely work late without asking for overtime pay. When required to go above and beyond for the company in the future, the employee will unlikely do so, unless he is rewarded for it.

I believe that there is also a difference between quantitative and qualitative norms, and just like social and market norms, the two do not mix well. Imagine two people host a dinner party for their friends. They make several appetizers, a delicious main course, and a tasty dessert. After dinner they play a new and entertaining board game with their guests.

Everyone has a great time and heads home happy and satisfied. Then, a week after the party, the hosts send an e-mail to the guests asking them to provide feedback on the event by rating different aspects of the party on a 1 to 10 scale. That would be incredibly weird, right?

It isn't just the fact that the hosts are asking for feedback, which is socially awkward, it is the fact that they are trying to quantify an experience that is inherently a matter of quality, which is incredibly bizarre. If I were to ask you to rate how much fun you had playing soccer with some friends, whether it was a 6 or an 8, it would seem out of place. Metrics too can taint the social dynamics and qualitative aspects of any organization. By evaluating employees against quantitative criteria, an organization can undermine all the nonquantitative aspects of the role they play in the organization. If you tell teachers they are evaluated on the test results their students achieve, you can undermine all the other qualities they bring to their role—inspiring students to be inquisitive, helping students learn to manage conflict and work with others, instilling a sense of life-long learning, or providing a positive role model.

This was evident in the laundry company's attendance reward example. When employees began to be quantitatively evaluated and rewarded on attendance, those employees who previously showed up to work on time, and didn't miss many days of work, soon changed their behavior. They began to miss work more often (remember, they were 5.5 times more likely to miss a second day of work in a month once they had missed a first), and they became less productive. Those aspects of their job that they did for intrinsic reasons all of a sudden became tainted by an evaluation system.

It would be interesting to conduct an experiment, much like the laundry company's example, where a quantitative system is put in place in a company, but this time no reward or evaluation system is tied to the measure. Nobody would be paid more, or even recognized, for their performance. The performance would simply be tracked and reported. I suspect that just the introduction of a quantitative reporting system itself can taint motivation. Quantification can undermine quality.

||||||||||

At the age of twenty-two, Fredrick Winslow Taylor started as a clerk at the Midvale Steel Company in Pennsylvania. He may have started as a clerk, but he quickly moved on to be a lathe operator, a gang boss, an engineer, and finally chief engineer of the works of the plant. Taylor's meteoric rise in the company was because of what he saw. Everywhere Taylor went, he saw inefficiency.

Taylor broke down every task undertaken in the plant—the shoveling of ore from railcars, the lifting of iron pigs, the inspection of ball bearings—and investigated how it could be improved. For Taylor there wasn't a process that couldn't be made more efficient. Work previously done by manual labor was replaced by equipment or machines. Workers were given breaks in order to counteract fatigue (both physical and mental). The process that Taylor brought to Midvale Steel was extremely successful. Efficiency of the plant increased dramatically (and not without conflict; workers made redundant by Taylor's efficiency improvements weren't happy to lose their jobs). The processes Taylor established would spread to all kinds of industries and processes, with variations and adaptations to his theories driving management practices for decades. The approach would become known as Taylorism, and later as scientific management.

The concept behind Taylorism and scientific management is simple: break down every process, relentlessly investigate how to make that process more efficient, and measure the results. Lather. Rinse. Repeat. The basis of Taylorism is still with us today. In most organizations departments, roles, processes, and tasks are broken down into constituent parts and given performance criteria, and managers and employees are measured and rewarded on those criteria.

There are few management practices or organizations that do not place metrics in a central, if not the sole, role in performance evaluation.

Countless consultants, management gurus, and advisors had made their living on claiming to improve metrics in the workplace and large organizations. The idea that everything can, and should, be measured, is pervasive in modern management practice. The first line of the book *How to Measure Anything* is "Anything can be measured." It is a bold claim. The book goes on to say that "the belief that some things—even very important things—might be impossible to measure is sand in the gears of the entire economy."[24]

Dean Spitzer, the author of *Transforming Performance Metrics*, claims that "measurement underlies every system in an organization."[25] These aren't claims that metrics are useful, that they can apply to most things, or that they are imperfect but can be improved upon. This is the assertion that anything and everything can be measured. Every activity, every quality, every process can be reduced to a number. If your company is struggling, it is because you don't have the right metrics. Employees not productive? You have the wrong metrics. Your products are failing to keep up with innovation from your competitors? You have the wrong metrics. Metrics are not only a tool for organizations to use, organizations *are* metrics. Metrics, especially in the world of business, are king. And few have dared to challenge the authority of the king.

The problem with this veneration of performance metrics, and rewards tied to them, is that they only seem to work well in situations where the jobs are relatively simple, the output is easily observed, and quality is not an issue. Windshield installation is the type of job where performance metrics can work.[26] If jobs are simple and straightforward, metrics may be a good way to measure and motivate performance. But the fact is, every job is complex.[27] Every job has multiple components and different objectives. Even a windshield installer has to work with others, respond to direction from management, and foster a safe work environment. If a windshield installer has 50 percent better productivity than her peers, yet alienates and stresses out her coworkers, undermines the authority of her leaders, and makes derogatory comments at work, would she still be a valuable employee? If you were to describe your job, would you be able to distill it down to a single task? Could you measure everything your job encompasses with a single performance metric?

For those jobs that are more complex than installing a windshield or riveting two pieces of metal together (although both require technical skill), performance metrics can in fact undermine productivity. Aspects of work that may involve creativity, social awareness, cooperation, or other nonlinear performances do not respond well to metrics or extrinsic motivation. This leaves managers at an impasse. How should leaders motivate employees if not through incentives? How can you manage something if you cannot measure it?

One theory in organizational psychology distinguishes between two types of leadership: transactional and transformative.[28] Transactional leadership focuses simply on the exchange of resources. Employees provide their labor, effort, and ingenuity to a task and are rewarded based on their accomplishment of measurable goals. It is Taylorism manifest. Transformational leadership, on the other hand, is the opposite. Transformational leadership is defined by leaders who inspire their employees by behaving admirably, displaying conviction, and appealing to their followers on an emotional level. Transformational leaders create a vision that is appealing and inspiring, communicate optimism, and provide meaning to their followers. They intellectually stimulate their followers, challenge their assumptions, take risks, and solicit ideas from their followers. Transformational leaders attend to their followers' needs, acting as a mentor.

What you'll notice about transformational leadership is that very few traits of leadership, or even the management process, are particularly fit for measurement. How do you measure charisma? Or inspiration? You could of course conduct surveys to ask employees the degree to which they are motivated, but surveys don't have the same degree of objectivity and certainty that, say, measuring how many hours an employee works or how many widgets employees create in a day does. As Margaret Wheatley and Myron Kellner-Rogers point out, behaviors such as commitment, focus, teamwork, learning, or quality are not produced by measurement. Those traits emerge when people feel connected to their work and to each other.[29]

Transactional leadership lives in the world of metrics. Exchange is conducted in a world of numbers: performance goals, bonus amounts, sales targets, hours worked. Transformational leadership lives in another world entirely. It doesn't set performance goals, or at least it doesn't make it the focal point of an organization. It strives for purpose and meaning. It seeks out challenge and growth. It recognizes that not everything can be reduced to metrics and simple transactions. It recognizes that much of what we do, whether in our work or personal lives, is built on something much bigger than just numbers. There is more to our lives than metrics.

The quantification of work and the use of metrics as motivation were tools that were developed in an era when most of the labor force was undertaking manual labor. Workers would do the same simple task again and again and again. The ball bearing inspector's job was to inspect ball bearings. A welder undertook the same weld day in, day out. Taylor developed his theories of management in a steel mill, not a marketing firm or a research department. In those former situations, measurement works well. It is simple. It is easy.

But as the economy has changed, our metrics haven't. We still insist that employees' contributions to work can be easily quantified, that every process in an organization can be broken down and optimized through measurement, and that in order to motivate people, we simply need to measure them in the right way and provide the right incentives. As long as we get the metrics right, the thinking goes, not only will we succeed, but there is no way we cannot.

In a knowledge economy, systems of production and value are fundamentally different from assembly line production. Motivating workers is no longer a straightforward system of measuring the right things and providing the right incentives. In the modern workplace, fostering productive, creative, and motivated employees may counterintuitively require management to step away from metrics and incentives and instead focus on the fuzzier aspects of inspiration, intellectual stimulation, challenge, and purpose.

When it comes to the softer parts of work—motivation, creativity, purpose, cooperation—measurement fall short. Sometimes, when it comes to work, measuring cannot capture what matters. Even the act of measuring can undermine the values and behaviors it is trying to nurture. Not everything that counts can be counted.

||||||||||

We are buried beneath the weight of information, which is being confused with knowledge; quantity is being confused with abundance and wealth with happiness. We are monkeys with money and guns.

—Tom Waits

In this book we have examined metrics in nearly every aspect of our lives. Test scores in schools, performance measures in healthcare, crime and enforcement statistics in law enforcement, productivity metrics in business, measures of energy efficiency, public health metrics, measures in academics, and measures in war. But we have not yet touched upon some of the most complex and influential metrics in our world: how we measure our economy and our well-being.

Measuring the economy has a long history. Ever since countries began collecting taxes, there has been a need to measure, at least roughly, how large the economy is. As history progressed, and as societies became more complex and data collection and sharing methods improved, the detail and completeness of these measures improved. By the sixteenth and seventeenth centuries, British and French tax collectors began to create estimates of the total income of their countries with the purpose of improving tax collection. Over time governments begun to piece together a better picture of the size of their economies.

But these measures were still very rough and based on incomplete, inaccurate, and unreliable information. It wasn't until the twentieth century, when better data collection and modern statistics combined to produce one of the most-used forms of economic measurement—one that shapes the policies of governments and the decisions of multinational corporations and affects the daily lives of everyone on the planet—Gross Domestic Product.

Gross Domestic Product (GDP), simply put, is a tally of all the economic activity conducted in a country every year. It is a summary of every product produced, service provided, improvement built, and income paid. The measure of GDP is based on various estimates and data that are maintained in each country's Systems of National Accounts, through census data as well as various surveys of retail sales, housing starts, and manufacturer shipments.[30] These estimates are continuously revised as more and more data become available. In short, GDP is the best attempt we have at measuring what the total wealth of a country is and how well off its citizens are.

GDP is the most widely used measure of our economic productivity and arguably the most focused on, researched, and used metrics in the world today. Created in 1934 in the United States by the National Bureau of Economic Statistics, GDP quickly became a widespread measure of economic productivity after the Bretton Woods conference in 1946. The Allied Powers, wishing to avert another war, believed that economic prosperity in Europe would stave off another disastrous conflict, and at the time, the best way to measure this prosperity was with raw economic productivity. GDP fit the bill perfectly.

Today GDP is used by governments across the world to prepare national budgets, by federal reserves to set monetary policies, by Wall Street and other centers of finance as an indicator of economic activity, and by various businesses for the purposes of investment, production, and employment planning.[31] Yearly, quarterly, and monthly estimates of GDP are produced and reported by national governments, the World Bank, the IMF, and various other organizations. The sheer amount of energy that goes into compiling, analyzing, and reporting the GDP is staggering. Almost every country has offices dedicated to calculating the metric.

While GDP is a widely used metric, it has been widely criticized by academics in both economics and noneconomics fields, cultural observers, nongovernmental organizations, and even governments themselves. The Kingdom of Bhutan actually switched the official measurement of its economic well-being from GDP to Gross Domestic Happiness.[32]

Criticisms of GDP range from neglecting activities outside the market economy, to failing to account for environmental destruction, to missing what really matters. GDP, as prevalent as it is, succumbs to nearly every criticism discussed in this book. Let's look at some.

First, many critics point out that GDP is basically an output metric. GDP, as previously explained, measures the amount of production within a country (it doesn't count production in other countries that are owned by companies in the subject country). Effectively GDP is a tally of the value of all the "things" produced in a country. This includes all goods and services. It is the value of all the hours billed by lawyers, toys sold, haircuts purchased, coffees drank, cars bought, smartphone app purchases, and nearly everything else imaginable in a single year in a country. It is, at least theoretically, an account of all the outputs of an economy. GDP measures these activities using various sources, including census data and surveys of manufacturers and retailers.

As discussed earlier in the book, output metrics fail because they do not account for outcomes. GDP is no different. Measuring raw economic activity speaks nothing to profitability, effectiveness, or what is achieved with all that activity. This is seen in how GDP measures various aspects of the economy. Healthcare, for example, is measured in the GDP by its inputs: doctors' wages, medical equipment, hospital rooms. According to

GDP, health care consists of how much resources we put into our health system and not how healthy our population is.

Another area where GDP fails is in missing the hidden parts of the economy. Anything that does not involve a monetary transaction that is tracked by the government (or reported), and therefore is not part of the market, is not accounted for by GDP. You are probably thinking about the black market, or other activities that are hidden for various nefarious reasons. But the bulk of nonmarket activities are actually incredibly mundane.

One example is housework. When household members do their own cleaning, laundry, and cooking, the services they provide for themselves are not accounted for in the marketplace. No money changes hands, so according to GDP, it doesn't exist. But when these tasks are provided for by the market, in the form of cleaning contractors, all of a sudden it appears as if something is being done that wasn't before. Take a hypothetical case where one member of the household's entire income goes to paying for household services. It appears as if an entire person worth of services just appeared out of nowhere, yet the same services are being provided.

Here is a rather ridiculous, but illustrative example. Imagine two people agree to clean each other's houses and pay each other the exact same amount to each other for the service. Both report it on their income and expenses for tax purposes. Prior to the arrangement, neither activity was considered part of the market. But once those two people decide to pay each other to clean their homes, and, more important, claim it on their taxes, both of their incomes increased. Yet nothing new was done. The two houses are being cleaned in both cases, and for both participants the effect on effective income is zero (actually less, as they would pay taxes on the income from the work).

Other examples include volunteering and leisure time. Spending time at a national park does not typically involve a monetary transaction (unfortunately it increasingly is), yet it confers benefits to the user.

Imagine if the government provided everyone in the country a tax credit for park visits and then charged the same amount for a yearly visit to a national park. Let's pretend every single person bought a park pass equal to the amount of the credit. All of a sudden, it looks like a bunch of economic activity is occurring, but nothing has actually changed.

This especially applies to how GDP measures income and consumption. Income is measured after taxes are taken out, and consumption is measured as expenditures on goods and services. But for services that are provided by the government, this doesn't enter into the equation.

Some services are provided by the private sector in one country but by the public sector in another. Healthcare and education are good examples. Take the hypothetical case where healthcare is provided by the market, through employer-provided insurance, in one country (country A) but by government, paid for through income taxes, in another (country B). Imagine two people living in either country, both receiving the same quality of healthcare. In country A, the person pays five thousand dollars less in taxes, but spends six thousand dollars on health insurance each year. In country B, the person pays five thousand dollars more in taxes, but does not have to spend anything on health insurance, as it is covered by the government. According to conventional measures of income and consumption, the person in country A is seen to be five thousand dollars "richer" (in terms of consumption and income) than the person in country B, when in fact person B has one thousand dollars more than person A in effective income.

Government provision of services distorts these measures in all manner of areas. Governments provide both collective services, such as security, and individual services, such as education and healthcare. Nearly all of these services are measured only as inputs (how many police officers, teachers and doctors, are employed and how much they are paid) and rarely as outcomes (levels of crime, feelings of safety, general health of the population, or educational achievement). It is not just services that are not provided by the market that GDP misses, it also omits all the costs to the environment that result from economic activity. GDP doesn't measure the health of our ecosystems, biodiversity, levels of pollution, soil degradation, deforestation, erosion, nor loss of habitat. Nor does GDP measure the depletion of resources from the earth. Oddly, the extraction of minerals and energy resources are seen as coming from nowhere; the only costs are those of extraction. Economists call these things "imputations," the things not provided for by the market, and they are incredibly difficult to measure and quantify. Yet they are incredibly important. But it is not just these difficult-to-measure activities that GDP miscounts. Other things it counts perversely.

||||||||||

Too much and for too long we seemed to have surrendered personal excellence and community values in the mere accumulation of material things . . . Gross National Product counts air pollution and cigarette advertising, and ambulances to clear our highways of carnage. It counts special locks for our doors and the jails for the people who break them . . . Yet the gross national product does not allow for the health of our children, the quality of their education or the joy of their play . . . It measures neither our wit nor our courage, neither our wisdom nor our learning, neither our compassion nor our devotion to our country, it measures everything in short, except that which makes life worthwhile.
—Robert F Kennedy, speech at the University of Kansas, March 18, 1968

Another failure of GDP is that it counts very different qualities at the same. Robert Kennedy eloquently illustrated this point. Expenditure on guns and alarm systems for our homes are counted as the same as trips to the zoo or buying a good book, yet the two categories have vastly different utilities. If you don't think so, just ask yourself if you would rather live in a country where you don't have to buy a gun or alarm system and can go to the zoo and read books instead.

This failure comes in two ways. The first is by measuring services by their inputs (as previously discussed), not their outcomes. By doing this, increases in efficiency—that is, providing greater outcomes with the same input—are seen as losses in productivity. If someone invented a new medical technology that achieves the same result at half the cost, it registers as a loss economically. Inventing a new dishwasher that costs a fraction of what the old dishwasher cost, shows up as a negative on the economic balance sheet.

The second way GDP treats different qualities as the same is by counting what we call defensive expenditures the same as other expenditures.

Two examples of defensive expenditures are commuting and security. People commuting are doing so to achieve another goal: getting to work. Commuting is not an economic end in itself. It is something undertaken to achieve something else. Someone who spends more on commuting than another person, in terms of gas, vehicle costs, insurance, and so on, is not really improving his or her quality of life—quite the opposite, actually. If another person was to walk to work, spending little more than what a good pair of shoes cost, and spent the rest of his or her money on more enjoyable things, he or she would be seen as having the same quality of life as the long-distance commuter, despite being able to afford more enjoyable things.

The same goes for security. Spending money on an expensive home security system, or on guns to protect yourself in your home is not an expenditure that is in itself enjoyable. The feeling of safety and security is what people are trying to achieve, and spending more on things that achieve this doesn't necessarily make you safer.

These distortions and errors in value make GDP a perverse metric that, as Robert Kennedy said, measures everything except that which makes life worthwhile. According to GDP, a country that works itself to death and where people spend their income on guns and alarms for protection, on nannies to take care of their children, on cleaning up pollution, and on healthcare because they are sicker, is better off than a country that spends less money but spends their income on books, dinner with friends, plants for their garden, tickets to a movie, or equipment to go hiking, and spends their time with their friends and loved ones learning new things or helping others.

Measures like GDP reduce all value to how well something can be monetized. If you can't be paid for something, according to GDP and similar metrics, it doesn't count. And when you can suddenly monetize something that was previously done outside of the market, GDP treats it as if something new has occurred. Don't get me wrong. Economic and material wealth are not bad things. Poverty is destructive and takes a terrible toll on people's well-being. Not having access to fresh water or affordable healthcare and living in substandard housing and unsafe communities are undesirable conditions. Increasing wealth and income does have a positive effect on well-being. Up to a certain point.

In 1974 the economist Richard Easterlin published a study that demonstrated that people's self-evaluations of their quality of life did not correlate strongly with income.[33] Other studies have shown that while high income individuals tend to have a higher quality of life evaluation than lower incomes in a country, the relationship doesn't hold across countries. While rich people tend to report a higher quality of life than poorer people, rich countries don't seem to be any happier than poor countries.[34] There seems to be a point beyond which increasing wealth no longer improves people's well-being. Once people have met their basic needs for shelter, safety, health, nourishment, and household necessities, having more stuff really doesn't make people happier. Yet our primary measurement of economic well-being is based on exactly that.

There are, however, proposed alternate measures to GDP. Some measures attempt to include or exclude various factors to account for what GDP misses, or wrongly includes, such as defensive expenditures. The

Genuine Progress Indicator (GPI) and the Green GDP are two such measures. Other measures account for our use of resources rather than what we produce, the ecological footprint being the most well-known. A few measures abandon the GDP methodology altogether and jump straight into measuring well-being directly, using methods such as subjective well-being surveys. Similarly, some measures try to measure well-being indirectly by measuring the things that are believed to lead to a better quality of life, such as the Human Development Index (HDI), which combines measures in education, life expectancy, and income.[35] These are just a few examples; there are many, many more.

While direct measures of well-being—basically asking people how they are doing—may seem overly subjective, they are the best metric of well-being we have. Critics will claim that not much can be learned from such measures, that without an objective standard, such measures are vague and unimportant. Many will argue that any measure should be objective. Yet, when it comes to well-being, objectivity is impossible.

Well-being is an inherently subjective phenomenon. What may be fulfilling, important, or meaningful to me, may not be to you. Any objective measure of well-being is forced to choose which subjective aspects to measure. While measuring income may be objective, the act of choosing income as the thing to measure is in itself a subjective choice.

Measuring well-being and happiness takes us right back to chapter 2. Most of our measures of well-being measure what we think are the causes of well-being: income, educational attainment, literacy, crime rates. But these are just the inputs. The real outcomes—a sense of satisfaction, happiness, contentment—are difficult to measure and are rarely done so. And there is no doubt that we should do better at measuring these things, or just start to measure them in the first place. But ultimately, no matter how much we improve measuring these things, they are, by their very nature, things that do not measure well.

Why is GDP still so widely used when faced with such criticism and when so many alternatives are available? Why do we not hear reports on how our GPI is increasing or decreasing this quarter? Or how the ecological footprint of India is changing? The answer comes from one of the greatest critics of GDP, and a very surprising one at that: the man who developed the metric himself.

Simon Kuznets was born in 1901 in Pinsk, a Belorusian city that was then part of Russia. In university, Kuznets studied economics at the University of Kharkiv in 1917 and subsequently the Kharkiv Institute of Commerce starting in 1918. He continued his studies there until the Russian Civil War broke out in 1920. In the aftermath of the civil war and the subsequent Soviet reorganization of higher education, Kuznets ended up in the Department of Labor of the Council of Trade Unions. Thankfully, Kuznets did not last long in Soviet Russia. In 1922 his family emigrated to the United States.

There he continued studies at Columbia University, completing his PhD in 1926 and moving on to the National Bureau of Economic Research in New York in 1927. It was here he built upon the work of previous economists to refine a measure that sought to account for all the economic productivity in a nation. His meticulousness and rigor set the standard for what eventually became GDP.

When called to present his work to Congress in 1934, Kuznets took the opportunity to elucidate the shortcomings of what he had worked so hard to develop. The measure, Kuznets cautioned to the Senate, did not include "services of housewives and other members of the family," "relief and charity," "services of owned durable goods," "earnings from odd jobs," and "earnings from illegal pursuits," among others.[36] Kuznets understood that not being able to include these things meant that GDP was lacking, as many have later pointed out.[37]

Kuznets also knew that GDP was, and always would be, flawed. He never intended it to be a measure of well-being, explaining that it was fundamentally a measure of productivity and not quality of life. Even then he understood the limitations as a measure of economic productivity.

In his deposition to Congress, Kuznets said something much more profound. He touched upon something that affects every measurement we deal with. A lesson that we should always carry with us:

The valuable capacity of the human mind to simplify a complex situation in a compact characterization becomes dangerous when not controlled in terms of definitely stated criteria. With quantitative measurements especially, the definiteness of the result suggests, often misleadingly, a precision and simplicity in the outlines of the object measured.

Almost one hundred years ago, the architect of one of the most rigorously and painstakingly calculated metrics in our society was telling us that we couldn't do the exact thing that he was proposing: easily reduce a complex phenomenon to a number. This was coming from a man who was legendary in his meticulousness.

Just because we can make a metric simplified and precise, no matter how detailed we are in measuring it, does not make the phenomena simplified and precise. Just because we can reduce education to scores on standardized, multiple-choice tests, does not mean that education is as simple or precise as test scores. Public health is not as simple as the number of cases of a disease or the average life expectancy of a population. Kuznets understood this. He understood that while GDP would be a useful metric (and I think it is, despite all the criticisms mentioned), we should approach it with caution and humility. Kuznets wasn't just talking about GDP. His language spoke to something greater. He was talking about all quantitative measurements. Every time we reduce learning to a percentage score on a test, every time we measure safety by the number of police we have, every time we count our work by the hours in a day, we distort the truth. We start to believe that the more precise, the more quantitative our measurements, the closer to the truth we get. But nothing is further from it.

Why do we still use GDP despite all its criticisms and limitations? Because it is a hard number. It is precise. It gives an air of certainty and authority to something that is by its very nature obscure, shifting, and subject to interpretation. Hard numbers are easy. Dealing with hard numbers is much easier than dealing with the vague, subjective, and ever-changing nature of our lives, values, and relationships.

Kuznets was warning us. He was warning us against the hubris of quantification. He was warning us not to be overconfident in our measurements. He knew that once we started putting numbers to things, we would start to believe that numbers actually exist behind the data. But we didn't hear the message. We rushed headlong into the twentieth century, embracing the pursuit of information with unchecked fervor. We began to measure anything and everything we could imagine: consumption habits, demographics, number of hospital beds, changes in values and beliefs, car crashes, military spending, children's test results, economic productivity, currency exchange rates, construction costs, crime rates, and nearly anything we could even remotely hope to quantify. We put our little ant heads to the ground, swung our antennae back and forth, and followed the trail.

With a newfound ability to collect, analyze, and report enormous amounts of data, we developed an information hubris. We started to believe that because we could quantify something, we could easily understand it. Not only did we believe that complex phenomena could be reduced to simple measurements, we started to believe that they should be reduced to a simple number. We took up Galileo's refrain, "Measure what is measurable and make measurable what is not so."

So we went forward, quantifying anything we came across. We demanded "hard numbers" for any activity. This became a laudable goal, even if we had no idea what the numbers meant. Managers, teachers, agencies, coaches, administrators, governments, businesses, and everyone in between were expected to produce quantifiable measures for what they did. Our obsession with metrics is so strong that some even claim that "unmeasured things cannot be easily replicated, or managed or appreciated."[38] Metrics were no longer a tool to understand the world;

the world couldn't be understood, or even appreciated, without metrics. The examples in this book, and uncountable other examples, show just how widespread our misunderstanding of metrics is. As Tom Waits said, "We buried ourselves beneath the weight of information, confusing it with knowledge."[39] At the same time respecting nuance, complexity, or competing objectives came to be seen as wishy-washy, imprecise, or lazy. When something couldn't be, or wasn't, quantified, it was neglected or ridiculed. Anything without a number attached was discarded or devalued. We started to truly believe that if it couldn't be measured, it couldn't be managed.

In this march toward an ever-increasing quantification of our world, all the things that cannot easily be quantified are being lost. Anything that can't be monetized in our economy loses value in our eyes. Activities at work that can't be easily measured or tracked are being discarded. Aspects of teaching that do not result in better test scores are abandoned. Ways of living that make people happier, but with less material wealth, are viewed with suspicion, disdain, or both.

All of this isn't to say that we shouldn't measure anything. This is not an argument for a defeatist approach to metrics. Far from it. Better measurement is important. Hopefully the lessons provided in this book illustrate that. Measuring and understanding how to evaluate progress toward our goals, values, and aspirations are incredibly important. Yet too much of what informs our ideas of measurement has come from the hard sciences: math, chemistry, physics, biology, and, to a lesser extent, economics. In these fields precision in measurement is always the end goal. A chemist who describes the ideal temperature of a reaction as "pretty hot" or a physicist who says a rocket needs to go "fast" won't last long in their job. Quantification drives everything in the hard sciences, and it should.

In the hard sciences, measurement is fairly straightforward. Measuring the velocity of a falling object, the boiling point of a solution, or the concentration of a protein in the body is a matter of instrumentation, not a fundamental question of whether the measurement is the correct one. When we want to know how much a ball weighs, we are only really concerned with how accurately we can measure that weight.

But the further outside we move from the hard sciences, the further we move into the inexact worlds of biology, psychology, economics, politics, and sociology. With the greater questions of who we are, what we should be, and what we value, the less metrics become straightforward. The fundamental problem with measuring human, social, and environmental phenomena is that there is no simple answer to what the right metric is. In the hard sciences, measurement is about instrumentation. In the social sciences, measurement is about value. Metrics in the messy world of education, healthcare, work, economics, sports, relationships, and well-being are not simply about instrumentation, yet we treat them as if they are. We try to find ways to more accurately measure GDP, but we put little effort toward figuring out if GDP is the right measurement in the first place, or even if there is a right measurement.

Many times, when designing and implementing a metric, the questions we ask are similar to those we would use in these fields: "How accurately can we measure this?" "How do we collect the data?" "What can we measure?" But these questions are misdirected. The first and foremost question we should ask is, "What is important?" Then we should work out how to measure it, if at all.

That is the fundamental flaw behind GDP. It is not just that GDP does not capture all the economic activity in a country, nor that it primarily measures inputs, nor that it is blind to environmental degradation or human health. It isn't GDP that has failed, it is us. The intent of GDP was never to measure well-being, but we treated it as such. Because GDP was able to provide definitive quantities, it took on an air of authority. Other considerations that were not as easily measured—mental well-being, population health, human rights, democratic values—took a backseat. We deluded ourselves into thinking that measuring the amount of production in a country meant anything other than just that, production.

What GDP measures is greatly divorced from what makes life worthwhile, yet that is what we use it for, because nothing else provides such a definitive value.

GDP is an exemplar of what metrics have become in our lives. As with GDP, we began to believe that our measures meant more than what they measured. We started to believe that anything could and should be measured; that every aspect of our work, our society, and our lives could be reduced to numbers and equations; that success in anything was as simple as getting our numbers higher. We started to believe that our lives were more like a video game—where we just had to get enough points to level up and get the right scores on our stats—than like poetry, whose meaning is subject to interpretation and whose importance defies measurement. We doubted anything that couldn't be expressed with a hard, objective measure. We convinced ourselves that the be all and end all of everything was a number; that once we quantified something, we made it real; that outside the realm of numbers, the world doesn't exist. We deluded ourselves with the idea that anything that couldn't be measured couldn't be understood or enjoyed or valued. We started to believe our own disillusion.

CHAPTER 9
THE MEASURE OF METRICS

Throughout this book, we have seen how metrics have been misused, abused, and misunderstood. But we have also seen how metrics can be improved, how we can avoid their pitfalls and shortcomings, and how we can learn from the mistakes of others.

Our obsession with metrics needs to end. The popular saying by Peter Drucker, "If you can't measure it, you can't manage it" needs to be challenged and rethought. We need to take a more thoughtful approach to what and why we measure. For while they can be useful, metrics can also obscure, disrupt, and distort systems.[1]

David Parmenter, an expert in developing and implementing performance measures for over twenty years, saw that metrics had become so abused that he wrote an article that asked, "Should We Abandon Performance Measures?" He saw that metrics can be gamed, as we noted with Goodhart's Law; can encourage teams to perform tasks contrary to an organization's strategic direction; and can use up valuable staff and management time. And metrics derived by consultants often yield little more than a "doorstop" report.[2]

At the beginning of this book, I introduced the reasons behind metrics. I discussed how metrics provide us with an understanding of truth, giving us a sense of certainty in what we are trying to understand. Metrics also provide us with simplicity by helping us reduce and comprehend complex systems into legible models. Metrics serve as a tool of verification where there is an absence of trust. Finally, metrics provide us with objectivity in situations where differing perspectives and values allow subjectivity to cloud our judgment.

Throughout this book we have seen how all of these purposes of metrics, rather than reinforcing the usefulness of measurement, have the potential to undermine and betray the usefulness of measurement. Let's look back at them.

COMPLEXITY

When it comes to complexity, metrics can be useful in helping distill a multifaceted system into a simplified model where decisions can be more easily made and relationships between different aspects of the system can be understood. The problem with complexity occurs when metrics are used to oversimplify the system. If you reduce the complexity too much, you end up losing a lot of what is important. As David Manheim said, "By reading the blurb instead of the book, you handicap your understanding."[3]

Take for example the need to create a simplified system to reward company executives. The trend to tie executive pay to performance through earnings allows boards of directors and shareholders to condense the complicated motives of executives into a single goal: maximizing profit. Knowing every single decision that an executive takes to benefit a company and how those actions lead to profit and shareholder value is too cumbersome to understand fully, so investors turn to a simple tool to evaluate success. Yet, by doing so, the compensation strategy oversimplifies the system. Short-term earnings are optimized, while long-term profitability is sacrificed. Aspects of a company that generate competitive advantages, such as marketing and research and development, are ignored or otherwise downplayed.

The downsides of simplifying a complex system was also seen in the shortcomings of using food miles as a proxy for the sustainability of food.

Our decisions of what to eat have impacts across the entire globe, from farms in Kenya, to freight yards in China, to our local grocery store, and finally to our dinner tables. Faced with such a complex, intertwined, and confusing network that is our food supply system, many chose to focus on a single metric to evaluate the sustainability of our food: how far it travels to reach our plate. This oversimplification blinds us not only to other aspects of our food system, it overemphasizes a component that barely makes up a twentieth of the emissions from the entire process. The oversimplification leads to perverse outcomes, where someone eating local food grown in a greenhouse believes he is doing good for the planet, when in fact he is doing the opposite.

Simplifying a system was also evident when looking at the public education system. Children learn a lot in schools. Not only do they attain scholastic knowledge, they learn life skills. Schools don't just teach math, language, and science, they teach children the skills of cooperation, focus, socialization, motivation, creativity, curiosity, and volunteerism and a love of learning. Yet, when it comes to evaluating our schools, the complex system of learning is boiled down to knowing arithmetic and grammar.

As John Ewing, an executive director of the American Mathematical Society for over fifteen years, put it "The end goal of education isn't to get students to answer the right number of questions. The goal is to have curious and creative students who can function in life."[4]

The desire for simplicity has two downsides. The first is that, when simplification goes too far, it results in the loss of a fulsome understanding of a system. Knowing how each of the components of a system works and how those components relate to each other leads to a better understanding of the entire system. Breaking systems down into components results in a loss of understanding of the complexity of the whole.

The second downside is that by focusing on just one aspect of a system, you de-emphasize the rest. This is referred to as a loss of dimensionality.[5] When academics are evaluated solely on the ability to publish,

publish often, and publish articles that are cited often, you deemphasize other aspects of an academic's contribution, such as teaching. When we measure the quantifiable aspects of an economy and society, such as economic productivity, we lose sight of other important aspects of well-being, such as security and freedom. As David Manheim put it: "When you make only part of a system stronger, it breaks the rest, unless the other parts are strengthened to compensate."[6]

OBJECTIVITY

One of the reasons we use metrics is because they provide objectivity. Metrics offer those much sought-after values in assessment: neutrality, impartiality, and detachment. As long as the numbers are accurate, arguments over the value of a metric are moot. The number is the number is the number. You want to prove you are more productive than your coworkers? Well, just measure your productivity, and the numbers won't lie. The numbers don't have bias.

Often we use metrics to avoid making a subjective judgment. We want our decisions to appear objective, unbiased, and dispassionate, so we use a seemingly objective measure for evaluation. It is a common defense for anyone advocating for one method of evaluation or another: "The numbers speak for themselves" or "It isn't my decision, I am just reporting what we measured." Yet when objectivity is pursued in the real world, it can have dire consequences.

In Vietnam, military commanders were faced with the most complex military confrontation in the history of the United States. Confronting both an invading army as well as a local insurrection, while dealing with political motivations of not only the North Vietnamese, but the local Vietnamese population and their own population back home, military commanders resorted to attempts to quantify the war. Surely if they could collect enough data, they could obtain an objective evaluation of the progress in the war. Subjective concerns—such as understanding the varying political, cultural, and social motivations driving both the insurgency as well as opposition at home—were largely ignored until they lost the Americans the war.

That same desire for objectivity erodes the purpose of fundamental research. Government officials, grant application reviewers, department heads, foundation chairs, and nearly everyone involved in funding academic research have to grapple with the challenge of trying to evaluate something that fundamentally escapes measurement. Will research into the protein of some bacteria result in a breakthrough in medicine? Will studying the people in extraordinary circumstances provide us with insights into human behavior that will lead to improved well-being? These are not easy questions, and not ones that everyone will agree on. But what is not up for debate is the number of citations an academic's last article received. That number doesn't change based on who you ask. So, too often, scientific research is reduced to the simple metric of how many publications and citations a work of research produces and receives. In the end, it hurts science.

An aversion to subjectivity is also what drives our need to measure well-being by other means. When the *Economist* magazine produces its yearly economic reports, or when governments report on the strength of their economy, they do not report the results on subjective surveys on quality of life, they report GDP. It would seem odd that a central bank or a government department of labor would report how well their citizens scored on a self-reported survey of well-being. Who is to say that someone in Nigeria evaluates his or her quality of life on the same scale that someone in Japan does? Or whether someone who is living below the poverty line has the same scale of prosperity than someone who is in the top 1 percent? Quality of life is a matter of opinion, a matter of perspective. What you feel is important in your life is different than what I feel. Why would anyone want to measure that, let alone report on it? What isn't a matter of perspective is the total economic output of France in 2017 (well, it is a matter of debate, but that is beside the point, at least the possibility of objectivity exists), so that is what countries resort to.

Yet, what really matters to people is not how much money their economy produced last quarter, or whether their country's growth in GDP kept up to similar countries. What they care about is whether they feel safe in their community, whether they feel they are secure in their health, and whether they can provide for the necessities of their families. They care about freedom from oppression and from indiscriminate violence, whether by their fellow citizens or by the state. They want to feel a sense of purpose in their lives and a sense of belonging. Yet, none of these things can be measured the same way economic productivity can be measured. So we fall back on it again and again.

Objectivity also played a part in undermining the Atlanta Public School system. Teachers bring numerous benefits to the students they teach, from inspiring creativity and curiosity to acting as a role model for students. They help students learn to cooperate with each other, to interact with people who are not like them, and to understand that they must compromise in order to achieve what they want. Yet none of these things are easy to objectively measure. How important was it that Damany Lewis provided an example of a positive male role model in the lives of his students, most of who were fatherless? That depends on who you ask. But what doesn't depend on who you ask is how well his students did on the Criterion Referenced Competency Tests. Those numbers aren't subject to bias or perspective. The numbers are the numbers. In the words of Alfred Kiel, the testing coordinator at Parks Middle School, the tests were paramount because data from a test "tells the truth. It's not what I think—and what I feel, and what ought to be, and how I perceive it—but how it actually is."[7]

The first problem of insisting on using objective measures is that it results in a neglect of anything that is, by its nature, subjective. This was the effect of the focus on metrics in Vietnam, in academia, in measuring the economy, or in evaluating teachers. The desirability for objective measures in all these arenas resulted in a neglect of what couldn't easily be objectively measured.

The other problem of objectivity is the appearance of objectivity itself. The measure is the measure, the numbers are the numbers. Individual perspectives, biased judgment, and personal opinion are removed, and only the objective numbers remain. But objectivity is an illusion. What many people fail to recognize is that choosing what to measure is itself a subjective choice. Choosing to test students on their knowledge of arithmetic and how much to weigh that test in the students' grade is a subjective decision. Each question on a test, and how it is worded, is a subjective choice about what children should be learning and how they should be evaluated on it. The same goes for any kind of evaluation. Even if choosing a purely "objective" measure, like the number of hours an employee works each day or how many lines of code he or she writes, the choice in the measure itself is subjective.

Subjectivity is unavoidable. Not in some postmodernist sense that everything is subjective and all points of view are valid, but in the real sense that our choice of any method of evaluation (or not choosing to measure something) is ultimately a choice about what we value. While a measurement itself may seem objective, in the sense that the data are quantitative, statistically sound, and collected in a neutral manner, it is the choice of the metric that is subjective. Deciding to measure, for example, employees' productivity by the number of hours they work is a subjective decision that claims, "The number of hours worked is important." Similarly, measuring a transportation project only by the delay in vehicle travel it causes is making a choice that vehicle travel time matters and not, for example, pedestrian safety.

We cannot simply measure something and then claim it is objective and dismiss any opinions to the contrary by pointing to the "objectivity" of the measurement. Choosing any measurement is a subjective decision. We have to think hard about the metrics we choose and defend why we use them. It is not good enough to simply say: "But that is what the numbers say." Yet this happens all too often. We have to justify why we chose to use those numbers in the first place. Proponents of metrics will often cite objectivity as the reason we need to measure something. Whether it is in program time lines, sales volume, successful surgeries, or raw economic productivity, the argument of many is that those measures give us an objective view on the situation. Often critiques of metrics will be responded to with, "Well, we need an objective measure, otherwise it is just a matter of opinion." Such responses either fail to recognize that the choice of the measure itself is a matter of opinion, or they are hiding their own perspectives and values behind the perceived objectivity of the measure. Objectivity is a cop-out, a way to avoid the difficult and often messy discussions about what matters and how to value it.

CERTAINTY

The desire for certainty, to know more than we knew before, and to be able to act with the confidence in our knowledge of the world, drives much of our desire for measurement. Nobody wants to admit to making decisions without any knowledge, let alone admitting to not even bothering to obtain that knowledge in the first place. We want to be sure of our actions and our decisions, and the only way for us to do so is to have the numbers to back it up.

In modern culture certainty often means quantification. It isn't enough to know something is true, we need to know how true it is. As Margaret Wheatley and Myron Kellner-Rogers point out, there is a belief that numbers are what are real. If you can give something a number, you can make it real. Once it is real, it is yours to manage and control.[8] Or as Peter Drucker's popular saying goes: "If it can't be measured, it can't be managed."

The quest for certainty can be useful. It can provide us with a better understanding of something we previously didn't know much about.

Often, knowing more about a situation, rather than less, results in us making better decisions. Yet, as David Manheim says, "Not attempting to measure something can be a much bigger mistake than accepting a fuzzy measure—but not always."[9] Sometimes, a little knowledge can be harmful.

The need for certainty was at the heart of the NYPD tapes scandal and the shortcomings of the CompStat system. Initially the system provided much needed data that was useful in assisting with crime analysis. The data provided the police with the information needed to target areas of high crime so that officers could be deployed effectively to combat crime and disorder. But the obsession with numbers in the end hurt the NYPD. The department's fascination with crime rates and enforcement actions meant not only that officers resorted to unethical behavior in order to maximize those numbers, but also that anything that wasn't quantifiable was neglected. Like Marquez Claxton, the director of the Black Law Enforcement Alliance, said, "There is no number which says I stopped seven burglaries today."[10]

This same obsession for numbers is what is at the heart of Dr. Aufricht and Shauna Thome's struggles with trying to demonstrate the benefits of the Crowfoot Village Family Practice (CVFP). Their model of patient-centered care that seeks to improve efficiency and reduce the burden on patients nonetheless faces an uphill battle when justifying why it exists. Despite focusing on long-term patient health and providing a more robust package of healthcare services, the clinic's model is based on doctors doing less.

Certainty is also at the core of sports metrics. Sports statisticians, enthusiasts, coaches, managers, and fans are obsessed with what can be measured. If it can be counted, you can bet that some sports stats aficionado has found a way to count it. Players are rated on their on-base percentage, field goal percentage, ball possession, and all manner of actions they take on the court, field, rink, or diamond. But what sports analysis has trouble with is everything players do when they aren't in possession of the ball or puck. By focusing so much on what they can count, sports analysts miss out on everything that they can't.

The need to quantify the world is also behind testing culture in education, and especially in the Atlanta Public Schools scandal. Beverly Hall's obsession with test scores, and the desire to show them continually going up, resulted in a culture not only where any method to improve them, however scrupulous, was condoned, but also a culture where anything that didn't contribute to test scores was devalued. While teachers and principals themselves tried as best they could to weather the storm and stomach the cheating so they could continue to focus on what they felt mattered in their teaching, those values wouldn't keep them in their job. Nearly 90 percent of principals in Atlanta were fired or quit under Hall's test-obsessed administration, many doubtless because they refused to sacrifice their values in order to meet test objectives. The result was a slow erosion of everything that makes teaching and education worthwhile. As Tim Callahan, the spokesman for the Professional Association of Georgia Educators, put it: "Our teachers' best qualities—their sense of humor, their love for the subject, their excitement, their interest in students as individuals—are not being honored or valued, because those qualities aren't measurable."[11]

Certainty also played a role in Vietnam. The strategy of attrition required the United States to kill more Vietnamese combatants than they believed the Vietnamese leadership was willing to bear. This obsession with statistics and veracity meant that body counts had to be verified, with shocking outcomes. Military commanders sent men to their deaths in order to verify a kill, despite the uselessness of the information. The faith that leaders like Secretary of Defense Robert McNamara and General William Westmoreland put into these stats also betrayed an unwillingness to deal with softer and more fuzzy measures in the war.

Uncertainty is also at the heart of short-termism. As we saw in chapter 4, intertemporal problems are ultimately caused by the fact that the future is unknown, while the present is more certain. That uncertainty causes us to undervalue things that will lead to long-term benefits if they have short-term costs. The concept of "short-term pain, long-term gain" is a challenge for everyone, because we know the pain will happen, but we can never be sure of the gain.

The desire for certainty is often driven by a desire to apply techniques from the hard sciences—math, physics, chemistry—to the world of humans. Applying statistical methods, algorithms, and equations works well in the world of pure numbers, and to a lesser extent, the world of particles, molecules, and substances. But when it comes to human beings and their emotions, relationships, values, social constructions, and belief systems, the numbers start to fall apart. As Megan McArdle put it: "The less you deal with things and the more you deal with human beings, the less useful productivity metrics are." When working with human minds and bodies "it is hard to know how much of the final result is a result of your labor."[12] This desire for certainty, to be able to put a number to anything, and to be sure in the knowledge of its truth, results in several shortcomings. The first is something called reification. This is when you start to believe that the measure, and not the thing you are measuring, is what is real.[13] Safety becomes crime statistics and enforcement actions. Healthy living becomes doctor visits. The value of a player is his or her statistics. Winning a war becomes a matter of counting bodies.

Reification has a strong appeal. It is tempting to simplify the world into easy to collect and calculate numbers, and to reduce the complex, nebulous, and fluctuating systems we live in to something we can enter into a spreadsheet and come out with a number. But that is not how the world works. The world of humans, values, and beliefs is not something that can be reduced to a calculation. Freedom isn't a number. Purpose isn't an equation. Creativity cannot be fostered by collecting data. As David Manheim said, "Measurement sometimes becomes a substitute, a way to cover your rear and an excuse for doing fun math and coding instead of dealing with messy and hard to understand human interactions."[14]

The other shortcoming to our desire for certainty is that it neglects those things that cannot be measured. Not only do we believe that those things that can be measured are what is real, we stop believing that those things that cannot be measured matter, or even exist. The more we move toward quantification and management by measurement, the more we move away from the qualities that escape easy measurement. This is common in the workplace, especially in large organizations where direct observation of employees' contributions is difficult. Because counting an employee's motivation, ability to cooperate, creativity, customer focus, or dedication are difficult to observe directly or measure, organizations often fall back on evaluating employees on hard numbers—the number of hours they work, their productivity, the number of processes they complete. But these measures can backfire. By neglecting to consider the soft contributions employees make, we undermine their other contributions, to the detriment of the organization. When organizations focus only on what they can directly count, they end up losing the people who are there for a greater purpose.

TRUST

Confucius said to his disciples that there are three things needed for government: weapons, food, and trust. If a ruler cannot provide all three, he should give up the weapons first and the food next. Trust should be guarded to the end.[15]

Do you trust your employees? Your coworkers? Your government? The teachers who teach your children? The doctors who look after your health? If you don't, how can you ensure they are providing you with the services, products, and outcomes you value? For many of us, when trust is absent, and we cannot directly observe something, we seek to verify, and verification in large organizations and systems more often than not means measurement.

Trust, or lack thereof, is at the root of nearly every measure we use when dealing with people. Virtually every performance standard, productivity report, activity requirement, and work evaluation is grounded in a basic, but often unstated, belief: We do not trust one another. The need for certainty stems out of a lack of trust. Why verify something if it is coming from someone or something you trust? The desire for objectivity also comes from the fact that we do not trust that someone else shares our perspective.

Trust, in essence, is at the root of why we choose to measure. In many organizations it is a scarcity of trust that drives the need to measure performance. Many companies simply do not trust that their employees will act in the company's best interest, so they measure them.

We saw in chapter 2 how a lack of trust drives many companies to measure employees based on the number of hours they work. Companies simply do not trust that employees will use their time efficiently if given control of it, so they measure them on it. It was no surprise that when Cali Ressler and Jody Thompson surveyed employees at Best Buy and asked about how to improve the work environment, the most common response was, "Trust me with my time."[16]

That same lack of trust is what drives health agencies to measure how many "billable activities" a doctor performs. It isn't enough to trust a doctor to provide the right amount of care for their patients, which may involve doing less, not more. Instead, we must measure them. We must ensure that they are being "productive." We would rather a doctor write a prescription or order a test than have him or her tell a patient to just wait it out, as the condition will improve regardless. That same lack of trust is what drives patients to request unnecessary tests and prescriptions from their doctors.

While trust (or rather lack thereof) drives much of our desire for measurement and verification, trust itself defies measurement. Trust is something that you have until you don't. Trying to measure it is like measuring whether a light is on or off. As the saying goes, "Trust takes years to build, seconds to break, and forever to repair." Once it is gone, it is hard to bring back.

In New York the obsession with crime statistics and enforcement metrics led to a deterioration of the trust the people of New York had in the police. While precincts were able to demonstrate year-over-year decreases in their reported crime rates, their actions led to a gradual erosion of trust in the community. As Al Vann, the councilman for Bedford-Stuyvesent, put it in a letter to Police Commissioner Kelly, "We believe that residents can no longer trust the precinct to protect and serve them," saying that residents felt the police "treat our community as if it were the subject of a military occupation."[17]

Trust in the police is not just a feel-good concept, trust makes for more effective policing. The police depend on cooperation from the public. They need citizens to identify and report crime and to provide information to police officers. In return, citizens must trust that the police will protect them when they serve as witnesses to crimes. When trust in the police is eroded in the community, crimes go unreported, assistance in identifying perpetrators and providing evidence is reduced, and fear increases. Trust is the most important asset a police department has.

What we often fail to understand is that by implementing performance metrics, we can undermine trust. Not only the trust that employees or civil servants place in their employers, administration, or leaders, but also the trust the community puts in our civil servants, the trust that employees place in corporate leaders, and the trust that citizens place in government. As Onara O'Neill points out, This lack of trust is not only at the root of many of our metrics, but it has resulted in a culture of "cover your ass." Doctors spend more time recording their activity, and less time with their patients. Police spend more time recording activities, preparing cases, and fewer criminals are brought to justice. Children spend more time preparing for exams and less time learning. All of this is part of a greater drive to accountability, which has resulted in a drive "toward defensive medicine, defensive teaching, and defensive policing."[18] I would add that we are also headed toward defensive working, defensive management and defensive governance, if we are not already there.

Metrics, when abused, can undermine trust. When we use a lack of trust to justify measuring employees on their performance, we inadvertently undermine the trust those employees had in the organization. Employees no longer trust that their employers value their contributions beyond what can be measured. Trust goes two ways. Ultimately, metrics cannot replace trust in our organizations, our society, or our lives. As O'Neill says, "Elaborate measures to ensure that people keep agreements and do not betray trust must, in the end, be backed by trust. At some point, we just have to trust."[19]

||||||||||

Throughout this book, we have seen how metrics can be abused, how they can distort, disrupt, and undermine our purposes. We have seen how metrics can blind us from what is really important, how they can shift our focus to unproductive or counterproductive actions. We have also seen how metrics can help bring greater clarity to our systems, organizations, and lives. Metrics are a powerful tool that, if used improperly, can cause irrevocable harm. It is prudent to review the lessons about metrics that we have learned in this book.

First, be wary about using metrics to assign any kind of praise or blame. The more praise or blame is assigned to a metric, the more rewards and punishments are doled out based on the results, the more the metric becomes susceptible to manipulation. One reason people game a metric is because they have no recourse to improve it by their own actions. In several examples in the book, we saw how results and outcomes may be beyond the control of any single individual. Patrol officers, let alone precinct commanders, have little control over the crime rates in their precinct. Salespeople are only one component of what it takes to sell a product. A teacher's instruction is only one component of what will make a child successful at learning. When praise or blame is assigned in these situations, it only leads to frustration, or worse, manipulation. If people cannot improve their performance in order to improve the metric, they will find other ways to achieve the standards required of them.

This is a defense against Goodhart's Law. Goodhart's Law says that when any measure becomes a tool for evaluation, it ceases to be a good measure, as people will learn to game the system. The greater that incentive is to meet the metric, the more pressure on achieving results, the greater lengths people will go to achieve that goal, and the more they will stretch their ethics to do so. One way to counter this is to reduce the pressure to meet the metric. Teachers will cheat if their jobs are on the line, but they probably won't if test scores are used simply as a method to identify areas for improvement. The less weight is put onto a metric, the less it will be used to evaluate individual performance and the less likely it will be gamed.

Throughout this book we examined numerous examples of Goodhart's Law. Teachers learn to manipulate test scores in order to meet standards. Police officers write up misdemeanors in order to meet quotas. CEOs manipulate earnings to increase stock value. Workers find ways to game any system of performance measurement they are subject to. But the greater danger is not in manipulating the data, or finding ways to maximize a metric, the real danger of metrics is that they change our focus on what really matters. The greater problem in education is not that teachers may cheat on students' tests, it is that they change the way they teach and neglect teaching the complex skills that students need. The real problem in police departments that have adopted stats-heavy analyses, such as Comp-Stat, is not that police officers fudge the stats by downgrading crimes, it is that they stop doing real police work. The crisis in academia and research is not that journals exist simply to up a researcher's h-Index, or that academics cite each other's work incessantly without reason, it is that a focus on publication and citation is anathema to fundamental research, inquiry, creativity, and the pursuit of new ideas. Goodhart's Law is a distraction from the real issue: Metrics fundamentally change the way we do things. The more we put emphasis on achieving a metric, the more people will shift their efforts away from what really matters to what is being measured.

Instead, metrics should be used to identify areas for improvement so that employees can work collaboratively with their leaders to do things better.[20] Here's one way to look at this: Measurement should be used as feedback rather than as a metric. Feedback differs from metrics in that the information provided can come from anywhere, the system is responsible for creating its own meaning, new ideas are encouraged, and the focus is on adaptability and growth. Metrics, on the other hand, are imposed, they are one size fits all, their meaning is predetermined, and they focus on stability and control.[21]

Second, as detailed in chapter 2, when using metrics, understand whether you are measuring inputs, outputs, or outcomes. In many cases measures should focus on the outcome, the thing you want to change. By focusing too much on inputs or outputs, you may only encourage inefficiency, or worse, counterproductivity. However, these are not hard-and-fast rules. In some cases measuring inputs or outputs can be useful. In academic research, for example, outcomes cannot be predicted when research begins. Discoveries are often serendipitous and unpredictable, yet can be groundbreaking. Trying to measure outcomes is like predicting whether you will get in a car accident or not. You cannot know for certain whether you might be hit by a distracted driver or hit a patch of black ice, but what you can do is learn to drive safely and according to the conditions of the road. Just as we shouldn't assign blame to someone who is a careful driver, yet is involved in an accident, neither should we measure scientists on their output. Instead we should measure them on their ability to think creatively and explore new areas of knowledge, their capacity to create an environment that fosters inquiry and ingenuity, and their adaptability to change.

Third, recognize whether your metrics are prioritizing the short-term over the long-term and vice versa. Chapter 4 discussed how measures such as earnings or publications in the corporate world and academia ultimately sacrificed long-term benefits for short-term results. Other measures have this potential to undermine long-term goals too. When cities measure operational expenses without reference to long-term maintenance of infrastructure, they are discounting the future. When governments seek to reduce taxes by cutting education or healthcare, they are sacrificing the future for the present.

Fourth, when measuring anything, understand the formula you are using to determine the measure. Sometimes using the wrong denominator (when using ratios) can skew and pervert the purpose of what you are trying to measure. In short, are you measuring what you think you are measuring?

Fifth, be cognizant of whether you are measuring just a part of the system you want to improve, or the entire thing. Some systems may seem too complex to fully understand, resulting in a desire to simplify. But that simplification may go too far, and the metrics you seek to maximize may undermine other things that matter.

Sixth, ensure you are measuring things of different quality differently. There is good reason to simplify the categories and qualities you measure, as no measure can capture every intricacy and dimension of everything. But this simplification can go too far. When you count every cause of death as the same, you disregard the vast differences in the nature of those deaths and end up focusing effort on the wrong things. The same goes for any measures where the quality can vary greatly. If you measure employees on how many "processes" they complete, but those processes can range from very high quality to very low, you may need to rethink your measures.

Seventh, be wary of focusing intently on those things that can be easily measured. Do not let your strategies devolve into a numbers game. In any organization there will always be those who desire to fall back on "management by metrics," an approach that seeks to measure anything and everything. Managers and leaders who focus on numbers, and only numbers, end up encouraging behavior that only knows how to respond to numbers. What you get is people who know how to play the numbers game. Not everything that can be counted, counts. As Dan Ariely said, "What you measure is what you'll get. Period."[22]

Eighth, remember that just because something is not easily measured does not mean that it is not valuable. This applies not only in the "softer" areas of our world, such as our personal lives or our society at large, but also in the seemingly quantitative areas of business or science. Traits such as motivation, cooperation, inspiration, creativity, and a sense of purpose are not created by measurement. Not everything that counts can be counted.

Ninth, understand that by measuring you just may well undermine the very motivation you seek to foster. As we saw in chapter 9, metrics and incentives do not necessarily motivate people in the way you think they might, and they can even demotivate them. When you measure and reward one thing, you should think about what that does to the value of other things. By building one thing up, are you tearing something else down? By putting one thing in the spotlight, are you relegating other things to the dark?

Tenth, understand that no single metric holds all the answers. Measure multiple things.[23] Throughout this book, we saw numerous examples or poor metrics, but we also saw some examples of good ones. No metric holds the entire truth or can solve all your problems, but measuring several things may help further your understanding and temper the shortcomings of individual metrics. Not only should you measure multiple things, but you should regularly question whether the metrics you are using are useful or relevant. What's more, you should also question whether there is anything useful or relevant that can be measured that you aren't measuring.

Eleventh, do not get carried away with measuring. Some metrics are useful, many others are not. Do not fall into the trap of measuring just for the sake of measuring. This was the error that Robert McNamara made in the first part of the war in Vietnam. The amount of data was so staggering that it ceased to have any meaning. Businesses also fall into this trap. Companies have over one hundred metrics that they can use to track Web traffic, but are all of them useful?

Twelfth, do not use metrics to make up for a lack of trust. Whether it is a trust that employees will be productive, teachers will educate our children properly, healthcare professionals will look after our well-being, or the police will protect us and keep us safe, metrics are not a replacement for trust. Trust is built through continued action and reinforcement of shared values and a sense of duty and accountability to each other. Using metrics to replace trust only shifts that accountability to the numbers themselves.

Thirteenth, rather than measure performance, focus instead on behavior. In many roles, especially those with complex tasks that involve many different groups of people, no single person can be held responsible for the outcomes of their work. There are just too many forces outside of their own actions that can influence outcomes. Employees can do all the right things but still not achieve the results they need. Performance metrics in these situations act as arbitrary dispensers of reward or blame, leading to frustration, disillusionment, and, sometimes, hopelessness. Instead, organizations should focus on teaching, encouraging, and rewarding behaviors. If an employee exhibits all the right behaviors—dedication, cooperation, ingenuity, problem solving, and more—but is just unable to achieve results because of factors outside their control, they should nevertheless be valued.

Finally, learn to be critical of metrics. The point of this book isn't to solve every problem of measurement that anyone may come across. Rather, it is to provide a basic understanding of the shortcomings of metrics and how to spot them. When faced with a measurement at work, in what you read, or in your daily life, ask what it means and question whether it is truly measuring what it says it is measuring.

Throughout this book there have been many heroes and a fair share of villains. The heroes were those who recognized the flaws of metrics and decided to do something about it. Adrian Schoolcraft exposed massive fraud and cover-ups in the NYPD. Dr. Peggy Aufricht saw the incredible inefficiencies of primary healthcare and worked tirelessly to create a whole new system that focused on patient health. Shauna Thome continues to advocate for a better way to operate and measure primary healthcare. Heather Vogell and John Perry exposed a cheating scandal in the Atlanta Public Schools system and revealed how an obsession with test scores led hundreds of teachers, principals, and administrators to cheat on students' exams. Randy Schekman started an open-source journal after seeing the perversity of bibliometrics and the emphasis on citations. Edward Lansdale and Bernard Fall saw the insanity that was the Vietnam War and the folly of counting bodies instead of understanding the people whose country they were fighting in. Simon Kuznets recognized the shortcomings of his economic measurement that came to dominate the world.

But the biggest character in these stories was rarely mentioned: the public. Behind nearly every flawed metric in this book are the people who just want to know the numbers. Shareholders who rely on earnings to understand the value of stocks instead of taking the time to look into the fundamentals of a company's competitive position. A public that looks to rising or falling crime rates as an indication of community safety while ignoring the questionable actions of police officers. A public that demands that healthcare professionals work hard to deliver the care we need, without thinking about whether that care makes us healthier. Parents who want to know that their children's school produces good test scores, but do not consider the other values and skills the school will teach them.

Many of the villains in this book are not really villains, they are just people working in a system that demands they produce the right numbers. Many of the police officers working at the 81st Precinct in New York were likely good people who wanted to do good in their community. But put into a system that valued quotas above all else, they responded as many of us would. The teachers at Parks Middle School and other schools throughout Georgia were mostly good people who wanted to make a difference in students' lives. Yet, when placed into a culture that stressed test scores no matter how they were achieved, they did what they needed to in order to keep teaching their students. Put good people in a bad system, and they will bend. Rather than blame the people, often it is better to change the system.

Metrics are a force all around us. They regulate our places of work. They determine our wages and benefits. We use them to evaluate our schools, our healthcare systems, and our economy. They are used to shape policies, business strategies, and government programs. Metrics permeate our lives like never before. But only if we let them.

There is incredible power in metrics, and that power is ultimately about choice. The great part of metrics is that we get to choose what we measure. We can choose to measure ourselves by how much money we make, or we can choose not to. We can instead choose to measure our lives by what we contribute to the betterment of our fellow humans. Someone can tell you he or she is faster, stronger, richer, or have more things than you, but those statements only have power over you if you choose to let them have it. Ultimately, we choose what we deem to be useful, important, and valuable. That is the last lesson we turn to in the final chapter.

CHAPTER 10
GATEWAYS NOT YARDSTICKS

Maria is writing a test. It is much like the tests discussed in chapter 2. The subject matter is the same. The same formulas, concepts, and tools she needs to use for this exam are the ones most students need. But that is where the similarities end.

Maria isn't in a gymnasium with hundreds of other students. She is not being timed. The questions she is answering are not designed to confuse her, or to punish her for taking too much time, but that does not mean they are easy. Some may be multiple-choice, but few, if any, are designed to test her memorization.

Maria is sitting by herself in front of a classroom computer, taking the test at her own pace. If she needs to think something through, she has the time to do so. If she is confused by a question, she can take the time to understand it. If Maria fails the test, there is no negative repercussion on her grade. The test won't impact her chances for college admission, at least not directly. Her school won't suffer funding cuts if Maria and others do poorly on this test. For, if Maria does poorly on this test, she can retake it. She can take it again tomorrow, or in a week if she wants, or again a month later. If she needs to, she can take the test ten times over.

This seems counterintuitive. A test that isn't timed? That can be written over and over again? A test a student writes on her own time, when she is ready for it? Surely such a testing system lowers standards and fosters an environment of mediocrity. What good can come from a test that is so lenient on students? The answer is simple. There is one thing that sets this test apart from most other tests. Maria doesn't just need to pass this test. She needs to ace it.

||||||||||

Salman Khan is smart by any measure. Born in Louisiana to a Bangledeshi father and an Indian mother, not only did Salman earn an MBA from Harvard Business School, but he also received three other degrees from MIT. Soon after completing college, he began working for a hedge fund. In 2004 he got married in New Jersey.

Salman went about his life in the financial industry and, if it wasn't for a wedding he went to in 2004, his life very well may have continued down that path. For at that wedding, he ran into someone who would change his life forever: his cousin Nadia.

After talking with Nadia, Salman learned that she had recently done quite poorly on a math placement exam. Salman found this strange, as Nadia had always been a high achiever. The test result came as a blow to her self-confidence. For Nadia, the test was a signal that perhaps she wasn't that good at math. But Salman refused to believe it; as she had demonstrated quite the opposite on several occasions. So, he offered to tutor her. And thus, with a single tutor and a single student, the Khan Academy was born.

With Salman in Boston and Nadia in New Orleans, the tutoring had to be done remotely. Using tablet computers and Yahoo Doodle, Salman began to tutor Nadia in math. What Salman learned was although Nadia was able to take on complex math problems, she had trouble with the basic concept of unit conversion (converting inches to feet, feet to miles, and so on). When Salman would ask her questions about the concept, Nadia would freeze up, unable to work through the problem. Like those who have trouble answering questions during a high-stakes test, the pressure to answer the question had paralyzed Nadia.

Not wanting to sound stupid, Nadia would not simply answer, "I don't know." Instead she felt compelled to give an answer, so she would guess. Then after finding out the answer was wrong, she would resign herself to the idea that she just wasn't good at that particular subject. If she hadn't gotten the right answer, she must just be bad at that subject. It had never crossed her mind that not understanding was perfectly normal. Picking up on this, Salman encouraged Nadia to say when she didn't understand what she was learning. He encouraged her to speak up when she was stuck so they could approach the problem in a different way or he could give her a different explanation of the concept. The message was: You are not expected to know every concept, but you are expected to want to learn it.

The tutorials Salman provided to Nadia were soon used to help other family members and friends. Due to the increased demand, Salman started recording his lessons on YouTube so students could view them any time. It wasn't just the convenience that the people using Salman's tutorials felt was useful, if they didn't understand something, they could go back in the video and go over the lecture again. And soon, it wasn't just close family and friends who were receiving tutoring from Salman, dozens and then hundreds and then thousands of others found Salman's videos on YouTube. They discovered the same benefits: They were able to control when, where, and how they viewed Salman's tutorial videos, which allowed them to learn at their own pace and focus their efforts on those concepts they found difficult. Salman had caught on to something. In 2009 he quit his job and began working on the Khan Academy full-time.

From this idea, that students shouldn't rush through concepts they don't understand, Salman changed the way he approached teaching. Salman began implementing the concept of mastery learning. Mastery learning differs from conventional educational approaches in one fundamental way. In a conventional school what is held constant is the amount of time each student has to learn a particular subject—two weeks on long division, two weeks on exponents, three days of valence electrons. In mastery learning the constant is the level of learning the student is expected to achieve. As Salman puts it, "Our schools measure out [students'] efforts in increments of time rather than in target levels of mastery. When the interval allotted for a given topic has run out, it's time to give a test and move on."[1]

If each concept was independent of all others, this would only be a minor problem, but concepts in every subject are related. As Khan says, "Concepts build on one another. Algebra requires arithmetic. Trigonometry flows from geometry. Calculus and physics call for all of the above. A shaky understanding early on will lead to complete bewilderment later."[2] The result of such a system, the conventional way we learn and test students, is what Salman calls "Swiss Cheese Learning"; a student's understanding is developed full of holes. As students rush from one subject to another, they leave little gaps in their understanding. Every subject that they don't fully understand builds a shakier and shakier foundation. Salman believes that many students are not intrinsically unable to excel at math or other subjects, but that, like Nadia, they are trying to learn something with an incomplete foundation. Teachers at Parks Middle knew this well. As Damany Lewis said, "We had two weeks to teach percentages, and if you're still on percentages at week three, because your kids don't get it yet, they'll say 'You don't teach well enough.'"[3] Tests in conventional schools, as we learned in chapter 2, are designed to sort and rank students. The tests are designed so that some students do well, and others do poorly. This is why only a certain amount of time is dedicated to each subject. If students were given a variable amount of time, they might all do similarly well on the test. If that were the case, there would be no way to evaluate if Samantha is smarter than Tom.

Following this reasoning, a test where every student does well is a poor test. How else can we sort students into grades from well-performing to falling behind? What is the use of a test that everyone does perfectly on? School curriculums and tests are designed to move the pace of learning beyond the reach of some students so that they won't do as well on the test. The way conventional tests are structured, schools are designed to make some children fail. And by doing so, they fail children. But Salman Khan decided to ask the opposite question: What is the use of an education that doesn't teach all the students to master each subject? What good is an education system that not only leaves some students behind, but is designed to leave them behind? Shouldn't the purpose of our education be to teach as many students as much as we can?

That is why Salman developed the testing practice, the type of test that Maria was taking at the beginning of this chapter, the way he did. He wanted to ensure that students not only understood a subject before moving on, but that they mastered it. And he wanted all students to master every subject. Salman let students take tests whenever they felt ready. They could take as much time as they needed, and they could take the test as many times as they liked. However, anything less than mastery of the subject matter was not acceptable. Salman decided that the initial criteria for passing a test would be as follows: For any concept, the student had to get ten questions right in a row at some point when answering fifty questions. Ten isn't some magic number. There isn't some mathematical formula showing that ten questions in a row somehow crosses a threshold of understanding. Salman Khan just thought it was a pretty good indicator of mastery. It would later be refined using more advanced techniques, but the concept was the same: Students need to master a concept before moving on to the next one.

For Salman, the purpose of the test is not to rank students or tell them they are poor at a subject. Rather, a test is an indication of whether or not students understand a particular concept or if they need more time and work to understand it. Tests at the Khan Academy are not yardsticks of ability, but gateways to new learning.

In 2007 Salman, with support from local teachers, was able to test his concept of mastery learning in a summer educational program in the Bay Area called Peninsula Bridge. Peninsula Bridge offers additional educational support to motivated students from underresourced schools in the area. Better-off schools donate their facilities, and the children are given the opportunity to improve their education, tuition-free, for a summer. Khan's program lasted six weeks, and the students were mostly in sixth to eighth grade.

What made the Peninsula Bridge experience interesting was that several teachers, rather than use the fifth-grade math curriculum, as Salman suggested, preferred to go right back to the very basics with their classrooms. Inadvertently, Salman had implemented a controlled experiment.

While some classrooms would start with curriculum just a year or two earlier than the grade level of the students in the classroom, others were going back to the very basics. These were sixth, seventh, and eighth graders going back to relearn $1+1=2$.

What the teachers found was interesting. While most students raced through the early curriculum, several students got stuck on some early concepts, such as two-digit subtraction or fractions. But once they got over those hurdles, their learning curve skyrocketed. It was like there was a broken component of an engine holding their pace of learning back, and once that component was repaired, the engine was able to go full throttle. Several students who started with later curriculums, on the other hand, still hit roadblocks on later concepts, struggling to understand or learn at a normal pace.

What was surprising to Salman was that the students in the classrooms that went back to the very basics, those who started with $1+1=2$, not only caught up to the "advanced class," they surpassed them in the curriculum. It was like they needed to go back and fix everything that was wrong with their engines before starting the race. This idea was illustrated by one seventh-grade student, who Salman calls Marcela. Marcela was one of the least advanced in the class at the start of the program. She was learning at a rate about half of the average student. She had hit a roadblock; she was struggling an incredible amount with adding and subtracting negative numbers. But the program let her struggle with that concept, not allowing her to advance until she understood it. Then, one day, it hit her, and it all made sense. Then, all of a sudden, Marcela just blasted through the curriculum. She went from nearly the bottom of the class to second best. All because she was allowed to not know something until she understood it.[4]

||||||||||

There is a lesson in the way the Khan Academy used their tests. Salman Khan understood that tests were no longer in the service of education, but that education was in the service of tests. He decided to change that.

When the focus of tests changed from ranking students to authentic learning, everything about them changed. If you are not interested in ranking students, the idea of only taking a test once seems silly. On a conventional test, if a student does poorly, the thought that follows is, "Well, Patrick is just not as smart as Helen, which is why he didn't do as well on the test." When tests aren't focused on ranking students, the response changes to, "Patrick doesn't understand exponentials, so we need to go back and help him work through it until he does." When we stop trying to rank students, we start to focus on teaching them.

When the focus of a primary health clinic changes from evaluating how much work doctors do to how healthy patients are, patient health improves. When we measure productivity at work rather than how much we work, companies do better. When we measure the full costs of transportation and housing, we make better decisions about where to live and how to get around. When we change how we measure diseases from how many people it claims to the full burden of that disease on life satisfaction and expectancy, we make better decisions on improving people's lives. When we measure our economies on how they affect our lives rather than how much stuff we produce, we improve the well-being of everyone. What you measure is what you get.

Measurement is the means, not the end. The goal of a school system is not to raise test scores, but to educate children. The point of education is to provide children with authentic learning and understanding, to challenge them to think, to have them question ideas and improve on them, to have them think critically, to have them learn how to learn, and to prepare them to help solve the problems we as a society face. Our school systems should focus on the best way to teach all of our students and not on evaluating which ones do better at what subjects.

A healthcare system should be about fostering a healthy populace, not keeping doctors busy. Our economy should be about creating authentic prosperity and improving the well-being of our citizens, not producing as much stuff as quickly as possible. Our measurements should reflect those aspirations, we shouldn't change those aspirations to fit what we can measure. Measurement is never the goal. The goal is always something else: a healthier populace, better-educated students, efficient transportation, better quality of life. When the metric becomes the goal, we lose sight of what really matters.

The Khan Academy teaches us that the role of metrics in our lives can be rethought. We can put metrics into the service of the goals we are trying to achieve, rather than being slaves to them. Salman Khan understood that education should be about teaching students to master all the subjects they were learning, and that they had to master each step before moving on to the next. He didn't seek the best way to evaluate students and then fit his teaching to that task. He wanted to find the best way to teach children and designed his tests to serve that purpose. As Margaret Wheatley and Myron Kellner-Rogers would put it, Salman Khan let the meaning define the measure, not the other way around.[5] Salman Khan wasn't looking for a better way to test children, he was looking for a better way to teach children. We are not slaves to the things we measure, they work for us. We are not ants.

The next time you want to measure productivity at work, or the effectiveness of a new fitness regimen, don't ask yourself, "What can I measure?" Instead ask, "What am I trying to do?" Asking that simple question may just change the way you do things and what you ultimately achieve. It is one of the most important questions you can ask.

When somebody who is overworked in a miserable job, spending too much on security systems to protect their family because their community is unsafe, too much on healthcare because their job and their lifestyle severely affects their health, and too little time with their family, is measured as better off than someone who lives in a safe neighborhood, works fewer hours at a more meaningful job, has more time for leisure activities, is healthier and will live longer, but makes less money, something is wrong. Something is wrong when a student who doesn't understand the material does better on a test than one who is thinking on a deeper level but can't answer a dumbed-down multiple-choice question with confidence. Something is wrong when those who show up early and leave late but don't do any meaningful work are valued more than those who get their work done quickly and efficiently but spend less time at work. When doctors spend more time doing unnecessary work than focusing on improving patients' health, something is wrong.

Test scores in our schools fail to measure authentic learning. Too many employers fail to measure genuine contributions to work. Too many employees measure their success at work by how much they make and not by how much enjoyment they get from their jobs, how meaningful their work is, or how much time their jobs leave them to spend with their friends and family. We evaluate our social relationships on how many Facebook friends, Twitter followers, or Instagram likes we have, not on how strong our friendships are, whether we have someone we can confide in, or how much we share our lives with others. What we can measure becomes what we do.

Our lives are not a tally of incomes, possessions, and educational degrees or the number of social media followers. We can't measure our happiness in the value of our homes or our cars, in the number of countries we have traveled to, the number of friends we have made, or the times we've won a game. All of these things may help improve the value of and meaning we get from our lives, but that is not the same thing as value and meaning. You cannot measure the value of sharing intimate feelings with another person, the beauty of a view from a mountaintop, the joy of seeing a child learn to walk, or the satisfaction of helping someone in need. Our lives are stories, not equations.

We should measure more in our lives, and I hope this book has demonstrated that. But we should never measure just for the sake of measurement and never without some thought toward what we are measuring and why. We should know that how and what we measure will affect what we do and how we do it. We should understand if we are measuring an input, output, or outcome, and why. We should keep in mind whether we are measuring short-term goals or long-term ones. We should choose the right denominator, one that reflects the phenomena we are trying to capture. We shouldn't misconstrue our measurements by omitting important aspects of a system. We should understand the different qualities of the things we measure and account for them. We shouldn't let our lives become number games, and we shouldn't neglect those things that can't be counted but really count.

With these measurements we shouldn't mistake precision for certainty, mistake data for understanding, nor mistake absence of measurement for absence of importance. Just because a metric uses a precise number, that doesn't mean it is true. Just because we can come up with a measure for something, it does not mean we understand it. Just because we can't measure something does not mean it does not matter. No metric is perfect, and most, in fact, are quite bad. We should be more critical of any measurements we come across in what we read and use at work and how we evaluate ourselves. We should put more thought into what we are measuring, what it means, and how it affects what we do. But more important, we should remember from time to time to not worry about evaluating everything, and we should simply enjoy the things that we just can't count.

If this book has taught you anything, hopefully it has taught you that not everything can be measured. Not everything that is worthwhile is worth measuring. The smile of a loved one, watching your children grow and learn, mastering a new skill, overcoming adversity, enjoying a sunset, showing appreciation for someone, engaging in meaningful work, taking on a challenge, understanding something deeply, feeling accepted, knowing someone intimately, finding value in giving to others, and creating a life full of experiences and emotions and memories and meaning are things that you just can't count. But they count for more than anything.

ACKNOWLEDGMENTS

A book is never written by just one person. This book is no different. There are countless people who helped write this book, whether by providing feedback and insight, pointing me in the right direction when I was stuck, introducing me to new topics for research, or just being a good support during the countless hours I spent on the book. First of all, my family. Thanks to my mom Elma, my dad Tony, my brothers Michael and David, and my sisters-in-law Andrea and Christa. You all were incredibly supportive during these last several years. All those Sunday dinner conversations provided a lot of ideas for this book, so thank you all for those. Special thanks to my mom, Andrea, and Christa for putting up with those unnecessarily loud dinner conversations every Sunday night; the Schryvers men are still learning that being louder doesn't mean be more right. Also thanks to my nephews Isaac, Alaric, Xavier, and Solomon. Your jokes, smiles, and hilarious antics always bring me joy.

There were many friends, colleagues, and classmates who helped me throughout the process who deserve thanks. Karol Cheetham for being the first person to agree to read my book, for giving me great feedback in the very early stages of this work, and for being a great friend. I think it's my turn to buy drinks. Josh Bourdage for introducing me to the world of organizational psychology and helping by sending me all those articles. Michael Bowerman for discussing the book with me and introducing me to the ideas of the logic model and the DALY. Michael Gestwick for his paper on energy use, which I found fascinating. Brandon Holterman and Sarah Kenny for letting me use their beautiful cabin in British Columbia to complete my book. I hope that squirrel doesn't come back. Holly Marisco for being so supportive of me while I worked on the book.

ACKNOWLEDGMENTS

Thanks for everything you did, especially for the cookies. Ryan and Candace Bjornsen, my best friends, without whose support I never would have been able to write this book. Thanks for all the conversations, climbing, wing nights, game nights and for letting me be "Mr. Pete" to your three beautiful daughters.

I must thank Peggy Aufricht and Shauna Thome from the Crowfoot Village Family Practice. Your dedication and passion to healthcare is truly inspiring. Heather White for her passion for community service. Special thanks to Chris Turner, who gave me the best advice before I started writing this book: This is a marathon, not a sprint. You were right, this was a marathon, but your advice helped me prepare for it. I also want to thank Dan Crissman and Katy Hamilton for providing editorial feedback on earlier drafts of the book.

Huge thanks to Jeff Shreve, my agent, for helping me learn the whole writing and publishing process and for being such a great advocate for this book. The writing process is incredibly daunting for first-time writers, and you helped me get to know the ins and outs of everything. Steven L. Mitchell and the rest of the team at Prometheus Books and Karen Ackermann and the team at Rowman & Littlefield deserve a big thanks for all their hard work in editing, marketing, and publishing this book, but mostly for believing in me. Thanks to Katie Sharp for the great work she did copyediting this book and making the writing a lot tighter and cleaner and for deleting probably a thousand superfluous commas throughout the book. Taking a chance on a first-time writer isn't easy, and the people at Prometheus Books and Rowman & Littlefield deserve a lot of kudos for taking a chance on this one.

Finally, to my mom. You deserve a second thanks. You have been such an incredible support throughout my life. This book is for you.

NOTES

INTRODCUTION

1. Bert Hölldobler and E. O. Wilson, *The Super-Organism: The Beauty, Elegance and Strangeness of Insect Societies*, (New York: W. W. Norton, 2009), 183–87.

2. Peter Minimum. "Digital Advertising's Perverse Incentives." *Marketingland* (April 21, 2017). https://marketingland.com/digital-advertisings-perverse-incentives-212180.

3. David Manheim. "Goodhart's Law and Why Measurement Is Hard." *Ribbon-Farm* (June 9, 2016), https://www.ribbonfarm.com/2016/06/09/goodharts-law-and-why-measurement-is-hard/.

CHAPTER I

1. Kate Taylor, "Principal Acknowledged Forging Answers on Tests for Students, Officials Say," *New York Times*, July 28, 2015; Laila Kearney, "NYC Grade School Principal Who Committed Suicide Had Forged Tests," Reuters, July 27, 2015.

2. Abby Jackson, "How a cheating scandal at a well-regarded public school in New York turned tragic," *Business Insider*, July 28, 2015.

3. Susan Edelman, Amber Jamieson, and Jamie Schram, "Principal commits suicide amid Common Core test scandal," *New York Post*, July 26, 2015.

4. Alan Singer, "The Results Are In: Common Core Fails Tests and Kids," *Huffington Post*, May 2, 2016.

5. Peter Sacks, *Standardized Minds: The High Price of America's Testing Culture* (De Capo Press, 2000), 128.

6. Alfie Kohn, *The Case Against Standardized Testing: Raising the Scores, Ruining the Schools*, (Portsmouth, NH: Heinemann, 2000), 2.

7. Bowers, Bruce C. quoted in Sacks, 9.

8. Kohn, *The Case Against Standardized Testing*, 7, 18.

9. The College Board. The SAT: Practice Test #5. https://collegereadiness.collegeboard.org/sat/practice/full-length-practice-tests.

10. Sacks, 205.

11. Sacks, 207.

12. Kohn, *The Case Against Standardized Testing*, 6.

13. Ibid., 4.

14. Ibid., 6.

15. Ibid., 93.

16. Sacks, *Standardized Minds*, 7.

17. Ibid., 211.

18. Ibid., 273.

19. Ibid., 8.

20. Jennifer Jennings and Jonathan Marc Bearak. "'Teaching to the Test' in the new NCLB Era: How Test Predictability Affects Our Understanding of Student Performance." *Educational Researcher*. Vol. 43, No. 8. (November 2014): 381–89.

21. Sacks, *Standardized Minds*, 129.

22. Ibid., 134.

23. Elizabeth A. Harris, "20% of State Students Opted Out of Tests in Sign of a Rising Revolt," *New York Times*, August 13, 2015.

24. John Perry, "Surge in CRCT results raises 'big red flag,'" *Atlanta Journal Constitution*. December 2008, updated January 19, 2012.

25. Rachel Aviv, "Wrong Answer: In an era of high-stakes testing, a struggling school made a shocking choice," *New Yorker*, July 21, 2014.

26. Ibid.

27. Christopher Waller and LaDawn B. Jones, *Cheating but Not Cheated: A Memoir of the Atlanta Public Schools Cheating Scandal* (LaDawn B. Jones, 2015), 181–97.

28. Aviv, "Wrong Answer."

29. Waller and Jones, *Cheating but Not Cheated*, 216.

30. Ibid., 110.

31. http://www.gadoe.org/Curriculum-Instruction-and-Assessment/Assessment/Pages/CRCT.aspx.

32. Aviv, "Wrong Answer."

33. Waller and Jones, *Cheating but Not Cheated*, 131.

34. Ibid., 138.

35. Michael Winerip "Ex-School Chief in Atlanta Is Indicted in Testing Scandal," *New York Times*, March 29, 2013.

36. Aviv, "Wrong Answer."

37. Ibid.

38. Ibid.

39. Waller and Jones, *Cheating but Not Cheated*, 141.

40. Michael Winerip "Ex-School Chief in Atlanta Is Indicted in Testing Scandal." *New York Times*, March 29, 2013.

41. Aviv, "Wrong Answer."

42. Waller and Jones, *Cheating but Not Cheated*, 201–3.

43. Aviv, "Wrong Answer."

44 Waller and Jones, *Cheating but Not Cheated*, 16.

45. Aviv, "Wrong Answer."

46. Waller and Jones, *Cheating but Not Cheated*, 144.

47. Aviv, "Wrong Answer."

48. Ibid.

49. Ibid.

50. Waller and Jones, *Cheating but Not Cheated*, 111.

51. Aviv, "Wrong Answer."

52. Waller and Jones, *Cheating but Not Cheated*, 116.

53. Aviv, "Wrong Answer."

54. Waller and Jones, *Cheating but Not Cheated*, 128.

55. Aviv, "Wrong Answer."

56. Michael Winerip "Ex-School Chief in Atlanta Is Indicted in Testing Scandal." *New York Times*, March 29, 2013.

57. Waller and Jones, *Cheating but Not Cheated*.

58. Waller and Jones, *Cheating but Not Cheated*, 132.

59. Aviv, "Wrong Answer."

60. Waller and Jones, *Cheating but Not Cheated*, 117.

61. Perry, "Surge in CRCT results raises 'big red flag.'"

62. John Perry, "Are drastic swings in CRTC scores valid," *Atlanta Journal Constitution*. October, 2009, updated July 5, 2011.

63. Ibid.

64. Ibid.

65. Aviv, "Wrong Answer."

66. Waller and Jones, *Cheating but Not Cheated*, 83.

67. Michael Winerip, "Ex-School Chief in Atlanta Is Indicted in Testing Scandal," *New York Times*, March 29, 2013.

68. Aviv, "Wrong Answer."

69. Winerip, "Ex-School Chief in Atlanta Is Indicted in Testing Scandal."

70. Waller and Jones, *Cheating but Not Cheated*, 72.

71. Waller and Jones, *Cheating but Not Cheated*, 171.

72. Valerie Stauss, "How and why convicted Atlanta teachers cheated on standardized tests," *Washington Post*, April 1, 2015.

73. Winerip "Ex-School Chief in Atlanta Is Indicted in Testing Scandal."

74. Aviv, "Wrong Answer."

75. Ibid.

76. Ibid.

77. Waller and Jones, *Cheating but Not Cheated*, 141.

78. Ibid., 145

79. Aviv, "Wrong Answer."

80. Waller and Jones, *Cheating but Not Cheated*.

81. Aviv, "Wrong Answer."

82. Valerie Stauss, "How and why convicted Atlanta teachers cheated on standardized tests" *Washington Post*, April 1, 2015.

83. Aviv, "Wrong Answer."

84. Ibid.

85. A similar observation by Donald T. Campbell occurred around the same time as Goodhart's work, and is termed "Campbell's Law." While there is debate around which researcher should claim credit for the phenomenon, this book will use the term Goodhart's Law.

86. Zeger Van Hese "Metrics—perverse incentives?" Test Side Story. https://testsidestory.com/author/zegervanhese/page/7/.

87. Robert Gibbons, "Incentives in Organizations," *Journal of Economic Perspectives*, Vol. 12, No. 4 (Autumn, 1998): 115-32.

88. David Parmenter, "Should We Abandon Performance Measures?" *Cutter IT Journal.* January 2013 http://cdn.davidparmenter.com/files/2014/02/Should-we-abandon-ourperformance-measures-Cutter-Journal-2013.pdf..pdf.

89. Megan McArdle, "Metrics and Their Unintended Consequences," *Bloomberg Opinion*, January 3, 2018 https://www.bloomberg.com/opinion/articles/2018-01-03/metrics-and-unintended-consequences-in-health-care-and-education.

90. Patrick Walker. "Self-Defeating Regulation." *International Zeitschrift*, April 2013.

91. John R Hauser and Gerald M. Katz, "Metrics: You Are What You Measure!," *European Management Journal*, Vol. 16 No. 5 (April 1998): 517–28.

92. Dan Ariely, "You Are What You Measure," *Harvard Business Review*, June 2010. https://hbr.org/2010/06/column-you-are-what-you-measure.

CHAPTER 2

1. Dr. Margaret Aufricht, interview with the author, February 2014.

2. Dr. Lisa Wyatt Knowlton, Cynthia C Phillips, *The Logic Model Guidebook* (Sage Publications, 2012), 4–6

3. Knowlton and Phillips, 6–7

4. Shauna Thome, interview with the author, November 2018.

5. Health Quality Council of Alberta, *2009 Measuring and Monitoring for Success* (Calgary: Health Quality Council of Alberta, 2009), 37.

6. Ibid., p. 38.

7. PerryUndem Research/Communication, *Unnecessary Tests and Procedures in the Health Care System: What Physicians Say About The Problem, the Causes, and the Solutions: Results from a National Survey of Physicians* (PerryUndem Research/Communication, May 1, 2014), http://

www.choosingwisely.org/wpcontent/uploads/2015/04/Final-Choosing-Wisely- Survey-Report .pdf.

8. Kaiser Health News, "Unnecessary medical tests, treatments cost $200 billion annually, cause harm," HealthCare Finance, May 24, 2017, https://www.healthcarefinancenews.com/news/unnecessary-medical-tests-treatments-cost-200-billion-annually-cause-harm.

9. Cali Ressler and Jody Thompson. *Why Work Sucks and How to Fix It: The Results-Only Revolution* (New York: Penguin Group, 2008), 4.

10. Ibid., 1.

11. Ibid., 16.

12. Ibid., 83–86.

CHAPTER 3

1. Imran S. Currim, Jooseop Lim, and Joung W Kim, "You Get What You Pay For: The effect of top executives compensation on advertising and R&D designs and stock market return," *Journal of Marketing*. Vol. 76 (September 2012).

2. Alfred Rappaport, "The Economics of Short-Term Performance Obsession," *Financial Analysts Journal*. Vol. 61, No. 3.

3. Currim, Lim and Kim.

4. Michael Mauboussin, "The True Measures of Success," *Harvard Business Review* (October 2012).

5. Rappaport.

6. Ibid.

7. Ibid.

8. Kevin J. Laverty, "Economic Short-Termism: The Debate, The Unresolved Issues, and the Implications for Management Practice and Research," *Academy of Management Review* Vol. 21, No. 3.

9. Razeen Sappideen, "Focusing on Corporate Short-Termism," *Singapore Journal of Legal Studies*. (December 2011).

10. Rappaport.

11. Ibid.

12. Sappideen.

13. Ibid.

14. Rappaport.

15. Ibid.

16. Laverty.

17. Ibid.

18. Sappideen.

19. Ibid.

20. Ibid.

21. Mauboussin.

22. Laverty.

23. George A Akerlof, "The Market for 'Lemons': Quality Uncertainty and the Market Mechanism," *Quarterly Journal of Economics* Vol. 84, No. 3 (August 1970).

24. Laverty.

25. Ibid.

26. Currim, Lim and Kim.

27. Mizik

28. Johnson and Kaplan (1987) cited in Lin Peng and Alisa Roell, "Managerial Incentives and Stock Price Manipulation," *Journal of Finance* Vol. LXIX, No. 2 (April 2014).

29. Currim, Lim and Kim.

30. Sappideen

31. Currim, Lim and Kim.

32. Natalie Mizik, "The Theory and Practice of Myopic Management," *Journal of Marketing Research* Vol. 47, No. 4.

33. Ibid.

34. Sappideen.

35. Laverty.

36. Mizik.

37. Ibid.

38. Currim, Lim and Kim.

39. M. P. Narayanan, "Managerial Incentives for Short-Term Results," *Journal of Finance* Vol. XI, No. 5 (December 1985).

40. Rappaport.

41. Currim, Lim and Kim.

42. Ibid.

43. Edward P. Lazear, "Compensation and Incentives in the Workplace," *Journal of Economic Perspectives* Vol. 32, No. 3 (Summer 2018).

44. Randy Schekman, "How Journals Like Nature, Cell and Science Are Damaging Science," *Guardian*, December 9, 2013, https://www.theguardian.com/commentisfree/2013/dec/09/how-journals-nature-science-cell-damage-science.

45. Marc A. Edwards and Siddharthta Roy, "Science Is Broken: Perverse incentives and the misuse of quantitative metrics have undermined the integrity of scientific research," *Aeon*, November 7, 2017, https://aeon.co/amp/essays/ science-is-a-public-good-in-peril-heres-how-to-fix-it.

46. Rahul Rekhi and Neal Lane, "Qualitative Metrics in Science Policy: What Can't Be Counted, Counts," *Issues in Science and Technology* Vol. 29, No. 1 (Fall 2012).

47. Steven Johnson, *Where Good Ideas Come From*, (New York: Riverhead Books, 2010), 229.

48. Rehki and Lane.

49. Ibid.

50. Yves Gingras, "The Abuses and Perverse Effects of Quantitative Evaluation in the Academy," *Academic Matters* (Winter 2017).

51. http://www.academiaobscura.com/super-specific-journals/ accessed February 7, 2019.

52. Hossam Zawbaa, *Journal Citation Reports 2018* (Thomson Impact Factor 2018). https://www.researchgate.net/publication/326212036_Journal_Citation_Reports_2018_Thomson_Impact_Factor_2018/download.

53. Gingras.

54. Ibid.

55. Ibid.

56. Alison Abbott, et al. "Metrics: Do Metrics Matter?," *Nature* Vol. 465 (2010): 860–62, https://www.nature.com/news/2010/100616/full/465860a.html.

57. Edwards and Roy, "Science Is Broken."

58. Ibid.

59. Ibid.

60. Gingras.

61. Marc A. Edwards and Siddhartha Roy, "Academic Research in the 21stt Century: Maintaining Scientific Integrity in a Climate of Perverse Incentives and Hypercompetition," *Environmental Engineering Science* Vol. 34, No. 1 (2017).

62. Edwards and Roy, Academic Research in the 21st Century."

63. Edwards and Roy, "Science Is Broken."

64. Edwards and Roy, Academic Research in the 21st Century."

65. N. Tomecko and D. Bilusich, "The Value of Input Metrics for Assessing Fundamental Research," 22nd International Congress on Modelling and Simulation, Hobart, Tasmania, Australia (December 3–8, 2017).

66. Ibid.

67. Edwards and Roy, "Science Is Broken."

68. Gingras.

69. Rehki and Lane.

70. Edwards and Roy, "Science Is Broken."

71. Tomecko and Bilusich.

72. Edwards and Roy, "Academic Research in the 21st Century."

73. Edwards and Roy, "Science Is Broken."

74. Pierre Azoulay, Joshua S. Graff Zivin and Gustavo Manso, "Incentives and Creativity: Evidence from the Academic Life Sciences," *RAND Journal of Economics* Vol. 42, No. 3 (Fall 2011).

75. Tomecko and Bilusich.

76. Ed Yong, "The Absurdity of the Nobel Prizes in Science," *Atlantic* (October 3, 2017).

77. Ibid.

78. Rehki and Lane.

79. Edwards and Roy, "Academic Research in the 21st Century."

80. Edwards and Roy, "Science Is Broken."

81. Azoulay, Graff Zivin and Manso.

82. Edwards and Roy, "Science Is Broken."

83. Azoulay, Graff Zivin and Manso.

84. Ibid.

85. Ibid.

86. Ibid.

87. Ibid.

88. Ibid.

89. Tomecko and Bilusich.

90. Rehki and Lane.

91. Edwards and Roy, "Science Is Broken."

92. Laverty.

CHAPTER 4

1. "Vancouver traffic congestion is the worst in the country: study," *Huffington Post* (March 22, 2016), https://www.huffingtonpost.ca/2016/03/22/vancouver-trafficcongestion _n_9524956.html?utm_hp_ref=ca-vancouver-traffic-congestion.

2. Kendra Mangione, "Vancouver is Canada's worst city to drive in study claims," *CTV Vancouver* (September 27, 2017), https://bc.ctvnews.ca/vancouver-is-canada-s-worst-city-to -drive-in-study-claims-1.3609105.

3. Mike Lloyd, "Vancouver nowhere near the top in global gridlock ranking." *CityNews* (February 6, 2018).

4. Joe Cortright, "Driven Apart: How sprawl is lengthening our commutes and why misleading mobility measures are making things worse" (CEOs for Cities, September 2010) http:// cityobservatory.org/wp-content/uploads/2015/08/Cortright_Driven_Apart_2010.pdf.

5. Ibid., 25.

6. Ibid., 25.

7. Ibid., 3.

8. Jing Cao, "Millenials Embrace Cars, Defying Predictions of Sales Implosion," *Bloomberg Business* (April 19, 2015).

9. Derek Thompson, "Millennials: Not So Cheap, After All," *Atlantic* (April 21, 2015).

10. Joe Cortright, "Young People are Buying Fewer Cars," *City Observatory* (April 22, 2015).

11. Urban Systems, Alta Planning Design, Acuere Consulting and Dr. Tarek Sayed P. Eng. "Pedestrian Safety Study: Final Report," Urban Systems, e-2.

12. Taras Grescoe, Straphanger: *Saving Our Cities and Ourselves from the Automobile* (New York: HarperPerennial (2013), 16.

13. Lorrie Goldstein, "Greenhouse gases? Not our problem," *Toronto Sun* (June 3, 2015).

14. Environment and Climate Change Canada (2017) Canadian Environmental Sustainability Indicators: Greenhouse Gas Emissions. Consulted on May 1, 2016, http://www.ec.gc.ca/indicateurs-indicators/18F3BB9C-43A1-491E-983576C8DB9DDFA3/GHGEmissions_EN.pdf.

15. Ibid.

16. Energiewende Outlook: Transportation sector. PricewaterhouseCoopersAktiengesellschaft Wirtschaftsprüfungsgesellschaft " July 2015, https://www.pwc.de/de/energiewende/assets/energiewende-outlook-transportation-2015.pdf.

17. United States Environmental Protection Agency, Sources of Greenhouse Gas Emissions, https://www.epa.gov/ghgemissions/sources-greenhouse-gas-emissions.

18. Railway Association of Canada, 2014 Rail Trends, http://www.railcan.ca/assets/images/publications/2014_Rail_Trends/2014_RAC_RailTrends.pdf.

19. http://ec.europa.eu/eurostat/statistics-explained/index.php/File:Inland_freight_transport,_2014_YB16.png.

20. Goldstein.

CHAPTER 5

1. Statistics Canada "The Daily—Survey of Household Spending, 2011," https://www150.statcan.gc.ca/n1/daily quotidien/130130/dq130130b-eng.htm.

2. Center for Transit-Oriented Development and Center for Neighbourhood Technology, "The Affordability Index: A New Tool for Measuring the True Affordability of Housing Choice" (Metropolitan Policy Program, The Brookings Institution, January 2006).

3. Barbara J. Lipman, "A Heavy Load: The Combined Housing and Transportation Burdens of Working Families" (Center for Housing Policy, October 2006).

4. Michael Hammer, "The 7 Deadly Sins of Performance Management (and How to Avoid Them)," *MIT Sloan Management Review* (Spring 2007): 19–28.

5. https://www.tradegecko.com/blog/zara-supply-chain-its-secret-to-retail-success.

6. Hammer.

7. Trade Gecko, Zara Supply Chain Analysis—the success behind Zara's retail success (Trade Gecko, June 25, 2018), https://www.tradegecko.com/blog/zara-supply-chain-its-secret-to-retail-success.

8. Angela Paxton, *The Food Miles Report: The Dangers of Long-Distance Food Transport* (Sustainable Agriculture Food and Environment Alliance, republished in 2011).

9. Paxton, 7.

10. Pierre Desrochers and Hiroko Shimizu, *The Locavore's Dilemma: In Praise of the 10,000-Mile Diet* (New York: Public Affairs, 2012), 103.

11. Christopher L. Weber and H. Scott Matthews, "Food Miles and the Relative Climate Impacts of Food Choices in the United States." *Environmental Science and Technology* Vol. 42, No 10 (2008).

12. "Sea fairer: Maritime transport and CO2 emissions," *OECD Observer* No. 276 (May–June 2008).

13. Paxton, 9.

14. Ibid., 7.

15. Robert G. Hunt and William E. Franklin, "LCA—How It Came About: Personal Reflections on the Origin and Development of LCA in the USA," *International Journal of Life Cycle Assessment* Vol. 1 (1996): 10.

16. Ibid., 5.

17. Ibid., 4–5.

18. Sevde Ustun Odabasi and Hanife Buyukguno,. "Comparison of Life Cycle Assessment of PET Bottle and Glass Bottle," Eurasia 2016 Waste Management Symposium Conference Paper (May 2016), https://www.researchgate.net/publication/314100348_Comparison_of_Life_Cycle_Assessment_of_PET_Bottle_and_Glass_Bottle.

19. Sarah Martin, Jonas Bunsen, and Andreas Ciroth, "Case Study: Ceramic Cup vs Paper Cup," *GreenDelta* (December 13, 2018).

CHAPTER 6

1. At the opening of the conflict, the Germans had about 3,300,000 soldiers against the Allies' 3,350,000 (France had about 2,240,000 soldiers serving in the north and the British had 500,000 soldiers with the Dutch contributing about 400,000 men and the Belgians 650,000). The Germans were also outgunned: The Allies had 3,383 tanks deployed in France, while the Germans only had 2,439 at their disposal. When it came to heavy artillery, the Germans were nearly at half the strength of the Allies with 7,378 guns compared to 13,974. Even in terms of mobility, the Germans were at a disadvantage. They had 120,000 vehicles, compared to France's 300 000. It was only in aircraft where the Germans were better equipped than the Allies, with 5,638 aircraft versus the Allies 2,935, https://en.wikipedia.org/wiki/Battle_of_France, http://www.newworldencyclopedia.org/entry/Battle_of_France.

2. American Cancer Society, "Cancer Facts and Figures 2018," https://www.cancer.org/research/cancer-facts-statistics/all-cancer-facts-figures/cancer-facts-figures-2018.html.

3. Ibid.

4. Dan Gardner, *Risk: Why We Fear The Things We Shouldn't—and Put Ourselves in Greater Danger*, (Toronto: Emblem, 2009), 255.

5. Dan Gardner, 251–73.

6. Cancer is the second-largest killer. The top ten are rounded out by chronic lower respiratory diseases, accidents, stroke, Alzheimer's disease, diabetes, influenza and pneumonia, nephritis and related diseases, and, sadly, suicide.

7. Ahmedin Jemal, et al. "Trends in the Leading Causes of Death in the United States, 1970-2002," *Journal of the American Medical Association* Vol. 294, No. 10 (September 14, 2005).

8. Daniel F. Sullivan. "Conceptual problems in developing an index of health," Vital and Health Statistics Series 2. No 17. (Bethseda, MD: National Center for Health Statistics, May 1966).

9. World Bank. *World Development Report 1993: Investing in Health.* (New York: Oxford University Press, World Bank, 1993), https://openknowledge.worldbank.org/handle/10986/5976 License: CC BY 3.0 IGO.

10. This is an oversimplification. Calculating years of life lost is actually quite complicated and can be done in various ways, such as "potential years of life lost," "period expected years of life lost," "cohort expected years of life lost," and "standard expected years of life lost," all of which use different assumptions and methods to calculate the life expectancy used in the calculation. The last methodology, "standard expected years of life lost," uses the highest observed life expectancy globally (for example using Japanese data for the life expectancy for women, which was the highest in the world in 1994 at 82.5 years). This methodology allows all deaths, even those above the average life expectancy to count toward the calculation. It is the methodology used in the Global Burden of Disease Study, discussed later.

11. C. J. L Murray, "Quantifying the burden of disease: the technical basis for disability adjusted life years," *WHO Bulletin OMS* Vol. 72 (1994).

12. Joshua Saloman, et al. "Disability Weights for the Global Burden of Disease 2013 Study" *Lancet, Global Health* Vol 3, No. 11 (November 2015), 712–23, http://www.thelancet.com/journals/langlo/article/PIIS2214-109X(15)00069-8/abstract.

13. Murray.

14. World Health Organization, "Global Burden of Disease 2004 Update: Disability Weights for Diseases and Conditions" (2004), http://www.who.int/healthinfo/global_burden_disease/GBD2004_DisabilityWeights.pdf ?ua=1.

15. GBD 2015 DALYs and HALE Collaborators, "Global, regional, and national disability-adjusted life-years (DALYs) for 315 diseases and injuries and healthy life expectancy (HALE), 1990–2015: a systematic analysis for the Global Burden of Disease Study 2015" *Lancet* Vol. 388 (October 8, 2016): 1603–58.

16. Ibid.

17. http://www.healthdata.org/united-states.

18. Stacy Dale and Alan B. Kreuger. "Estimating the return to college selectivity over the career using administrative earnings data," National Bureau of Economic Research. Working Paper 17159 (June 2011).

CHAPTER 7

1. Nicole Gelinas, "How Bratton's NYPD saved the subway system" *New York Post* (August 6, 2016), https://nypost.com/2016/08/06/how-brattons-nypd-saved-the-subway-system/.

2. William J. Bratton, "Great Expectations: How Higher Expectations for Police Departments Can Lead to a Decrease in Crime," Measuring What Matters: Proceedings from the Policing Research Institute Meetings. Ed. Robert H. Langworthy (National Institute of Justice and Office of Community Oriented Policing Services, July 1999).

3. Graham A. Rayman, *The NYPD Tapes: A Shocking Story of Cops, Cover-Ups and Courage* (New York: Palgrave MacMillan, 2013), 15.

4. Bratton.

5. George Kelling, "Measuring What Matters: A New Way of Thinking About Crime and Public Order," *City Journal* (1992).

6. Alan Finder, "Chief of Transit Officers Resigns After 21 Months," *New York Times* (January 17, 1992), https://www.nytimes.com/1992/01/17/nyregion/chief-of-transit-officers resigns-after-21-months.html.

7. George L. Kelling and James Q. Wilson. "Broken Windows. The Police and Neighborhood Safety," *Atlantic* (March 1982).

8. Ibid.

9. Bratton, 9.

10. Rayman, 15–16.

11. Bratton.

12. Ibid.

13. Rayman, 16.

14. Ibid., 17.

15. Bratton.

16. Rayman, 21.

17. Ibid., 17.

18. Bratton.

19. https://en.wikipedia.org/wiki/Uniform_Crime_Reports.

20. Rayman, 18.

21. Ibid., 16.

22. Ibid., 19.

23. Bratton.

24. Rayman, 24.

25. Ibid., 6–10, 12–14, 22–23, 33–38, 41–42, 44, 47, 49–50, 54, 68, 71–72, 76, 78, 93, 108, 108–9, 122, 132, 142–51, 153–59, 163, 167.

26. Ibid., 92.

27. Ibid., 97.

28. Ibid., 186.

29. Ibid., 66.

30. Ibid., 62–65.

31. Ibid., 234.

32. William K. Rashbaum, "Retired Officers Raise Questions on Crime Data," *New York Times* (February 6, 2010).

33. Rayman, 25–27.

34. David N. Kelley and Sharon L. McCarthy. The Report of the Crime Reporting Review Committee to Commissioner Raymond W. Kelly Concerning CompStat Auditing, April 8, 2013, https://www1.nyc.gov/assets/nypd/downloads/pdf/public_information/crime _reporting_review_committee_final_report_2013.pdf..

35. Rayman, 28.

36. Ibid., 65.

37. Ibid., 27–28.

38. George Kelling and William Bratton, "Why We Need Broken Windows Policing," *City Journal* (Winter 2015).

39. Rayman, 92.

40. Andrew Guthrie Furguson. *The Rise of Big Data Policing: Surveillance, Race, and the Future of Law Enforcement.* (New York: New York University Press, 2017).

41. Rayman, 219.

42. Furguson.

43. News Release, "1990s Drop in NYC Crime Not Due to CompStat, Misdemeanor Arrests, Study Finds," New York University (February 4, 2013).

44. Rayman, 226.

45. Ibid., 250.

46. Kelling.

47. Kelling.

48. Kelling.

49. Kelling and Wilson.

50. Kelling.

51. Rayman, 234.

52. David Sklansky, quoted in Malcolm Sparrow. *Handcuffed: What Holds Policing Back and the Keys to Reform* (Washington, DC: Brookings Institute Press, 2016), 101.

53. Gregory Daddis. "The Problem of Metrics: Assessing Progress and Effectiveness in the Vietnam War," *War in History* Vol. 19, No 1 (2012).

54. Ibid., 32.

55. Ibid.

56. Ibid.

57. Tim Darling. "The Whiz Kids: How 10 Men Saved America (and Then Almost Destroyed It)," synopsis of John Byrne, "The Whiz Kids: Ten Founding Fathers of American Business—and the Legacy They Left Us). http://www.amnesta.net/other/whizKids/.

58. Daddis.

59. Ibid.

60. Ibid.

61. Ibid.

62. Ben Connable. *Embracing the Fog of War: Assessment and Metrics in Counterinsurgency* (RAND Corporation. 2012), 100.

63. Daddis.

64. Ibid.

65. Connable.

66. Daddis.

67. Connable.

68. Ibid.

69. Daddis.

70. Ibid.

71. Connable.

72. John E. Mueller, "The Search for the 'Breaking Point' in Vietnam. The Statistics of a Deadly Quarrel," *International Studies Quarterly* Vol. 24, No. 4 (December 1980).

73. Ibid.

74. Scott Sigmund Carter and Marissa Edson Myers, "Body Counts and 'Success' in the Vietnam and Korean Wars," *Journal of Interdisciplinary History* Vol. XXV, No. 3 (Winter 1995).

75. Ibid.

76. Ibid.

77. Mueller.

78. Connable.

79. Ibid.

80. Mueller.

81. Carter and Meyers.

82. Connable.

83. Systems Analysis Office assessment from Alain C. Enthoven and K. Wayne Smith, "How Much Is Enough? Shaping the Defense Program, 1961–1969" (New York: Harper and Row, 1971), 295, referenced in Daddis.

84. Connable.

85. Ibid.

86. Daddis.

87. Connable.

88. Ibid.

89. Mueller.

90. Connable.

91. Mueller.

92. Connable.

93. Mueller.

94. Connable.

95. Ibid.

96. Ibid.

97. Mueller.

98. Mueller.

99. Kinnard, D. *The War Managers* (Hanover, NH: University Press of New England, 1977), quoted in Mueller.

100. Mueller.

101. Connable.

102. Ibid.

103. Ibid.

104. Carter and Meyers.

CHAPTER 8

1. Nina Munk, "How Levi's Trashed a Great American Brand While Bob Haas pioneered benevolent management, his company came apart at the seams," *Fortune* (April 12, 1999), http://archive.fortune.com/magazines/fortune/fortune_archive/1999/04/12/258131/index.htm.

2. Greg Johnson, "Troubles at Levi Strauss Revealed in SEC Filing," *Los Angeles Times* (May 5, 2000), http://articles.latimes.com/2000/may/05/business/fi-26752.

3. Michael Streeter and Roger Trapp, "Levi's pounds 500m bonus aims to keep staff riveted with joy" *Independent* (June 14, 1996), https://www.independent.co.uk/news/levis-pounds-500m-bonus-aims-to-keep-staff-riveted-with-joy-1336924.html.

4. "Levi to cut 6,400 jobs," *CNN Money* (November 3, 1997), https://money.cnn.com/1997/11/03/companies/levis/.

5. Munk.

6. Ibid.

7. Johnson.

8. The Associated Press, "Levi's Profit Fell Sharply in '99," *New York Times* (May 8, 2000), https://www.nytimes.com/2000/05/08/business/levi-s-profit-fell-sharply-in-99.html.

9. Johnson.

10. Victor H. Vroom. *Work and Motivation* (New York: Wiley, 1964).

11. Steven Kerr, "On the folly of rewarding A, while hoping for B," *Academy of Management Executive* Vol. 18 (1975).

12. Edward P. Lazear, "Compensation and Incentives in the Workplace," *Journal of Economic Perspectives* Vol. 32, No. 3 (Summer 2018).

NOTES

13. Edward L. Deci, "Effects of Externally Mediated Rewards on Intrinsic Motivation," *Journal of Personality and Social Psychology* Vol. 18, No. 1 (1971).

14. Daniel Kahneman. *Thinking Fast and Slow* (New York: Farrar, Straus & Giroux: 2011), 53.

15. Mark R. Lepper and David Greene, "When Two Rewards Are Worse Than One: Effects of Extrinsic Rewards on Intrinsic Motivation," *Phi Delta Kappan* Vol. 56, No. 8 (April 1975).

16. Timothy Gubler, Ian Larkin and Lamar Pierce, "Motivational Spillovers from Awards: Crowding Out in a Multitasking Environment," *Organizational Science* (February 12, 2013), https://papers.ssrn.com/sol3/papers.cfm?abstract_id=2215922.

17. Erik Canton, "Power of Incentives in Public Organizations When Employees Are Intrinsically Motivated," *Journal of Institutional and Theoretical Economics* Vol. 161 (2005).

18. Ibid.

19. Ibid.

20. Marc A. Edwards and Siddhartha Roy, "Academic Research in the 21st Century: Maintaining Scientific Integrity in a Climate of Perverse Incentives and Hypercompetition," *Environmental Engineering Science* Vol. 34, No. 1 (2017).

21. Dan Ariely, et al., "Large Stakes and Big Mistakes," *Review of Economic Studies* Vol. 76, No. 2 (April 2009).

22. Dan Ariely. *Predictably Irrational* (New York: HarperCollins, 2008), 75–102.

23. Ibid., 79.

24. Douglas W. Hubbard, *How to Measure Anything: Finding the Value of "Intangibles" in Business* Second Edition (Hoboken, NJ: Wiley, 2010).

25. Dean R. Spitzer, *Transforming Performance Metrics: Rethinking the Way We Measure and Drive Organizational Success* (New York: American Management Association, 2007), 13.

26. Lazear.

27. John P. Campell et al., "A Theory of Performance," in N. Schmitt & W. C. Borman (Eds.), *Personnel Selection in Organizations* (San Francisco, CA: Jossey-Bass, 1993).

28. Bernard Bass, "From Transactional to Transformative Leadership: Learning to Share the Vision" *Organizational Dynamics* Vol. 18, No. 3 (Winter 1990): 19–31.

29. Margaret Wheatley and Myron Kellner-Rogers, "What Do We Measure and Why: Questions About the Uses of Measurement," *Journal of Strategic Performance Measurement* (June 1999).

30. Robert Costanza et al., "Beyond GDP: The Need for New Measures of Progress, Pardee Papers No. 4 (Bosont University, January 2009), 4.

31. Costanza et al., 8.

32. Joseph E. Stiglitz, Amartya Sen and Jean-Paul Fitoussi, *Mis-Measuring our Lives, Why The GDP Doesn't Add Up* (New York: The New Press, 2010); Mark Anielski, *The Economics of Happiness: Building Genuine Wealth* (British Columbia: New Society Publishers, 2007); The Centre for Well-being, *The New Economics Foundation, Measuring Our Progress: The Power of Well-Being* (New Economics Foundation: London, 2011); Costanza et al.

33. Easterin, Richard A. "Does Economic Growth Improve the Human Lot? Some Empirical Evidence" in Paul A. David and Melvin W. Reder (eds.), *Nations and Households in Economic Growth: Essays in Honour of Moses Abramovitz* (New York: Academic Press, Inc., 1974).

34. Justin Fox, "The Economics of Well-Being," *Harvard Business Review* (January–February 2012), https://hbr.org/2012/01/the-economics-of-well-being.

35. Costanza et al., 11–22.

36. Ibid., 8.

37. Simon Kuznets, "National Income, 1929–1932" (National Bureau of Economic Research Inc, 1934), https://www.mysciencework.com/publication/download/cd57cc170990 d63a4e9c7d7fde09154d/b6f8e72d183ef69e56e66d41709bf682.

38. Spitzer, 11.

39. https://www.npr.org/sections/allsongs/2008/05/an_interview_with_tom_waits _by.html.

CHAPTER 9

1. David Manheim, "Goodhart's Law and Why Measurement is Hard." Ribbon-Farm (June 9, 2016), https://www.ribbonfarm.com/2016/06/09/ goodharts-law-and-why -measurement-is-hard/.

2. David Parmenter, "Should We Abandon Performance Measures?" *Cutter IT Journal* (January 2013), http://cdn.davidparmenter.com/files/2014/02/Should-we-abandon-ourper-formance-measures-Cutter-Journal 2013.pdf..pdf.

3. Manheim.

4. Rachel Aviv, "Wrong Answer: In an era of high-stakes testing, a struggling school made a shocking choice," *New Yorker*, July 21, 2014.

5. Manheim.

6. Ibid.

7. Aviv.

8. Margaret Wheatley and Myron Kellner-Rogers, "What Do We Measure and Why: Questions About the Uses of Measurement," *Journal of Strategic Performance Measurement* (June 1999).

9. Ibid.

10. Graham A. Rayman, *The NYPD Tapes: A Shocking Story of Cops, Cover-Ups and Courage* (New York: Palgrave MacMillan, 2013), 32.

11. Aviv.

12. Megan McArdle, "Metrics and Their Unintended Consequences," *Bloomberg Opinion*, January 3, 2018, https://www.bloomberg.com/opinion/articles/2018-01-03/metrics-and -unintended-consequences-in-health-care-and-education.

13. Manheim.

14. Ibid.

15. Onara O'Neill, "A Question of Trust, Lecture 1: Spreading Suspicion," Reith Lectures 2002 (BBC Radio 4, 2002).

16. Cali Ressler and Jody Thompson. *Why Work Sucks and How to Fix It: The Results—Only Revolution* (New York: Penguin Group, 2008).

17. Graham Rayman, "NYPD Tapes 5: The Corroboration," *Village Voice* (August 25, 2010), https://www.villagevoice.com/2010/08/25/nypd-tapes-5-the-corroboration/.

18. Onara O'Neill.

19. Ibid.

20. Michael Hammer, "The 7 Deadly Sins of Performance Management (and How to Avoid Them)," *MIT Sloan Management Review* (Spring 2007): 19–28.

21. Wheatley and Kellner-Rogers.

22. Dan Ariely, "Column: You Are What You Measure," *Harvard Business Review* (June 2010), https://hbr.org/2010/06/column-you-are-what-you-measure.

23. Hammer.

CHAPTER 10

1. Salman Khan, *The One World Schoolhouse: Education Reimagined* (New York: Twelve, 2013), 83.

2. Khan, 83.

3. Rachel Aviv, "Wrong Answer: In an Era of High-Stakes Testing, a Struggling School Made a Shocking Choice," *New Yorker*, July 21, 2014.

4. Khan, 139–47.

5. Margaret Wheatley and Myron Kellner-Rogers, "What Do We Measure and Why: Questions About the Uses of Measurement," *Journal of Strategic Performance Measurement* (June 1999).

INDEX

INDEX